GEOFF DUKE
THE STYLISH CHAMPION

Drawing by
David Boarer

GEOFF DUKE

THE STYLISH CHAMPION

MICK WALKER

First published in Great Britain in 2007 by
The Breedon Books Publishing Company Limited
Breedon House, 3 The Parker Centre,
Derby, DE21 4SZ.

Paperback edition published in Great Britain in 2012 by The Derby Books
Publishing Company Limited, 3 The Parker Centre, Derby, DE21 4SZ.

Dedication

To the new arrival in the Walker household:
Rascal, a border collie pup.
Any omissions to the life of Geoff Duke may well be found
in Rascal's digestive system!

ISBN 978-1-78091-218-9

Printed and bound by Copytech (UK) Limited, Peterborough.

Contents

Preface 7

Chapter 1 Early Days 8

Chapter 2 Norton Motors 19

Chapter 3 World Champion 72

Chapter 4 Gilera 1953–1954 109

Chapter 5 Gilera 1955–1957 145

Chapter 6 Going it Alone 179

Chapter 7 BMW, NSU and Benelli 200

Chapter 8 Scuderia Duke 222

Chapter 9 Industry Politics 236

Chapter 10 A Place in History 244

Appendices 248

Index 253

Every so often a unique snapshot of times gone by is discovered in a dusty vault or in shoeboxes in an attic by an enthusiastic amateur photographer. They are living history. Each and every one of us cannot resist the temptation as we marvel at the quality of the images, to let our mind drift back to the good old days and wonder what it was really like.

We at Mortons Motorcycle Media, market-leading publishers of classic and vintage titles, own one of the largest photographic archives of its kind in the world. It is a treasure trove of millions of motorcycle and related images, many of which have never seen the light of day since they were filed away in the dark-room almost 100 years ago.

Perhaps the biggest gem of all is our collection of glass plates – almost two tons of them to be precise! They represent a largely hitherto unseen look into our motorcycling heritage from the turn of the century. Many of the plates are priceless and capture an era long gone when the pace of life was much slower and traffic jams were unheard of.

We are delighted to be associated with well known author Mick Walker in the production of this book and hope you enjoy the images from our archive.

Terry Clark,
Managing Director,
Mortons Media Group Ltd

Preface

This, the fifth in a series aimed at covering the careers of the world's greatest motorcycle racing champions, highlights the man who was the first post-war superstar on two wheels – Geoff Duke.

Geoff Duke – The Stylish Champion is the story of someone who set new standards and dominated the World Championship scene, first on British Nortons and later on Italian Gileras during the first half of the 1950s.

Geoff Duke was the first rider to win three 500cc World Championship titles in succession, the first motorcyclist to win the coveted Sportsman of the Year award, and only the second motorcyclist to be honoured with an OBE (Order of the British Empire). In addition, he set new standards for smoothness which remain unsurpassed to the present day. He was also the last rider to win a world solo crown, in road racing, on a British bike.

But there was much, much more to Geoff Duke's list of achievements, including that of a brilliant off-road rider – in both trials and motocross – successful businessman, consultant, team manager, clerk of the course at the ISDT, and also the small matter of no less than six world road-racing Championship titles.

The list of good people who helped me compile Geoff Duke's story, by providing either information or photographs – or in some cases both – is lengthy. These include: David Boarer (who also did the excellent drawing at the beginning of this book), Ian and Rita Welsh, Wolfgang Gruber, Mick Woollett, Jim Blanchard, Peter Reeve, Vic Bates, Pooks Motor Bookshop, Jukka Helkama, Stu Rogers, Dave Kay, Piaggio, Avon Tyre Company, BMW, the late Don Upshaw, David Pike and Bill Lomas. Mortons Media Group Ltd, who house the archives of *The Motor Cycle* and *Motor Cycling* magazines of yesteryear, helped in their usual way.

I really enjoyed researching and writing Geoff Duke's story – here was a man who reached the very top in his chosen sport and then, for many years thereafter, was seen by many as an ambassador for it the world over.

Mick Walker, Wisbech, Cambridgeshire.

Chapter 1

Early Days

GEOFFREY Ernest (Geoff) Duke was born in St Helens, Lancashire, on 29 March 1923, the youngest son of a baker and shop owner in the town. World War One had been over less than five years, but already peacetime had returned with a vengeance, and so young Geoff was able to enjoy his formative years in the family household without fear of his father going off to war, as so many had experienced only a short time previously.

As Geoff was to describe in his autobiography *In Pursuit of Perfection* (Osprey, 1988), his motorcycle life was:

> *triggered early one Sunday morning back in 1933, when I caught a whiff of the now-rare aroma of Castrol R. Lying in bed I heard the steady thump of open exhausts outside bringing the delicious smell of 'R' in through the open window. The machines were the road bikes of two local enthusiasts; one was a camshaft Velocette and the other a Blackburne-engine Cotton. Little did I imagine then the exciting future in motorsport that lay ahead for me.*

During that same year older brother Eric bought his first motorcycle. This was a brand new 248cc ohv unit-construction New Imperial for the sum of 33 guineas (£34.65), and, as Geoff said, 'this began my own lifelong love affair with motorcycles'.

An introduction to the sport
Geoff's first experiences of motorcycle sport came with visits to nearby Wallasey and Ainsdale for sand racing, and to Parbold for path racing on the pillion seat of Eric's New Imperial which 'had me thrilled'.

But these visits were to be all too short, before Eric suffered a serious road accident when a woman drove out of a side turning in a Humber car, hitting the unfortunate Eric. Actually, Geoff, returning home from school, saw a group of people gathered around a crashed motorcycle and its rider, who was lying on the pavement, but 'not having a macabre curiosity, I continued home, little realising that the injured person was my brother'.

The crash brought to an end Eric's own racing ambition, as he had sustained no less than 22 fractures to his right foot and ankle. As Geoff described, 'the surgeon at the hospital requested our parent's permission to amputate Eric's foot. They refused, though, and fortunately so, for the surgeon set about rebuilding the shattered limb, doing a superb job.'

Even so, it was a worrying time for the Duke household, not helped by the leg having to overcome gangrene where a spindle, on which weights had been suspended to stop the leg shortening, passed through Eric's ankle.

After the incident, Geoff's parents forbade 'the mere mention of motorcycles'. However, Geoff's two-wheel interest was not to be extinguished, and, as he later recalled, 'it was around this time, too, that a visit with two friends to a local garage revealed a number of old motorcycles'. These machines were ones amassed by the dealership over many years, which had been bought in for repairs but never collected. One of these was a 1923 belt-drive Raleigh, which the youngster found hidden under a 'heap of worn-out tyres.' As Geoff described, 'we asked if it was for sale and the answer was yes – we could have it for the sum of 10s (50p). So, off we went to count our collective savings, returning the next day to buy the machine and wheel it home.'

Geoff with his mother after winning the 1951 Senior TT in the Isle of Man. After joining the Norton factory in 1948, his elevation to a world-class star was meteoric to say the least.

A 1923 belt-drive Raleigh of the type that Geoff and his friends purchased for the princely sum of 10 shillings (50p) in the mid-30s.

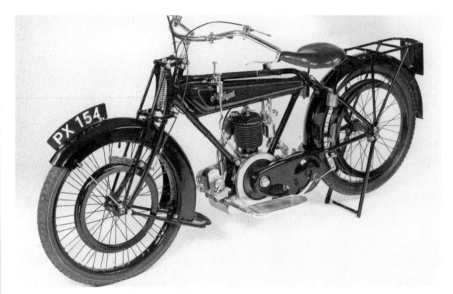

However, the Raleigh could not be taken to the Duke's home. But, as Geoff says, 'my two friends, Alec and Tom Merrick, the sons of a local doctor, lived not far from my home in a big house'. At this time, neither Geoff's mother and father or the Merrick's parents knew of their sons' purchase – as the Raleigh had been hidden in one of the outbuildings at the latter's residence.

But, of course, in time news leaked out, and as Geoff says 'reluctantly, they accepted the situation and permitted us to keep the machine'.

An engine overhaul was carried out by the boys, ably assisted by the doctor's chauffeur. Thereafter, the trio had a considerable amount of enjoyment – and not a few spills on the bike. Geoff describes it as 'wonderful fun'. Except, of course, when, one day, he managed to tear off a fingernail when 'practising alone'. This episode resulted in the boys being 'exiled to a farm at Garswood where farmer Hamilton, who supplied eggs and milk to the Merrick household, promised to keep a wary eye on us'. Geoff continued 'even the five-mile push to the farm failed to dampen our enthusiasm for the old Raleigh and Alec, Tom and I spent many enjoyable Saturdays riding our Raleigh up and down the half-mile track which connected the farm with the East Lancashire Road'. But, as time went on, the trio's quest for 'more speed' saw another visit to the aforementioned St Helens dealership, where they purchased a 1928 side-valve Triumph single (with chain drive!) in running order for the princely sum of 15 shillings (75p).

As Geoff recalled, 'the advent of this much more powerful machine inevitably introduced a keener competitive atmosphere to our racing scene, and we were soon timing each other over a one-mile, there-and-back course with an old alarm clock!' Geoff went on to describe this track in the following manner: 'it was rutted and bumpy like a scramble course. From the farm it went downhill for about 300 yards and then levelled off before a tight S-bend; it then continued along a straight until reaching the end. Here we would turn, using the adjoining field, before returning to the farm.'

The Triumph was followed by a seizure-prone Dunelt two-stroke and a BSA seven-fifty v-twin, the latter hitched to a sidecar. Eventually, as before, news filtered through to Geoff's parents of his activities. As he went on to say, 'they were not happy about it, but, presumably because I had not been hurt, decided to do no more that plead with me to be "very careful".'

During 1936 Geoff's father fell seriously ill with arthritis of the spine. His doctor advised a move to a different climate and so the shop was sold and the family moved to Blackpool. This also saw Geoff leave the local St Helens grammar school (he was 13 years of age) and get a job in his new home town with an estate agent to help the family's finances.

Then, in 1939, the family moved back to St Helens; the following year Geoff gained a job with the Post Office engineering department in Prescot as a telephone maintenance engineer. Irregular hours meant that having his own transport was essential. Reluctantly, his parents agreed to his purchase of a very second-hand DOT 175cc – Geoff's first road bike.

It was while employed at Prescot telephone exchange that the young Duke 'received', as he later put it, 'my first lesson in the importance of machine preparation and the need for concentration'. This came about in the following way: 'my DOT machine's rear tyre was totally devoid of tread which, at that time, did not bother me too much – in any case, I could not afford a replacement, however, this would be my undoing.' He continued, 'on the morning in question, though, full of the joys of spring – but unaware that overnight work on a drain had deposited a fine coating of sand on the road – I banked over the DOT at the usual angle, only to be dumped unceremoniously in the road, while my precious machine slid on for another 50 yards or so. Embarrassed but unhurt, I picked myself up and sheepishly looked around for anybody who had seen my downfall. To my relief, nobody was in sight, and fortunately my machine had suffered only a bent footrest. It was a salutary lesson, however.'

Next, in 1941 Geoff was transferred to an automatic exchange in St Helens, where he met twin brothers Alan and Don Whitfield, the proud owners of a camshaft Norton single. The young Duke was 'occasionally allowed' to occupy the saddle. It is also worth noting that, in Geoff's opinion, Alan was 'a superb rider' who after the war entered the 1947 Manx Grand Prix, but he unfortunately suffered a practice crash which brought an end to his racing career.

A BSA v-twin was another machine (hitched to a sidecar) which Geoff rode during his schooldays.

World War Two had begun at the beginning of September, when the Germans had invaded Poland, and soon afterwards Great Britain and France declared war on Hitler's Nazi regime after it failed to respond to a plea made by the Allies to leave Poland. As for the young Geoff Duke, after replacing the ageing DOT with a 1934 New Imperial Grand Prix two-fifty, he volunteered for military service in 1942, just prior to his 19th birthday – even though as a 'reserved occupation' his Post Office job meant that he was not automatically called up. However, as Geoff put it, 'I really did not enjoy the Post Office work'. So he chose the army, because the magazine *Motor Cycling*, via its then editor Graham Walker (Murray's father), ran a scheme for voluntary enrolment of DR's (Dispatch Riders) into the Royal Corps of Signals.

At first Geoff's application was rejected, and he was advised that 'my alternative would be to enrol as an instrument mechanic, in the hope of transferring to the motorcycle section'.

This Geoff did, and, after some six weeks of the traditional 'square bashing', was posted to Catterick Camp in North Yorkshire, where 'at the very first opportunity, I requested an interview with the Training Officer'. After listening to Geoff's plea for a transfer, this officer openly expressed his 'surprise' at the youngster's wish to become a dispatch rider – at the time considered 'a very low form of life in the Signals Corps'. But not to be put off, Geoff 'finally convinced him that I would not be put off and he then gave me the broadest of hints that, if by chance,' he was to fail his mechanics course, he would 'probably be demoted to DR'.

And so it transpired, and soon Geoff was one of a squad of some 20 riders under the watchful eye of a certain Sgt 'Nobby' Clark, with whom Geoff says he got on with 'like a house on fire'. Describing Sgt Clark in his autobiography as 'a fine rider', although he was one of the few regular army instructors in the unit, he bore no resentment towards the 'civilians' who were 'gradually taking over as instructors from the regulars'.

After passing his course with a 96 percent mark before going on leave, Sgt Clark informed Geoff that he had 'recommended me to be retained as an instructor on my return'.

Hugh Viney

However, upon his return to Catterick, Geoff was initially 'disappointed' to discover that he was not to report to 'Nobby' Clark, but instead to B.H.M. Viney. But, this soon disappeared as he found Sgt Hugh Viney was 'the most outstanding rider in the unit'. Geoff went on to describe:

Hugh Viney (pictured here in 1948) was not only a brilliant trials rider, but played a major role in Geoff's progress as a motorcyclist during his army service.

he was a brilliant trials rider and set the standard which I attempted to attain through his example, but never quite did. Nevertheless, for 2½ years I modelled myself on him – his machine preparation and riding technique. This experience was to stand me in good stead in later trials riding, and even my subsequent road racing career.

As proof of Hugh Viney's abilities as a trials rider is to recall that when the legendary Scottish Six Days returned in 1947 after a break of eight years, due to the international situation, it was Viney (riding an AJS) who was victorious. He then went on to record three further wins in the event in 1948, 1949 and finally in 1953. He was also to win several ISDT gold medals and be a member of the winning British Trophy team on more than one occasion. Geoff was later to refer to Hugh Viney as 'a shining star of the first magnitude'.

Speedway

In 1944, while still stationed at Catterick, Geoff tried his hand at speedway, first at Belle Vue (Manchester), which remained open during the war, and later at Odsal and Middlesbrough, riding a Rudge which he had purchased; the Rudge was later replaced by what Geoff was to describe as a 'JAP-engined track spare'. However, although doing many laps of the various speedway circuits, he never actually took part in a competitive race.

Charles Markham

Geoff met Charles Markham (then a Corporal in the Royal Signals) for the first time shortly after the former had arrived at Catterick Camp in 1942. As Geoff was subsequently to recall, 'when later I was retained as an instructor, a bond of friendship was established between Charles, a fellow Lancastrian, and myself'.

Originally a DR, Markham (a pre-war racer at Donington Park) was also an accomplished artist as well as a writer. In his spare time he produced 'amusing cartoons' for *Motor Cycling* and wrote many articles as well. As Geoff is the first to admit, Charles Markham was to play a vital role in Duke's early competitive career, as will become clear later.

This is how Geoff described Charles in the 22 December 1960 issue of *Motor Cycling* following his retirement from racing earlier that year:

Geoff first met Charles Markham at Catterick Camp in 1942. Originally a DR (Despatch Rider), Charles was also a former racer, an accomplished artist and journalist (for *Motor Cycling*).

He [Markham] was slightly built, much shorter than I in stature, but full of boundless energy, and had a ready wit which never deserted him. He appeared to be completely fearless on a motorcycle, yet he had a dread of heights.

Geoff continued:

Perched on the back of a '350' ridden by Charles over the deserted moorland roads between Lancashire and Yorkshire, I was 'schooled' in the art of road racing and high speed judgement by a master in his own right – an introduction, which, along with the trials experience which I had gained during my five years in the army, enabled me, at 25, to burst into the post-war racing scene.

Another Catterick colleague was Harry Johnson, who Geoff described thus: 'was to become my lifelong friend and mechanic, looking after my post-war racing machines at most events other than the Grand Prix'.

Promotion

In 1946 Geoff was promoted to sergeant and took over as chief instructor when Hugh Viney was demobbed, the latter joining AMC (Associated Motor Cycles) in South East London as leader of the works AJS trials team.

As for our hero, as he recalled in his autobiography, 'I managed to persuade my commanding officer to allow me to take part in a few civilian trials. To help prepare my machine I wrote to Bert Perrigo, the competition manager at BSA, who kindly provided a 21in front wheel and trials tyre, and a 4.00x19 tyre for the rear wheel, plus sprockets to lower the gearing of my army M20 BSA.' And Geoff went on to say, 'this helped tremendously, but the M20 side valve weighing some 360lbs was hardly an ideal trials machine – which I soon discovered when I rode it in the Scott Trial.' Even though he finished, Geoff said he was 'somewhat weary' by the end.

Geoff began his civilian trials career with a 1947 BSA three-fifty, similar to the one shown here.

Demob

Geoff was demobbed from the army on 1 July 1947 – his final two weeks in the service being spent at the Royal Tournament at Olympia in London. This is how he described the event:

I was with the Royal Signals motorcycle display team and one of my 'tricks' was to enter the arena at high speed and, with the aid of a ramp, jump over the prone bodies of a number of my teammates. On landing, it was necessary to lay the machine almost on its side and broadslide around the 'tar' speedway fashion to avoid hitting the fence at the end of the arena. We were using Triumph twins specially prepared for these events and the footrests were fitted with rubber sleeves with large bulbous ends, these were only for appearance purposes, and after a week of broadsliding they split and hinged upwards when the machine was laid over in a slide.

But as Geoff went on to explain:

prior to the last jump of the week, and unbeknown to me, the Triumph factory mechanic, anxious to have his wards in pristine condition for the finale, replaced the footrest rubber… also, as it was the finale, I wanted to put on my best performance. I made my best-ever jump, laid the machine over into its usual broadslide, and the footrest dug into the tar! The machine flipped back upright and I was catapulted into the guard fence. I was unhurt, but extremely embarrassed.

Geoff Duke could just as easily have been a champion trials rider (seen here in 1949), scrambler or road racer. He was a true all-rounder.

A civilian again

Upon leaving the army, not only did Geoff return to St Helens, but the other initial move was to purchase a brand new BSA B32 trials bike with his savings. He had also already written again to Bert Perrigo at BSA about the possibility of the latter finding Geoff work at the Small Heath, Birmingham, factory. Then, shortly after winning the Cheshire Centre Championship and the Northern Experts' Trial, Geoff received the offer of employment in the experimental engine department – Jack Amott taking him to Birmingham, where Bert Perrigo introduced Geoff to BSA's leading trials and scrambles star, Ulsterman Bill Nicholson. Not only this, but Bill 'persuaded Mrs Pearson, his landlady, to allow me to share Bill's room in her Charles Road home'.

A factory BSA rider

After more successes on his own privately-owned B32, Geoff was promoted to the BSA factory trials team, alongside Bill and Fred Rist.

By the time the Scott Trial came around in mid-November 1947, the name G.E. Duke was fast becoming a major figure in the trials world – finishing runner-up (a tie with fellow BSA rider R.B. Young) behind the winner, Hugh Viney (AJS).

A week later and Geoff, together with Nicholson and Rist, took the Manufacturer's Team Prize at the John Douglas Trophy Trial organised by

At BSA Geoff came into close contact with Bill Nicholson (seen here in the centre), together with the company's competitions team manager, Bert Perrigo (left).

the Bristol club, and only lost the trial to Hugh Viney on the special test. Add to that an eighth place at the prestigious British Experts, and G.E. Duke was on his way.

Signing for Norton

In the 22 January 1948 issue of *The Motor Cycle* it was announced that 'the new works rider for Norton in trials is G.E. Duke, who last year won the 350cc cup in the John Douglas Trial'.

However, this simple statement hid a much more complex set of events.

While practising for the Scott Trial the previous year, Geoff met Artie Bell, then the top rider in the Norton road-racing team. And around the same time Geoff was also contacted by his old army pal and mentor Hugh Viney – who wanted to know if he would be interested in joining him at Associated Motor Cycles. Geoff 'was interested', so Hugh arranged a visit to the London works. As Geoff describes in *In Pursuit of Perfection*, 'during this visit, I was taken into the racing department where Hugh Viney introduced me to Les Graham, the AJS road-racing team leader.' But Geoff was taken aback when 'in my conversation with Les, I mentioned my ambition to ride in the 1948 Isle of Man Clubman's TT. Les immediately replied that if I joined AMC the company directors would not allow me to compete.' The reason given was that the public would believe Geoff had works support and that would have been 'bad for the company's image'. It should be explained that the 'Clubman's' was exactly that: a race for normal club members on their own motorcycles. However, in practice, there were several dealer-entered machines – and manufacturers, particularly BSA – who sent service teams.

But even though Geoff had been somewhat surprised by Les Graham's comments, 'I virtually agreed to join AMC', but, as he went on to say, 'fate was to intervene'. This was because upon his return to Birmingham there was a letter from Artie Bell. Essentially it said that he had been impressed with Geoff's riding at the Scott Trial and that Nortons were about to produce a new 500cc trial mount, designed by Artie's Belfast pal (and business partner) Rex McCandless. As Geoff was later to reveal:

He, Artie, had spoken of me to Norton's technical director and racing manager, Joe Craig – and that Joe had expressed an interest in meeting me to discuss the possibility of my joining the Norton trials team! I could hardly believe my eyes! An opportunity to join the world's most famous racing marque was beyond my wildest dreams – even though the offer involved only trials.

Seeking advice

Although having in principle agreed to join AMC after the tour of their South London facilities and subsequent interview with old friend Hugh Viney (and Jock West), Artie Bell's letter put Geoff in a quandary. As he recalled in 1960:

Torn between my reluctance to let down Hugh Viney and the desire to join a firm famous the world over for its racing activities, I turned for advice to Charles [Markham]. His argument convinced me that it was policy to accept the Norton offer, although at that time racing didn't enter into the picture.

And so Charles Markham subsequently contacted Joe Craig, added his recommendation, and a meeting was arranged at the Victoria Hotel, Birmingham, which resulted in Geoff leaving BSA (which he described as 'a brief, but unsettled three months at Small Heath'). As Geoff went on to describe, 'This meeting was a success, and Joe offered me a job at the Norton factory and with it the chance to ride the new trials 500T model.' His salary was to be decided at a later date with the managing director Gilbert Smith.

As he said in *In Pursuit of Perfection*, Geoff was 'overjoyed' and, after leaving the Norton interview with Charles Markham, then 'broached the subject of my visit to AMC and how best to break the news of my "change of heart" to Hugh Viney – to whom I owed so much.' Charles told Geoff 'There is no alternative. You must ring Hugh Viney first thing tomorrow morning and put your cards on the table. Mention your disappointing conversation with Les Graham regarding the possibility of riding in the Clubman's TT, and the opportunity that could stem from joining Nortons, and trust he will understand.' This Geoff did, but 'Hugh told me of his displeasure and it was some time before we were back on friendly terms.'

At the subsequent meeting with Gilbert Smith, Geoff was 'offered a job to create a small competition department at the Bracebridge Street factory and to ride for Nortons in trials at a salary of £700 a year, plus expenses'. When one considers that the average British worker of the time received around £7 a week, this gives an idea of his remuneration.

And, unlike Les Graham's comment, before leaving Geoff mentioned his desire to race in the Clubman's TT to Gilbert Smith – this being greeted with 'positive enthusiasm'.

And so the great adventure began.

Chapter 2

Norton Motors

When Geoff first joined Norton Motors at the start of 1948, he was 'given a small area on the first floor' of the Bracebridge Street factory where he worked alone, preparing 'my trials and scrambles machines'. At this time he 'saw little of Joe Craig'. And to complete 'my limited paperwork, I based myself in the office of Norton's former chief designer, Edgar Franks, who was then concerned with answering Norton owners' complaints and queries. As a new boy in a strange environment, Edgar and his secretary were most kind and helpful.'

Off-road

It may come as a surprise to readers, but Geoff Duke's original ambition was to be a trials rider, not a road racer. And Norton's main interest – besides road racing – was the feet-up sport. Even after Geoff became a full works road racer, he continued in trials and later scrambles for several years.

The first of the 1948 season national trials was the Colmore Cup, which, *The Motor Cycle* reported in its 26 February issue, 'coincided with the first blast of real winter'. The area of Shipston-on-Stour, Warwickshire, was reported as 'snow covered', and it appeared to be 'the centre of the keenest sub-zero winds and blizzards that Britain has experienced for many a year', while the 'roads were as slippery as ice-bound rivers, and the hazards were nearly all so frozen as to be entirely changed in character from that associated with their names'.

But the Colmore was not to prove a notable debut for the Duke/Norton combination, Geoff being outside the first-class awards.

Next came the Kickham Trial the following weekend, and again the name G.E. Duke was not among the first-class awards – although *The Motor Cycle* mentioned his speed as one of the fastest laps.

Much better was the Hurst Cup Trial held on the beautiful Clandeboye Estate near Bangor, Northern Ireland, in early March. Six laps of a 7½-mile course had to be covered and, on each circuit, 22 sections were observed.

Harold Daniell, one of the many great riders who rode works Nortons. Harold is pictured here with a Lancefield tuned model during the late 1930s.

The Norton Company

During the first half of the 20th century, Norton was by far the most successful name in motorcycle racing. James L. 'Pa' Norton was born in Birmingham during 1869, the son of a cabinetmaker and wood carver. But, as events were to prove, his talents lay in an entirely different direction. From a young age, anything and everything mechanical fascinated him, and, what is more, his practical abilities in this direction were quite remarkable, as he demonstrated when he constructed, at the age of 12, a working model steam engine.

On leaving school, the 15-year-old Norton was apprenticed as a toolmaker. But, at the age of 19, he contracted rheumatic fever severely, and, although he visited New York aboard one of the new ocean-going liners, on the instructions of his doctor, his health was never very good afterwards. His continuing poor health aged him prematurely, which was why he was known as 'Pa', even while still a relatively young man.

In 1898, at the age of 29, James L. Norton established his first business, supplying components for the then-thriving bicycle trade – known as the Norton Manufacturing Company. He produced his first motorcycle in 1902 and the 'Energette', as it was called, was soon entered in reliability and speed trials.

But the big breakthrough really came when a Peugeot-engined Norton, ridden by Rem Fowler, had the distinction of winning the multi-cylinder class at the very first Isle of Man TT in 1907. This was followed by more success in both racing and record breaking at the famous Brooklands track in Surrey, where men such as Percy Brewster, Jack Emerton and Daniel O'Donovan (nicknamed the 'Wizard' due to his tuning skills) helped establish the Norton name at this venue.

In 1920 Norton moved to Bracebridge Street (still in Birmingham), which was to remain the company's home for the next 43 years.

Up to 1922, Norton motorcycles had been powered by side-valve engines, and it was at Brooklands on 17 March that year that the first overhead-valve model made its bow. This soon became the Model 18 (which was to remain in production for many years).

With James L. Norton's health rapidly deteriorating, 1924 saw the arrival of Walter Moore as chief engineer. Although 'Pa' Norton passed away in April 1925, this was not before he had witnessed double TT victories (Senior and Sidecar) the previous year.

Next came Norton's first overhead-cam engine, the CS1 (Cam Shaft One), which made a debut victory in the 1927 Senior TT (ridden by Alec Bennett, who had also won the 1924 Senior).

And so Norton continued to enhance its reputation as a manufacturer of superb racing models, the 1930s seeing the breed refined further with the Arthur Carroll-designed engine, and the Birmingham marque becoming increasingly famous for its racing exploits thanks to the efforts of team manager (and former Norton racer) Joe Craig and riders such as Tim Hunt, Jimmy Simpson, Stanley Woods, Jimmy Guthrie, Freddie Frith and Harold Daniell.

Behind the scenes technical developments during this period included features such as hairpin valve springs (1934), a megaphone exhaust system (1935), plunger-type rear suspension (1936), twin overhead camshafts (1937) and telescopic front forks (1938).

Norton chose not to enter a works team during 1939. Instead, under the guidance of Gilbert Smith, it prepared itself for another battle – World War Two, which commenced at the beginning of September that year. During the conflict more than 100,000 of the famous WD (War Department) 16H side-valve singles left the Bracebridge Street production lines.

Post-war Norton were struggling both commercially and in competition. However, two events changed their fortune. First the Bert Hopwood-designed Dominator twin sports roadster. And secondly, and more important to the Geoff Duke story, the McCandless Featherbed frame.

The latter enabled the Norton dohc single to carry on much longer than would otherwise have been possible, thus providing Geoff Duke with his early World Championship success.

As for the company, it was swallowed up by AMC (Associated Motor Cycles) during 1953. Then, in late 1962, the famous Bracebridge Street works was closed, with production moving to AMC's South East London facilities in Woolwich. AMC went into liquidation during 1966, but the Norton name lived on, thanks to Denis Poore and Manganese Bronze. This allowed a new version of the Norton twin, the Commando, to become a bestseller for the next decade, before NVT (Norton Villiers Triumph) hit the financial rocks itself at the end of the 1970s.

The 1980s and 1990s saw something of a rebirth, when a new company based in Shenstone, Warwickshire, built limited numbers of a rotary (Wankel) engine machine for both racing and road use.

A 1949 Norton advertisement exclaiming, 'A reputation built on reliability and racing successes'.

A REPUTATION BUILT ON RELIABILITY AND RACING SUCCESSES

THE UNAPPROACHABLE
Norton
THE WORLD'S BEST ROAD HOLDER

Each of the 50 riders, therefore, had the prospect of concentrating on a feet-up performance at 132 sections during the event. The top award went to BSA works star Ulsterman Bill Nicholson (BSA twin), followed by Hugh Viney (AJS), Ernie Lyons (AJS), Phil Alves (Triumph) and Geoff Duke.

Then came what *The Motor Cycle* described as 'Muddy Victory Trial', going on to report 'Mud predominated in last Saturday's 53-mile open Victory Trial held by the Birmingham MCC.' Once again Geoff secured a First Class Award (losing a total of 31 marks compared with the winner's 21).

In the Bemrose Trial, held in early April, Geoff dropped 11 marks, compared with Phil Alves (Triumph) who conceded eight. But by finishing ahead of star names like Nicholson and Viney, the Norton rider was justly proving his worth, his performances being described by *The Motor Cycle* as 'outstanding'.

Even better was his performance in the following week's Cotswold Cup Trial, when he topped the first class awards list with four marks lost, compared with the winner, Bill Nicholson, who was clean (zero marks conceded).

A scrambles debut

Mid-April 1948 saw Geoff take part in the Sunbeam Point-to-Point – the first of the season's major scrambles events. In the Senior race Geoff came home an excellent third, behind the winner Bill Nicholson (BSA Gold Star) and Phil Alves (Triumph Tiger 100). He was also part of the winning Birmingham Club team.

Geoff taking part in a scramble event at Ashgrove, near Cheltenham, summer 1948.

At the beginning of the race, Geoff's Norton (with rear springing – as against the trials model's rigid frame) was described as 'going very quickly albeit luridly and after being about 15th on the second lap had worked up to sixth place by half distance.' The report went on to say 'Duke continued to gain places and was riding so energetically that one wondered whether he could continue to stay aboard his leaping, swerving, bucking Norton' – but he did!

For the Open Travers Trial Geoff rode a three-fifty model, but although his riding was praised he was outside the awards. And it was on the same machine that he rode in the famous Scottish Six Days in early May with the number 37, between the third and eighth of the month inclusive. The Scottish – one of the very toughest of motorcycle competitions in the world – covered no less than 650 miles in the six days, with a total of 86 competitors facing the starter on the first day. And Geoff was to complete the event with a Special First Class Award for his efforts, one of 27 given.

Moto-Cross Des Nations

On 8 August 1948 Geoff took part in his first foreign dirt-bike meeting, the international Moto-Cross Des Nations in Belgium, as part of the official 12-man-strong British team, riding a 490cc Norton. The 2½-mile long La Fraineuse circuit at Spa was set up in a park and comprised virtually every type of going. *The Motor Cycle* report, dated 12 August, described the course in the following manner: 'There are narrow, woodland paths, short climbs and dips, ruts, mud, leafmould, adverse cambers and open grass-covered fields.'

In practice Geoff took a tumble – bruising his leg and arm. But as *The Motor Cycle* said, 'he made light of the damage, however, and was in good spirits throughout.' And although Belgium was to emerge the overall winners of the event, Geoff showed his potential at this level of competition by coming home in a superb fourth position against the cream of British and European stars.

1948 Moto-Cross Des Nations, Spa, Belgium

1st	N. Janson (499cc BSA)
2nd	M. Cox (498cc Triumph)
3rd	B.H.M. Viney (498cc AJS)
4th	G.E. Duke (490cc Norton)
5th	A. Milhoux (499cc BSA)
6th	B.W. Hall (498cc Matchless)

The Alan Trophy Trial

Two weeks later, on Saturday 21 August, Geoff formed part of the Manufacturer's Award-winning team at the Alan Trophy Trial, which began and ended at Bridge End, Dalston, near Carlisle. He was also a member of the winning club team (Middlesbrough and District) – and winner of the 1000cc Cup – quite a haul!

Disappointment

But there had been disappointment, which Geoff described in *In Pursuit of Perfection*:

> *with working for the most famous road-racing marque in the world, my thoughts soon turned towards road racing and, on the strength of*

a promise of support from managing director Gilbert Smith, I entered for the 1948 Senior Clubman's TT – but was turned down! The entry had been oversubscribed, and as I had no road-racing experience, my application was rejected.

Even so, Geoff did manage to gain 'the promise of the loan of a standard 350cc Manx Norton for the September Junior Manx Grand Prix – where my entry, surely one of the first submitted, was accepted.'

As Geoff readily admits:

my first-ever lap around the famous 37.73-mile TT Mountain circuit certainly made me realise the challenge it represented to a newcomer to road racing, having had so little time to learn the sequence of bends around the world's second-most-difficult road-racing circuit. Only the Nürburgring is more demanding.

As Geoff went on to say in his autobiography, 'determined to leave nothing to chance' he arrived in the Isle of Man a full week prior to the start of practice, having ridden up to Liverpool on 'my scrambles bike, suitably fitted with road tyres and higher gearing'. As for the motorcycle he was to use in the race, this was 'still on the assembly line at the Bracebridge Street factory at this time and was due to follow me by train from Birmingham, via Norton's Liverpool agent, Victor Horsman.'

A thorough preparation

Compared with most novice riders, Geoff Duke's preparation for his first race was thorough to say the least. He described this in the following manner:

In attempting to learn the circuit, I decided to go over it in three sections – from the grandstand to Kirkmichael, Kirkmichael to Ramsay, and from there back to the start. He continued: *Allowing myself two days for each section, I set off on my scrambles machine and stopped at every significant bend to study the general surroundings, walking back and forth along an imaginary racing line… and when a meal time came due or as darkness fell, I would complete the lap and then continue from the same place at the next session. Endeavouring to remember every bend from the start line to the finish, by the end of that first week I knew in my mind exactly where I was on the course at any given time.*

Isle of Man TT

For many years, certainly during the Geoff Duke era, the Isle of Man TT was the world's premier motorcycle racing event. First employed in 1911 (though in slightly different guise), the legendary Mountain Course measured 37.73 miles in length and comprised roads which were the normal traffic arteries of the Isle of Man. To avoid too much interference with everyday trade on the island the pre-race practice periods largely took place in the early hours of the morning. Closure of the roads for both practice and racing required a separate Act of the Isle of Man Parliament every year.

The start, grandstand, scoreboard and pits were situated in Glencrutchery Road, high above the town of Douglas. Soon after leaving the slight rise of Brown's Hill, followed by the drop to Quarter Bridge, a slow right-hander necessitated hard braking, engagement of bottom gear and usually the use of the clutch.

Bradden Bridge was the next landmark, a spectacular S-bend over the railway and river, then on to Union Mills three miles from the start; winding and undulating, the course dropped down to the Highlander and through the bends at Greeba to Ballacraine (7.25 miles) – a sharp right-hander.

The course was now very much out in the country, with the road twisting and turning through the leafy tunnel of the Neb Valley, past Laurel Bank and Glen Helen, then up the 1-in-10 rise of Creg Willey's Hill on to the heights of Cronk-y-Voddee. The descent of Baaregarroo before the 13th milestone section was generally held as being the fastest part of the course. It was followed by a tricky section ending with Westwood's Corner, a relatively fast left-hander.

Soon riders reached Kirkmichael (14.5 miles), with its second gear right-hander, followed by a trip through the narrow village street, after which there was a winding but fast stretch to Ballaugh – with the famous humpback bridge where both wheels left the ground. Left, right, left – the trio of Quarry Bends were taken in the region of 100mph or more, the bends leading out on to the start of the famous mile-long Sulby Straight, with, at its end, an extremely sharp right-hand corner at Sulby Bridge (20 miles). Then came hard acceleration up to and around the long, sweeping left-hander at Ginger Hall. Through wooded Kerromoar and the foot of Glen Auldyn, the circuit wound its way on to the town of Ramsey, where riders flicked right and left through Parliament Square in the very middle of the town. Then came the beginning of the long mountain climb, the road rising up May Hill to the testing Ramsey Hairpin (24.5 miles) and up again to Waterworks Corner and the Gooseneck.

Still climbing, riders passed Guthrie's Memorial and reached East Mountain Gate (28.5 miles), where the long gruelling ascent at last began to flatten out. A further mile on led to a quartet of gentle bends at the Verandah section, followed by the bumpy crossing of the mountain railway tracks at the Bungalow. The highest point on the course was at Brandywell, a left-hand sweep beyond the Bungalow, and from there the road began to fall gently, through the aptly-named Windy Corner, a medium fast right-hander and the long 33rd milestone bend.

Kate's Cottage (300 yards past Keppal Gate) marked the beginning of the flat-out, exhilarating sweep down to Creg-ny-Baa (34.5 miles). Still dropping, the course swept towards the left-hander at Brandish Corner and down yet more to the fast right-hander at Hillberry.

With less than two miles to the finish, there followed the short climb of Cronk-ny-Mona and the sharp right-hand turn at Signpost Corner. Bedstead Corner and The Nook followed in swift succession, and within a quarter of a mile it was a case of hard on the brakes for Governor's Bridge – an acute hairpin – which was the slowest corner on the course. The short detour through the hollow was a link to earlier days when it formed part of the main road. Once out of the hollow, riders accelerated into Glencrutchery Road less than half a mile from the grandstand and pit area.

In essence, the course remains the same today, when, at the beginning of the 21st century, the TT has long since lost its World Championship status. However, it still remains one of the most famous venues in motorcycle racing, attracting huge crowds every June; it was also the setting for some of Geoff Duke's greatest ever triumphs.

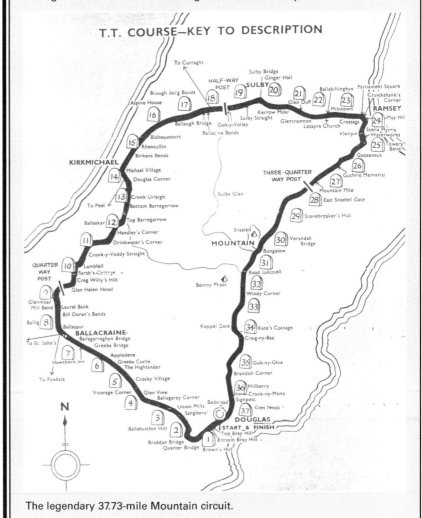

The legendary 37.73-mile Mountain circuit.

The three-fifty Manx (a standard production model) arrived on the eve of practice week, and as Geoff described when interviewed by Mick Woollett for the April 2003 issue of *Classic Bike* 'just the bike, no mechanic and no spares. And as a newcomer I was given a stern talking to by my chief marshal Doug Hanson on the lines of not trying to run before I could walk.'

And when practice finally commenced, as Geoff recalled later 'there I was, a brand new rider on a brand new Manx. It was the first time I'd ever ridden a road-racing machine of any kind! I tended to roll it off down the straight because I didn't want to burst the engine.'

The Motor Cycle dated 9 September 1948 reporting the final days of practice said 'scanning through the "Who's Who" in the programme, one sees that of the individual entries, well over 50 are newcomers to the Isle of Man circuit. Is there a potential star among the new men?' If only they had known!

With a fastest lap in practice of 'about 33 minutes', Geoff was 'way off the pace but I was happy because I knew I could go faster'. Even so, official practice times show Geoff to have been modest, as on the Friday, 3 September, Geoff had tied for third quickest (with Dickie Dale), with a lap of 32.23. And *The Motor Cycle* reported 'On his Junior Norton, G.E. Duke was riding in a party with two other machines at Union Mills, one of which he passed just after the top bend. Duke appeared to be one of the fastest men.' Another report said 'G.E. Duke was fast, neat and steady.'

Postponed

The 1948 Junior Manx Grand Prix was postponed from the scheduled Tuesday until the following day, Wednesday 8 September, owing to bad weather conditions, *The Motor Cycle* commenting 'The island was enveloped in searing rain, with visibility only a few yards.' And what a difference 24 hours made, the next day saw blue skies and soon dry roads all around the course.

And so the race got under way for a scheduled six laps (226.38 miles), and as *The Motor Cycle* commented 'This race is a departure for Duke, whose name is usually associated with trials and scrambles. If he shows the same aptitude for racing, he has a brilliant future.'

And Geoff immediately showed his potential by coming through at the end of lap one in third position – what a start to his career as a tarmac racer! By the end of the next lap he was joint second, and at the end of lap three he sensationally led the race. Then came the disappointing news that Geoff had retired at the Mountain Box with a seized engine caused by a split oil tank. But with Norton's managing director Gilbert Smith and race supremo

Joe Craig on the island he had, in three laps, shown enough of his prowess to mark him as a future star.

But as Geoff was to reveal later, Bill Clark (who worked as mechanic for Eric Langton, a top speedway star of the era), who was over on holiday, was 'manning my pit to give me signals... and we agreed that he would just give me my previous lap time – no race position or anything like that'. So even when Geoff had come in to refuel at the end of the third lap, Bill did not tell him his real position, saying only 'you're doing alright'. Geoff said 'I think he was afraid to say anything else in case I tried to go quicker and fell off.'

Back to the dirt

After the Manx GP, Geoff returned to dirt-bikes, winning the Frank Jones Cup for the best over-350cc performance at the Kidson Scramble at Bluith Wells towards the end of September, on his 490cc ohv Norton.

And trials were not forgotten, with a First Class Award being gained in early October in the Liverpool Motor Club's Reliance Trial on a three-fifty Norton. Another First Class Award came later that month in the Southern Trial – and also part of the winning Birmingham club team (with Bill Nicholson and Norman Vanhouse). This was followed by more success in the John Douglas Trophy Trial.

Geoff also competed in his second-ever road race, at the Ansty airfield circuit near Coventry. And what a performance he put in, finishing fourth in the 350cc final behind Ted Frend (AJS), and Velocette riders Bob Foster and David Whitworth.

More scrambling

The famous Lancashire Grand National Scramble was certainly a highlight in Geoff's 1948 dirt-bike season and not only did he record a magnificent third overall, and first in the 350cc machine awards, but also the coveted Ashes Casket for the top-performing rider in the Lancs versus Yorks contest. Also the North beat the South in both legs to make Lancashire boy Geoff a happy man.

Then, at the end of November came the British Experts' Trial, where Geoff (riding a 348cc Norton) lost 35 marks, compared with the winner Hugh Viney's (347cc AJS) 10, to finish 10th overall; still an excellent performance when one considers that virtually every top-trials man took part.

Solo champion of the North

Geoff rounded off 1948 by winning the Northern Experts' Trial in the week leading up to Christmas, his first major victory in a competitive motorcycling event. In the 23 December issue of *The Motor Cycle*, coverage of the event began:

> *In the Northern Experts' Trial held near Buxton on Sunday, that up-and-coming young man Geoff Duke added further to his stature, and still more firmly consolidated his reputation as the number-one trials rider of the North.*

However, in the same issue came news of Charles Markham's death in a road accident at Great Brickhill, south of Bletchley, while on his way from London to Birmingham on 13 December. Aged 36, Charles was at the time the Midland editorial representative for *Motor Cycling*.

Geoff Duke had lost not only a great friend, but a valuable mentor.

And so came to an end Geoff's first year with Norton, one of both highs and lows, but one in which he had built a number of important foundations for his future career.

At the beginning of 1949 it was announced that the official works Norton riders for the coming season on Norton trials and scrambles machinery would be Geoff, plus A.J. Blackwell and R.B. Young on solos, and A.J. Humphries on sidecar.

Around the same time it was reported that Geoff had been experimenting with a set of flywheels from the 596cc side-valve Big 4 Norton, these being some 4lb heavier than those normally to be found in Duke's ohv 490cc trial mount. But although the ploy worked, in Geoff's own words, he found 'the traction of the trials Norton so smooth in mud that there was no "bite" at the rear tyre'. Moreover, when he shut off, the momentum of the heavier flywheels prevented the engine from slowing down quickly, and the result, strange as it may seem, was still more spin. Really heavy flywheels in trials models, he thought, 'might be justified on dry, rocky going' such as the Scottish Six Days, but in mud – it was not for him.

Road racing

After competing in Derbyshire at the Bemrose Trial on Saturday 3 April 1949, Geoff Duke travelled south to race at Haddenham on a 348cc Manx machine. Huge crowds witnessed Geoff's first road-racing victory, when he beat none other than Les Graham (who had told him there was no chance of racing at AMC, see Chapter One) in the 350cc final, Les then being the leader of the AJS works team – and the man who would later that year become the first-ever 500cc world champion. Graham was mounted on an AJS 7R.

Les Graham won the first ever 500cc World Championship title on an AJS Porcupine in 1949. Later he joined the Italian MV Agusta team and was largely responsible for helping develop the four-cylinder model into a competitive machine. He was fatally injured when he crashed in the 1953 Senior TT.

Les Graham

Born on 14 September 1911, Robert Leslie Graham spent what would undoubtedly have been his greatest racing years in the service of his king and country. He won the DFC (Distinguished Flying Cross) for his wartime exploits as a Royal Air Force bomber pilot, but he was also a skilled engineer and, perhaps most importantly, in his post-war racing career, a man of considerable bravery and skill, and a born leader.

During the early 1930s he dearly wished to race, but his meagre resources restricted these dreams to an occasional outing at a grass-track or short-circuit event. And it was not until 1936, when he rode in the Ulster Grand Prix, that his name figured on the entry list at an international meeting. At the end of 1937 he joined the OK Supreme factory, both as a rider and to oversee the building of the overhead camshaft road and racing models. And so, on an OK Supreme, Les made his debut in the 1938 Lightweight (250cc) TT, in which he finished 12th. Then, on the eve of war in 1939, Les rode the CTS (Chris Tattershall Special) in the Lightweight, but was forced to retire with gearbox trouble on the sixth lap.

Then came the war, where he rose to the rank of Flight Lieutenant. When he finally left the service in 1946, his urge to race was even greater. And so he joined AJS as one of its official teamsters. But ill luck was to dog him repeatedly and, although then aged 37, he became the first holder of the blue riband 500cc World Championship title in 1949 (on an AJS Porcupine twin) – a Senior TT victory was to elude him. For example, that same year Les was leading the race comfortably on the final lap when at Hillberry he was forced out, with only a couple of miles to the finish line, with a fractured magneto armature spindle. He pushed in, where, as *The Motor Cycle* race report said, 'he was cheered every yard of that arduous two miles', to finally finish 10th.

At the end of 1950 Les signed for the Italian MV Agusta company. And

LES. GRAHAM

the Englishman played a major role in the subsequent development of both the four and single-cylinder designs. Because of this, success did not come until 1952, when he finished runner-up behind the combination of Masetti and Gilera.

The first round of the 1953 Championships was the Isle of Man TT; Les won the 125cc event, and many expected that he would enjoy victory in the Senior event a few days later and also have world title prospects. However, these hopes were to end in tragedy when MV's team leader lost control of his Earles-forked five-hundreds MV four at the bottom of Bray Hill. In the ensuing crash he was killed instantly. Following his death, MV Agusta abandoned the bigger classes until almost the end of that season, and development of the four did not really get back on track until John Surtees joined the team for the 1956 season.

Les was survived by his wife Edna and sons Stuart and Christopher. Stuart went on to become a top liner, riding works bikes for both Honda and Suzuki.

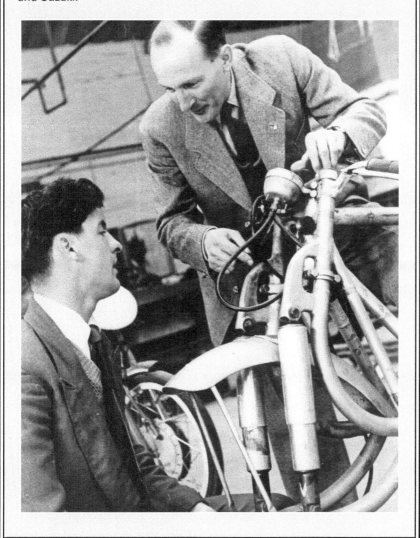

Les (right) and the 1952 125cc world champion Cecil Sandford discussing the Ernie Earles-designed front suspension used by MV on their fours from mid-1952.

Norton 500T

In January 1948, the same month Geoff Duke joined the Norton company, a new off-road model made its bow; this was the 500T (Trials), developed by Artie Bell and Rex McCandless. As the 29 January 1948 issue of *The Motor Cycle* reported, 'In their latest design of 500cc trials machine (still in prototype form), Norton have managed to save about 60lb in weight. They have also shortened the wheelbase to 52½in and increased ground clearance to nearly 7½in.'

Major among the changes was the re-introduction of the frame type employed on the pre-war models 16H and 18. Norton sources said they 'hoped that the first production models will appear in the spring'. Actually, the 500T did not go on general sale until much later that year – for the 1949 model year.

So how had the weight been saved? First, the diamond-type frame was considerably lighter than the triangulated cradle variety. Next, there was a lightweight (steel) petrol tank (with a capacity of 2½ gallon), and the method of fixing was, said *The Motor Cycle*, 'entirely new'. One single bolt was employed, this being centrally disposed at the rear end of the tank, with a rubber bush to fight vibration. On the top tube of the machine there was a lug with a tapped boss, into which this fixing bolt was screwed – after it had passed through the rear end of the tank. The front of the tank was held in place thanks to two locating points, comprising two circular horizontal extensions at the top of the front downtube, while at each side of the tank there were rubber bushed sockets into which the aforementioned extensions matched up. The tank, therefore, was fitted on to the front mountings and then locked into position by the way of the single rearward bolt; it was a simple and speedy way of both fitting and removal.

The wheelbase of the 500T was reduced by shortening the rear frame stays and fitting new fork yokes, the latter bringing the fork tubes back in line with the steering column.

Introduced at the same time as Geoff Duke joined the Norton company in January 1948, the 490cc 500T was a purpose-built trials model upon which the young Duke was to gain a string of successes.

It must be said that the engine was an extremely tight fit in the frame, so tight in fact that the rocker box of the 490cc (79 x 100mm) ohv single could not be removed without taking the cylinder head off first!

The gearbox was the old pre-war Sturmey-Archer pattern, as Roy Bacon said 'tucked into the small space left for it between the back of the crankcase and the rear wheel'. The 'box was equipped with wide rations and a folding kickstart lever'.

The engine was essentially the standard production overhead-valve type, but with a bi-metal aluminium head and linered cylinder barrel of the same material. Internally, components such as the cams and flywheels were stock ES2 components, while the three-ring piston had a compression ration of 6:1.

Considerable attention had been applied to general weight-saving; this included the fitment of several alloy items, such as mudguards, engine plates and the lightning of the 5½-inch front brake, which also came with an alloy brake plate.

As for the exhaust, this was tucked in close to the offside (right) crankcase, below the timing cover, and then rearwards to a silencer of special lightweight construction.

Even, as Geoff Duke said, 'my trials riding was only moderately successful as I found the 500T Norton much more of a handful than my previous 350 BSA'.

Next, on Easter Monday 18 April 1949, Geoff was in action at Blandford Camp, Dorset, in front of some 25,000 spectators. Here again he tasted victory, when he won his heat from none other than Harold Daniell, riding one of the very latest factory Nortons (our hero riding a standard Manx model running on alcohol fuel). In the final Geoff was forced to accept second best to Les Graham on the AJS, but the runner-up spot was still a superb performance.

In early May 1949 Geoff competed in the Scottish Six Days Trial for the first time.

The Scottish

In early May Geoff competed in the Scottish Six Days for the first time. He was consistently up with the leaders all week, finally finishing with a mere 38 marks lost against that of the winner, Hugh Viney, with 18 marks conceded. Geoff rode a works 500T machine. In addition, the Manufacturer's Team Prize went to Norton (A.J. Blackwell, R.B. Young, plus Geoff). By now it was becoming obvious that in all three disciplines of the sport the name G.E. Duke was equally successful, whether it be road racing, scrambling or trials. In 1949 Geoff could truthfully have been described as the most promising all-rounder in British motorcycle sport. It seemed everywhere he went he was immediately on the pace.

The Scottish Six Days Trial

All premier trophies were again won on

DUNLOP

The North West 200

Next Geoff crossed the Irish Sea to Ulster for the annual North West 200 road races, held over the 11-mile triangular Portstewart–Coleraine–Portrush circuit.

The racing was held in 'near-ideal conditions' (*The Motor Cycle*), and with works entries from not only Norton but also AJS and Velocette the competition was tough to say the least.

It is worth pointing out at this stage that Joe Craig had been replaced as team manager of the Norton squad for the 1949 season (to enable him to liaise with the Bourne, Lincolnshire-based BRM company concerning the four-cylinder racing engine). His replacement was the well respected Norton tuner Steve Lancefield (who also happened to be Harold Daniell's brother-in-law).

Unlike the official Norton works men (Daniell, plus Johnny Lockett and Artie Bell), Geoff Duke was riding his standard production 1948 Manx Grand Prix machine in the 350cc class at the North West. And with his bike he travelled by train from Birmingham to Liverpool, as Geoff says 'walking the bike to the Belfast boat for the night crossing'. On arrival he was met the following morning by the local Norton distributor 'who kindly provided transport to get me and my machine to Portstewart'.

During practice the inlet valve seat was damaged 'by a small stone' that had been sucked in by the carburettor. Unfortunately, Geoff 'possessed only a limited tool kit'. However, as he described in *In Pursuit of Perfection*:

> *The factory mechanics, all friends of mine, allowed me to use a corner of the garage where I could remove the cylinder head and repair the damaged valve seat with the aid of their comprehensive tools. While in the process of doing this, I went off for lunch – only to return to find my Norton with all its bits and pieces out on the pavement. The mechanics told me that Mr Lancefield had arrived and, seeing my machine in the corner, had simply uttered one word: Out!*

Luckily the weather was good, so Geoff continued his repairs out in the street, with 'occasional unofficial words of encouragement and advice from the works mechanics'. The damaged valve seat 'really needed recutting', but as no suitable equipment was available Geoff was forced to complete the job 'with elbow grease and grinding paste'.

By the time all this was complete and the engine re-assembled, practice was over, so it was a case of having to go direct into the race.

Geoff himself describes the 76-strong entry for the 350cc race as 'formidable'. And this is no understatement, with Harold Daniell, the Velocette pairing of Freddie Frith and Ken Bills, plus Reg Armstrong and Bill

Doran on AJS machines – all official works entries with the very latest machinery.

At the end of lap one Daniells led from Frith, Doran, Armstrong, Bills and Geoff. *The Motor Cycle* report said '50 yards covered all six men'. After Bills crashed (suffering a broken collar bone) and Doran was forced out with gearbox gremlins, it was, as *The Motor Cycle* described:

Duke's opportunity – he had been riding with the aplomb of a star of long experience. He had an advantage of nearly one minute over Armstrong, but was, of course, well out of touch with the leading pair – Daniell and Frith – who were still circulating as if in tow.

In the end, the race went to an extra lap due to no chequered flag being shown. And, after the additional lap, Daniell won by a machine's length in what *The Motor Cycle* said 'must have been one of the closest finishes ever seen in a near-200-mile international road race'.

And a rostrum position – on a new circuit, with a standard motorcycle, when confronted by highly-experienced riders on full factory models – put the name of Geoff Duke on everyone's lips that day.

350cc North West 200 – 17 laps – 188 miles

1st   H.L. Daniell (Norton)
2nd   F.L. Firth (Velocette)
3rd   G.E. Duke (Norton)
4th   R. Armstrong (AJS)
5th   J.F. Kentish (AJS)
6th   A.E. Moule (Norton)

The Clubman's TT

Next on Geoff's schedule came the Clubman's TT – in effect a year later than it should have been in the up-and-coming rider's career. Practice for this was to be held on Saturday 4, Thursday 9 and Friday 10 June, from 4.45am and on Monday 6 and Tuesday 7 June, from 6.30pm.

And his machine? A 490cc overhead cam International single, loaned by the factory, Geoff's race number being 23 in the 500cc race.

During the very first practice session for the Clubman's TT competitors, Geoff showed he meant business. This is an extract from *The Motor Cycle* report:

Signpost Corner, that difficult right-angle turn after Cronk-ny-Mona,

Clubman's TT

The Clubman's TT ran for a decade, from 1947 through to 1956, and it was to prove a stepping stone for several future stars including Geoff Duke and Bob McIntyre.

It was in January 1947 that the ACU (Auto Cycle Union) announced that it was to stage the first-ever Clubman's TT in its Isle of Man programme. At the time some details had yet to be decided, but sufficient information was released so clubs and clubmen could begin to make their plans. The race was to be staged over four laps of the famous 37.73-mile Mountain course and would be open to nominated clubmen riding machines between 251 and 1000cc which were catalogued models, fully equipped. However, the exact definition of these last two words had yet to be fully clarified. For example, *The Motor Cycle* in their 16 January 1947 issue wondered if a racing machine such as a Manx Norton would be eligible.

Practicing was to be undertaken at different times to that of the Junior, Senior and Lightweight international TTs. And an interesting feature was that there would be compulsory refuelling during the race. A club entering a rider would be called upon to declare that the motorcycle concerned was according to the manufacturers' catalogue, which had to have been printed and published prior to the date on which entries closed. Some changes would be allowed, but only related to components such as spark plugs, tyres and chains.

As for the entry fee, this was to be two guineas (two pounds, two shillings), and the club entering the winning rider was to receive the Clubman's Tourist Trophy and the rider a replica of this trophy.

The following month, February 1947, *The Motor Cycle* columnist 'Ixion' had this to say: 'The Clubman's TT is a bold experiment. The success or sudden death of the Wednesday race mainly pivots on (a) the enthusiasm with which clubs support it, and (b) the success of the officials in eliminating camouflaged trade machines (the terms "amateur" and "standard" are any organisers nightmare).'

In total, 65 entries were made for the inaugural Clubman's TT, held in June 1947. Several of these riders were to become well-known names in the sport during later years: Arthur Wheeler, Les Archer, Eric Cheney, Fron Purslow, Denis Parkinson, Allan Jefferies, Don Crossley, Phil Heath and Syd Lawton to name but a few. The three class winners were to be Eric Briggs (Senior), Denis Parkinson (Junior) and Basil Keys (Lightweight).

Twelve months later the Clubman's entry list had swollen to 101 – a full house as regards the number allowed in a TT at that time. The winner of the Senior event (riding a 998cc Vincent) was J.D. Daniels.

By 1949 there were now simply too many entries for a single race to cope with. The Juniors (now referred to as the 350cc) ran concurrently with the 1000cc machines, whereas the 500cc bikes had their own event, as did the Lightweights – the latter being given their own two-lap race. The 1949 Clubman's was notable on two counts: it provided future world champion Geoff Duke with his first major road-race victory (in the 500cc on an International Norton) and the BSA Gold Star scored its first TT win (Harold Clark, three-fifty).

In 1950 a ballot had to be held for the forthcoming Clubman's TT, so large were the entries. By now the 350cc class had become most popular. In the race six of the first 12 were Gold Stars, including first and second (B.A. Jackson and I. McGuffie).

By the time entries closed for the 1951 Clubman's races there were virtually full houses for both the Junior and Senior events, but those for the 250 and 1000cc were so poor that these later classes were axed from the calendar.

Of the 41 finishers for the Junior race, over half were mounted on BSA Gold Stars, with the winner being Brian Purslow. His time for the four-lap, 150.92-mile race was 2 hours 10 seconds (75.36mph). The fastest lap was set by Norton-mounted K.R.V. James in 29 minutes 35 seconds (76.54mph). The Senior event was won by I.K. Archer (Norton), with Ivor Wickstead (Triumph) setting the fastest lap at 81.06mph.

When the 1952 Clubman's TT regulations were published in January that year, a new rule had been introduced: 'After Thursday 29 May, any machine bearing racing number plates, whether observed or not, must not be used on any Isle of Man public highway except during practice hours and during the 15 minutes immediately before and after the official periods.' This directive also went on to say that any rider guilty of a breach of this regulation would be fined £5 and might be excluded from the races. Machines had to comply with local road fund licence and insurance requirements. This measure, it was said, had been forced on the organisers by what *The Motor Cycle* of 17 January 1952 described as 'those thoughtless few who, in past years, have caused annoyance to the Isle of Man police and residents, by riding at high speeds on open roads.'

When entries closed, there were a total of 105 riders for the Junior Clubman's, including reserves. No less than 75 of these were BSA Gold Star mounted.

And another name destined for future greatness made his Isle of Man debut in the 1952 Clubman's Junior TT: Glasgow Mercury Club member R. McIntyre. But although Bob had the distinction of setting the fastest lap in 28 minutes 16.4 seconds (80.09mph), he did not win the race. Instead, this honour went to Chesterfield's Eric Houseley, who completed the four-lap event in 1 hour 54 minutes 28.2 seconds, averaging 78.92mph. Both Bob and Eric rode BSA Gold Star machines, as did the fourth, fifth, seventh, eighth, ninth and 12th men home.

The Clubman's TT was destined to continue for another four years – even then it was the success of the BSA over other marques which finally sealed its fate. But it was responsible for producing two of the world's greatest racing stars during its 10-year history.

was chosen as the vantage point this morning. It proved to be an exciting one! Riding was very patchy, and approximately one in three of the riders on the course had to make use of the slip road. Many of the others only just scrapped round. However, there was also riding worthy of being described as brilliant. Outstanding was G.E. Duke.

It was Geoff who put in the quickest lap, in 30 mins 7 sec, and next came the vastly-experienced Allan Jefferies on a Triumph Tiger 100. And as the

Geoff's first Isle of Man victory came in June 1949, in the 500cc Clubman's TT. He is seen here at Governors Bridge on a 490cc International Norton. He not only set a new class record average speed of 82.97mph, but also a record lap of 83.70mph.

practice week progressed, it was these two riders who were being tipped as the most likely pair for the Senior Clubman's race.

But behind the scenes Geoff was far from happy with his machine, later describing the 1949 Senior Clubman's as 'one of my most worrying races of my career'. He described his bike in the following words: 'Although distantly related to the production racing Manx, in having an overhead-camshaft engine with an alloy cylinder head and barrel, that is really where all similarity between an International model ended.' He continued: 'The International was both heavy and equipped with near-useless brakes.'

If all the above was not enough, the Clubman's race regulations stipulated that the engine had to be kick-started at the fall of the starter's flag; as he found it difficult to kick over, Geoff modified the length of the kick-start lever by some two inches, by welding in an additional piece of steel tubing. As Geoff said, 'The greater swing this provided was sufficient to carry the piston over compression and solved any problem.'

Besides the inadequate brakes and weight, the International engine had suffered from excessive cam lobe wear when run for sustained periods at high speeds. And so a lubrication modification had recently been introduced, by providing a central oil feed to the cambox. However, Geoff was not sure if this change was acceptable by the ACU (the sport's governing body), and:

Here Geoff shakes hands with 46-year-old
Cyril 'Pop' Taft, after the former's 1949
Clubman success. Taft had won the
Clubman's Lightweight event.

because I worked at Nortons it was forbidden for my engine to be modified, but when I presented the machine, the chief scrutineer, Vic Antice, commented "what, no central oil feed to the cambox?" Apparently, the modification was acceptable, and I could hardly wait to push my machine to the Norton service depot in Ford Street to have the work carried out.

In *The Motor Cycle's* Clubman's race report it stated:

G.E. Duke has long been whispered as an embryo Handley, Woods, Guthrie, Frith and Bell... His riding today wrung breathless stammering plaudits from the microphone observers around the course, who acclaimed him as 'in a class by himself' among the clubmen.

And so it was, with Geoff leading from beginning to end, completing the race distance in 1 hour 21 minutes 53 seconds, an average speed of 82.99mph; he also set a new class lap record of 27 minutes 3 seconds (83.70mph), the latter being over 1mph quicker than the previous Clubman's TT lap record set by George Brown in 1948, riding a 998cc Vincent v-twin.

500 Clubman's TT – 3 laps – 113.19 miles
1st	G.E. Duke (Norton International)
2nd	A. Jefferies (Triumph Tiger 100)
3rd	L. Starr (Triumph Tiger 100)
4th	P.H. Carter (Norton International)
5th	T.P. Crebbin (Triumph Tiger 100)
6th	E. Andrew (Norton International)

Ansty revisited

Geoff made a return to the Ansty circuit (he had ridden there the previous autumn) on Saturday 25 June 1949 and put in a performance which can only be described as outstanding. Riding his three-fifty Manx Norton, he won both his heat and the final against highly-rated opposition, including the likes of Australian star Harry Hinton (Norton) and Scarborough specialist S.T. Barnett (AJS). *The Motor Cycle* described Geoff as riding 'in a very, very stylish manner.' And there is absolutely no doubt that his had been an exceptional performance that late June day.

An unexpected setback

At the beginning of July, some two and a half weeks after his Clubman's TT victory, Geoff had entered the Skerries 100 in the South of Ireland, a meeting organised by the Dublin and District Motorcycle Club, with Geoff riding his three-fifty Manx. But after setting the fastest 350cc lap at 74.52mph, Geoff suffered his first serious racing accident. This is how he described the incident himself:

> *I had a battle royal with Manliff Barrington on Francis Beart's Lightweight Norton, and was leading until disaster struck. Going through a fast S-bend, which had a grass verge on the left and a high hawthorn hedge on the right-hand side of the road, I caught my left footrest on an obstruction in the grass. This lifted the machine upright and I was catapulted off and through the top of the hedge. Meanwhile, my riderless machine carried on through the hedge as well!*

The result of this incident was a broken left leg, the plaster of which was only to be removed 'a few days before practice began for the Manx Grand Prix in September.' But Geoff says he 'felt fine and was raring to go, although push-starting was rather difficult'.

But even as late as Saturday 3 September there was press speculation as to whether Geoff would be riding, as besides his leg injury it had been rumoured that his back had been giving him trouble, to quote the man himself: 'lots of razor-sharp thorns had pierced my leathers and embedded in my very bruised back.'

Practice begins

Monday 5 September saw the 1949 Manx GP practice begin with Geoff taking his Junior Norton out (he was also entered for the first time on a 499cc Manx machine). During the session things began to dry out all around the course, after a wet start. *The Motor Cycle* reported: 'Seen at Governor's Bridge, Geoff Duke was very neat.' Bill Lomas (Velocette) was the fastest of the three-fifties that day, with Geoff fifth.

Out on his Senior mount for the first time, on Wednesday 7 September, Geoff once again posted the fifth-quickest time at 29 minutes 36 seconds – almost two and a half minutes slower than the fastest man, Crommie McCandless, riding a Beart Norton. Geoff's five-hundred had only been finished after he had left Birmingham for the island. He described his first outing as 'disconcerting, to say the least', going on to explain 'it was quite a handful, and when braking hard for Sulby Bridge, the machine weaved so

badly I thought it would throw me off!' However, when back in the workshop after practice it:

> *revealed twice the correct amount of oil in one front fork and none in the other. I suppose a tea-break at the factory must have intervened after the required amount of oil had been poured into one leg; the worker had probably forgotten which side he had filled and, without checking, had poured a second dose into the same leg, leaving the other side empty. After draining and refilling both sides correctly, though, the handling expected from a Norton was once again restored.*

And by the next practice on the five-hundred Geoff was fastest, with a lap of 27 minutes 23 seconds and a speed of 82.69mph. Conditions were both windy and wet, the latter at certain parts of the course.

On Friday, Geoff took his Junior Norton out and was reported as 'pretty to watch'; later it was learnt that he had stopped at the end of Sulby Straight to take a plug reading.

By the end of the practice week the name G.E. Duke was being banded about as a possible Senior winner, together with Crommie McCandless. *The Motor Cycle* commenting: 'Both have a touch of real genius in their riding and it would seem that if both have mechanically trouble-free rides, a battle royal will develop.'

And *The Motor Cycle's* prediction was pretty much spot on – with McCandless emerging victorious in the Junior and Geoff second. However, that was only half the story, because with a starting number of 97, Mr Duke had to contend with the problems of overhauling and passing masses of slower riders. And on the fifth lap this was to prove decisive, when he was forced to take avoiding action to prevent a collision, eventually dropping his machine, bending the left footrest and rear brake pedal, and stalling the engine. But so, even without a rear brake and clutch problems, he still came home runner-up at the end of the six-lap, 226.38-mile race. One commentator described Geoff's performance as 'tigerish'.

A Manx Grand Prix victory

Geoff was able to reverse the result in the Senior race, held two days later on Thursday 15 September, not only this but in the process winning at a record speed of 86.063mph – setting a new lap record for the Manx Grand Prix on lap two in 25 minutes 53 second, at a speed of 87.480mph. The duel between Crommie McCandless and Geoff was described in *The Motor Cycle* as being 'brilliant'. Conditions were near perfect, with the sun shining

Later in 1949 Geoff returned to the Isle of Man for the Manx Grand Prix. He won the Senior – again breaking race and lap records.

on the grandstands as the riders formed up for the start, while the wind had abated and was now best described as a breeze.

McCandless started number two, with Geoff at 23. By the end of the first lap Duke was the fifth man on the road, and both he and McCandless had broken the Senior Manx Grand Prix lap record (held since 1938 by Ken Bills – who then had the advantage of petrol-benzole fuel).

Perhaps the most significant thing about Geoff's 1949 Senior Manx GP victory was that his average speed for the race of 86.063mph was only 0.865mph outside the 1949 Senior TT average of 86.928mph!

Another interesting fact was that Geoff had been part of the winning club teams for both the Junior and Senior races. In both cases it was the BMCRC (British Motor Cycle Racing Club) A team.

A winning double at Scarborough

In a season of outstanding performances Geoff's debut at the North Yorkshire Oliver's Mount road circuit at Scarborough, over Friday 23 and Saturday 24 September, can only be described as incredible, when, under slippery conditions, he circled the 2 miles 780 yards in 2 minutes 31.6 seconds (58.09mph) to set a new outright lap record for the tortuous course. The previous record, held by George Brown riding a 998cc Vincent, had stood at 2 minutes 31.8 seconds (57.94mph). Not only this, but Geoff won the 350 and 500cc races. And although the meeting did not hold

Geoff seen here sitting astride his race-winning 1949 Senior Manx GP machine, with Crommie McCandless (who finished runner-up); Francis Beart (with darkglasses) is centre.

international status, several well-known foreign stars took part. There were three heats for the 350cc race, with Geoff winning his from Bill Doran (AJS) and Dickie Dale (Velocette); the Belgian champion Auguste Goffin (Norton) was sixth. The other heats were won by Jack Brett (Norton) and E. Andrew (AJS). In the final, run over 20 laps, *The Motor Cycle* race reporter said it all: 'Duke, riding with brilliance, increased his lead'. No one else could get near him; the finishing order was as follows:

350cc Scarborough – 20 laps – 48 miles

1st	G.E. Duke (Norton)
2nd	S.T. Barnett (AJS)
3rd	A. Goffin (AJS)
4th	J.P.E. Hodgkin (AJS)
5th	R.H. Dale (Velocette)
6th	P. Monneret (Velocette)

In the 500cc class the heat winners were J. Brett, R.H. Dale and R.F. Walker (all riding Nortons), with Geoff placed second behind Dale in Heat two.

In the final, held in far from perfect conditions, Geoff took the lead from S.T. Barnett on the third lap. Then on his sixth circuit, Duke set a new circuit lap record of 2 minutes 31.6 seconds. 'How did he do it in such conditions?' *The Motor Cycle* report asked. 'One can only say that here was a master, riding with inspiration.'

500cc Scarborough – 20 laps – 48 miles

1st	G.E. Duke (Norton)
2nd	R.H. Dale (Norton)
3rd	S.T. Barnett (Norton)
4th	J. Brett (Norton)
5th	A. Goffin (Triumph)
6th	G. Monneret (348cc AJS)

The awards on the Saturday evening were made by the well-known radio star of the time Wilfred Pickles.

Joining the works team

It was only after his Senior Manx Grand Prix victory that Geoff was asked if he would like to join the Norton works racing team for the 1950 season, the official announcement being made in the press on 20 October 1949. But

Four times world sidecar champion, Eric Oliver was champion in 1949, 1950, 1951 and 1953.

Eric Oliver

Englishman Eric Oliver was a teammate of Geoff Duke's during the latter's factory Norton racing career. And even though the two only rode together as part of the successful record-breaking team at Montlhéry in 1950, the two men had a genuine respect for each other and both won multi world titles in the same team, albeit, in Eric Oliver's case, on three wheels not two.

Born in 1918, Eric rode solo bikes before concentrating his efforts on three wheels following World War Two, and is remembered for his never-say-die, forceful racing style.

A tough, independent character, Eric Oliver paid great attention to every detail of his racing: studying other teams, practising his starts and racing techniques, and not forgetting the mechanical preparation of his highly successful Norton machinery, on which he won countless races and no less than four World Championship titles.

Eric's first experience of racing came in pre-war days, and in 1937 he competed in the Isle of Man, as he did the following year in both Senior and Junior events. His best solo performance in the Isle of Man occurred in 1948, when, on a Velocette Mark VIII KTT, he came home eighth in the Junior race, averaging 76.94mph (he also rode the same bike to 10th in the Senior race a few days later).

Already a member of the 'Continental Circus' by the time the first World Championship series was staged in 1949, Eric and his passenger Denis (Jenks) Jenkinson won two of the three rounds on their dohc Norton single and Watsonian sidecar. The pairing gained victories in Switzerland and Belgium, then, at the final round in Italy, they finished fifth.

In 1950, this time with Italian Lorenzo Dobelli as ballast, Oliver thwarted a serious challenge from Gilera (who had won the final round in 1949). Dobelli was again the passenger when Eric gained his third consecutive

Eric in typical racing pose. All his world titles were won on Norton machinery.

title in 1951 and might well have done so again the following year, but an accident in France, combined with a retirement through a sidecar wheel problem, cost him dearly.

In 1953, with new partner Stan Dibben, Oliver became champion for the fourth and final time. Although he won the first Sidecar TT since the 1920s, in 1954 he finally had to give way in the continental GPs to the additional power of the factory-entered BMW twins.

He retired the following year to concentrate on his Staines, Middlesex, motorcycle dealership, where he was a main agent for several marques, including, of course, Norton.

Then, in 1958, he made a famous comeback to the sport, when, passengered by Mrs Pat Wise, the pair drove to 10th place in the Sidecar TT, with a near standard road-going Norton Dominator 88 pushrod twin and Watsonian Monaco sports chair. It was generally agreed to have been an incredible achievement, both for driver and machine.

Then it was back to his business. Eric died in 1981 after suffering heart problems for several years, aged 63.

Record breaking at Montlhéry, October 1949.

Norton's record-breaking team at Montlhéry, just south of Paris, France, in October 1949. It was Geoff's first event as part of the works racing team.

his first taste of being part of this exclusive club came not in road racing, but instead at Montlhéry, record breaking. Montlhéry, some 12 miles south of the French capital Paris, with its high-speed banking, had been considered the number-one venue for many years in continental Europe, and with the demise of Brooklands, it now enjoyed a similar status with the British.

As Geoff explained in his autobiography:

At that time, the Norton team, with the machines, used to travel around the Continent by rail, utilising their local agent's road transport on arrival at the nearest railway station to the race circuit. On this occasion, however, it was decided that Artie Bell and I would take two machines plus spares and equipment over to France in my Ford V8 van. Joe Craig and the mechanics (Charlie Edwards and Frank Sharatt) travelled by train and boat, while the third rider, Eric Oliver, met us in Paris at the premises of the Norton agent, Monsieur Garreau, where final preparation of the machines was to be carried out.

And for around a week this little party waited for favourable conditions before making the record attempt. Finally, on Tuesday 27 October Eric Oliver got things under way when he wheeled out the 596cc-engined sidecar outfit. As *The Motor Cycle* reported in its 3 November 1949 issue, 'He thundered off, intent on putting the one-hour sidecar record up to 100mph.'

Strangely, although Eric managed to break other records, the one-hour sidecar record (which stood at 92mph, set by the Frenchman Amort on a 574cc Ghome-et-Rhone at Montlhéry in 1934) was not broken, as two attempts ended in failure due to the rear tyre wearing out on both occasions before the hour was up, when the Norton outfit had been averaging in excess of the 100mph mark.

The following day, Wednesday, was too windy for any attempt. Instead, as *The Motor Cycle* revealed:

> *therefore, of making onslaught against records in the solo 350cc class, Bell, Duke and Oliver (who was also the third solo rider) were to be found with Joe Craig and the mechanics in one of the neat workshop-garages housed beneath the high banking of the track.*

Conditions were much improved on Thursday, and so the same three riders between them broke six world records in the solo class. These new records were as follows:

2 hours	101.05mph
3 hours	101.10mph
4 hours	100.19mph
5 hours	100.09mph
500 kilometres	101.04mph
500 miles	100.106mph

Friday was another successful day. The five-hundred Norton was taken out, and the solo 500cc two-hour record raised to 111.85mph. But then further attempts in this class were abandoned owing to a footrest coming loose. However, Eric Oliver took out the 596cc sidecar machine and proceeded to shatter three more world sidecar records, to add to the three records he had already achieved on the first day.

In total the team broke 21 world speed records, with Joe Craig commenting:

> *All the records we have just put up were world records; the engines have been measured and checked. Officials here have*

Artie Bell, Eric Oliver and Geoff (pictured left to right) at Montlhéry.

The Montlhéry banking seen during Norton's successful attempt – the team broke no fewer than 21 world speed records.

been very co-operative. A thing that struck us all is how useful it would be if one had such a track as Montlhéry at home.

The 500cc solo record applied also to the 750cc and 1000cc classes, while the sidecar record established new figures in the 1000cc as well as the 600cc class.

The following equipment was used on each motorcycle:
Norton: frame, fork, engine and gearbox
Wellworthy: piston rings
Terry: valve springs
Amal: carburettor
KLG: spark plugs
BTH: magneto
Esso: fuel
Castrol: oil
Dunlop: tyres, saddle and racing pad
Ferodo: brake and clutch linings
Renold and Coventry: chains

Telcalemit: grease nipples
Bowdenex: cables
Smith's: rev counter

It is worth pointing out that the above companies were known as trade barons (and in modern speak would be called corporate sponsors), and Nortons racing, record-breaking, trials and scrambles teams were largely funded by these companies rather than Norton themselves.

Coming virtually at the same time as London's Earls Court Motorcycle Show, Nortons record-breaking efforts provided excellent publicity for the famous Birmingham marque and their sponsors.

Swinging-arm rear suspension
There was a 'powerful rumour' *(The Motor Cycle)* among the racing fraternity at the show, that there would be swinging-arm rear suspension on the factory racing Nortons for the 1950 season. This was the first time that the public knew what they might be seeing soon.

More of the dirty stuff
On his return from France, Geoff Duke's name next appeared in the programme for the Lancashire Grand National Scramble at Holcombe Moor, near Bury. Besides finishing in eighth position, Geoff also won the Ray Bailey Cup (for the fastest North West Centre resident).

Grand National Scramble – Holcombe Moor, near Bury

1st	C.M. Ray	(497cc Ariel)
2nd	B.H.M. Viney	(347cc AJS)
3rd	R.K. Pilling	(490cc Norton)
4th	S.B. Manns	(498cc Triumph)
5th	B.G. Stonebridge	(499cc BSA)
6th	W.J. Stocker	(346cc Royal Enfield)
7th	T.H. Wortley	(498cc AJS)
8th	G.E. Duke	(490cc Norton)

At the end of November 1949 Geoff competed in the British Experts' Trial in South Devon. As *The Motor Cycle* said in its report of the event in the 1 December issue:

It was the first occasion that this event had been disputed over the 'West of England' terrain and the change proved highly satisfactory.

The 60-odd mile course, embracing 18 separate observed sections, was enjoyed by competitors and decided the winners in both the solo and sidecar classes without the special test coming into the reckoning.

The best solo performance was achieved by L.A. Ratcliffe (347cc Matchless) with seven marks lost, whereas Geoff conceded 21 marks, finishing 12th overall. When one considers that Hugh Viney lost 24 marks, our hero's performance was all the more notable.

As in the previous year, Geoff brought 1949 to a close with an outing in the Northern Experts' Trial at Brierlow Bar; *The Motor Cycle* dated 22 December described his performance as 'effortlessly fast', and with only 11 marks lost he finished third, with only the winner G.E.H. Godber-Ford (seven marks) and R.B. Young (nine marks) in front – all three rode 490cc Nortons.

It had been a year of rapid progress for our young, but hugely talented, individual. Outstanding performances in any one branch of the sport would have been judged top rate, but in three – road racing, scrambles and trials – one can only describe Geoff Duke as the supreme all-round motorcyclist of his generation, and on the verge of taking the world by storm.

On Saturday 18 March 1950 Geoff was part of the winning Norton team in the Cotswold Cup Trial, and also won the Gibb Trophy on his 500T machine, conceding only 11 marks.

A victorious Victory Cup Trial

If one would have expected Geoff Duke to quit trials now that he had been signed up by the road-racing team, one would have been wrong. Because at the second trade-supported 'national' of the year, the Victory staged on Saturday 18 February 1950, not only did the name G.E. Duke appear in the entry list, but he emerged victorious. Held over a 60-mile course in the Shropshire Highlands, with its start and finish at Church Stretton, Geoff scored a perfect sheet – no marks lost. When one considers that virtually all the top feet-up stars were taking part, this was a notable performance. He even beat his old mentor Hugh Viney! Then, on Saturday 18 March Geoff was part of the winning Norton team at the Cotswold Cups Trial and also won the Gibb Trophy (for the best solo 351 – 500cc) on his 500T Norton, conceding 11 marks.

The one-piece leather suit

Up to 1950, a two-piece leather suit was the traditional attire for road racers. But while record breaking at Montlhéry the previous autumn Geoff had noticed that Artie Bell's close-fitting leathers (still two piece) provided a speed advantage, even though Artie was heavier. As Geoff recalled later:

> *If the fit of one's leathers made such a difference to lap times around Montlhéry, then it must also be the same in road racing. Also, I realised that the double thickness of the material, where the jacket overlapped the trousers at the waist, could become restrictive and uncomfortable when lying in the prone position to reduce wind resistance. In addition, there was little need for pockets and excessive padding. The answer was a lightweight, one-piece, close-fitting suit.*

So Geoff put the idea to the manufacturers of his conventional two-piece leather racing suit, who told him 'they would make what I wanted if I could provide a pattern'. So, his next approach was to his local tailor in St Helens, Frank Barker, who agreed to make the necessary pattern. But this interested him so much that having made the pattern, 'Frank said he would like to have a go at making up the suit'. As Geoff was to recall, 'For a tailor used to working with cloth and without any special equipment, he did a magnificent job for me.' The finished suit weighed less than 5lb and was ready for the 1950 TT. Later, when studying a photograph of himself during the 1950 Senior TT, Geoff noticed the effect of wind pressure on his racing boots. So, 'Frank, therefore, made me a pair of close fitting, zip-up boots using the same lightweight leather as the suit'. So almost overnight the old two-piece leathers and bulky, heavy boots became 'obsolete', and Frank Barker was so 'inundated with orders' that his 'traditional tailoring all but ceased'.

Testing the McCandless prototype

But before the new riding gear came a new motorcycle. As Geoff said in his autobiography, 'To be included in the Norton team in 1950 on an equal footing with Bell, Lockett and Daniell was really something, but to be fortunate enough to start my professional career on the "new-look" McCandless Norton was a heaven-sent opportunity.'

Geoff's first ride on the prototype was in the Isle of Man, when, in January 1950, Artie Bell and himself rode 'illegally' around sections of the

A little remembered fact is that even after he became a world-class road racer, Geoff continued to take part in trials, as this October 1957 photograph of him on an Ariel 250 shows.

Besides being a skilled engineer, Rex McCandless was also a more than capable rider. He is seen here at the North West 200 (number 77) the man looking on (centre) is Artie Bell.

Rex McCandless

By the end of the 1949 racing season it had become patently obvious to all concerned at Nortons, from Joe Craig and Gilbert Smith down, that something drastic was needed if the company was to have any real chance of winning either the 350 or 500cc World Championship titles.

Strangely, the answer to the company's prayers was not destined to come from within the Bracebridge Street factory itself, but from across the Irish Sea in the backstreets of Belfast, Northern Ireland. Back in 1944, while the war was still raging, *Motor Cycling* carried a two-page story detailing how a well-known 20-year-old Irish rider, Rex McCandless, had come up with an interesting new frame design and rear wheel suspension system which had been in the process of development in Ulster over the pervious couple of years. In fact, as far back as 1942, *Motor Cycling's* Belfast correspondent, who was then serving in the Royal Air Force, had visited the journal's London office and talked with 'immense enthusiasm' of a new type of suspension that a couple of his fellow citizens had been 'playing around with'. One of these was McCandless and the other Artie Bell, who, in 1939, was just beginning to attract factory interest as a rider of great promise. As related elsewhere, Artie was subsequently signed up by Joe Craig, and later still was joined by Geoff Duke, the two becoming great friends and teammates.

During the war years both Bell and McCandless were engaged in aircraft work at the Short Brothers factory in Belfast. There, the two men became engaged in a heated and lengthy debate over just what was needed to constitute the ideal motorcycle, McCandless being of the opinion that with ever-increasing power outputs from engines it was frame design which had been lagging behind. Bell had to agree, pointing out that, as racing motorcycles existed in 1939, the big weakness was that the rear of the machine was apt to attempt to take over control from the rider. In other words, as *Motor Cycling* so aptly described the condition, 'the tail was prone to wag the dog'.

Unlike the majority of designers, Rex McCandless had one big advantage: he was also a top-class competitor in the Irish racing world. And he saw, clearly, that a key problem in the average motorcycle of the late 1930s was over-hard or non-existent rear suspension, which meant that both the machine and its rider were subjected to a truly awful pounding and the roadholding and handling were badly affected, particularly on uneven road surfaces. McCandless therefore reasoned that if he could smooth out the bumps and thereby obtain improved roadholding, he would be able to make for greater use of the additional power which he foresaw would be achieved in the post-war era.

So he set about designing such a rear suspension for his self-tuned Triumph Tiger 100-engined machine, *Motor Cycling* referring to the subsequent designs as a 'spring heel'. This proved so successful that the

The original 1949 Featherbed prototype, in Belfast.

next stage was to come up with an equally effective frame. And perhaps this was in truth the most vital development of all, for it certainly established Rex McCandless as not just a successful rider, but also a gifted, forward-looking designer.

Although there had been spring frames before, to obtain the best results he believed that the main-frame and rear wheel springing had to be designed as a whole.

And so, to fund his concept he first of all, in the early post-war days, marketed the McCandless rear suspension (which could be fitted to existing rigid frame or plunger frame designs). This project was so successful that, together with Artie Bell his partner, the McCandless conversion business was sold to Midlands businessman James R. Ferriday.

This allowed Rex McCandless to set about the design and creation of applying his idea on a complete frame and suspension system together with a Norton racing engine.

Success did not come instantly, but instead many months of hard work and experiment were needed before the definitive chassis could be shipped to the Norton factory in Birmingham.

But, as explained elsewhere, before the racing machine came the design of a frame and cycle parts for the Norton 500T trials bike – on which Geoff Duke was destined to begin his Norton career in early 1948.

The racing frame arrived at the end of 1949, with tests being carried out by Artie Bell, plus Harold Daniell and Geoff Duke. The resulting machine proved a huge step forward in frame and suspension design, putting Norton on a new level for the 1950 season. The Featherbed (so named by Harold Daniell during a test session, because it reminded him of the comfort of a 'Feather Bed') had arrived!

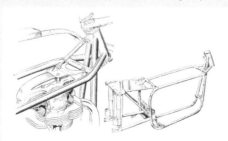

The McCandless Featherbed frame in its original guise with bolt-on sub-frame and remote reservoir rear shock absorbers. The detailed view displays head steady and tank strap.

Geoff's fellow solo team member in the 1950 Norton racing squad: Artie Bell, Johnny Lockett and Harold Daniell. The man on the far left (in the hat) is Harry Louis of *The Motor Cycle*.

TT course. He soon realised 'that this machine set an entirely new standard in roadholding'. Then, two weeks later, with Rex McCandless, Joe Craig, plus Artie and Geoff, they travelled to Montlhéry where 'the new model could be tested under very arduous conditions', but a broken primary chain (which damaged the sprockets) caused the squad to return to Birmingham. Next came further extensive testing at MIRA (Motor Industry Research Association) facilities near Nuneaton, Warwickshire.

After this it was decided to build 'a completely new machine incorporating all the new ideas which he (Joe Craig) and Rex had evolved from the various tests carried out.'

Getting the season under way

Bob Foster, Tommy Wood, Noel Pope and Geoff Duke were, as *The Motor Cycle* dated 6 April described, 'the stars to be seen at Blandford, Dorset, road race held last Saturday (1 April) in dry, though cloudy, weather.' In the 350cc event, Foster and Wood (both riding Velocettes) sandwiched Geoff between them. However, in the 500cc race the Norton teamster won from Wood (Norton) and Les Archer (Norton), completing the 16-lap, 50 mile-long race in 35 minutes 26.8 seconds, a speed of 85.06mph.

Next came a visit to Thruxton, near Andover, Hampshire, for the first-ever meeting at this new airfield venue. At that time the circuit, which was staged over the runways and perimeter road, measured 1.89 miles to a lap, embracing three straights on the runways and what *The Motor Cycle* called

Geoff's early rides on a works Norton, in 1950, were aboard the 1949 type 'Garden Gate' bikes with plunger rear suspension; seen here finishing runner-up to world champion Bob Foster (Velocette) in the 350cc event at Blandford on the 1 April 1950.

'some entertaining swerves on the perimeter track'. Organised by the Southampton and Bishop Waltham clubs, Geoff's performance was from the top drawer, with victories in both his races on his 350 and 500cc Nortons. He also set the fastest lap of the meeting in 1 minute 34.6 seconds, a speed of 72.15mph.

In the 20 April 1950 issue of *The Motor Cycle*, George Wilson described Geoff as 'today's most polished all-rounder'. The three-page feature charted Geoff's career to date, but it was how Wilson saw Geoff that was the most revealing, saying:

> *What of the man? He is probably the most likeable of all racing, trials and scrambles men – for he is, of course, all three! So quiet and unassuming is he that when we chatted to collate the material for this article I had repeatedly to bring him to order, since he would insist on singing the praises of Viney, Frith, Artie Bell and Joe Craig, and keeping mum about his own achievements. And apart from motor cycling, he has no hobbies – he says he has no time for anything else since racing, particularly, is a full-time job.*

Soon after George Wilson's piece had been published, Geoff was back in action, this time at *Motor Cycling's* Silverstone Saturday meeting. *The Motor Cycle* report said it all: 'That irrepressible young man, G.E. Duke, riding 350 and 500cc Nortons, dominated the race meeting.' It continued 'He won the first of the 25-mile 350cc "experts" races by 33 seconds and the 500cc "experts" race, over 50 miles, by 1 minute 26.5 seconds.'

Additionally, it was Silverstone which played a vital role in Geoff debuting the new McCandless-framed racer shortly afterwards (it should be recalled that until the international Blandford races a week later, none of the Norton team had actually raced with the new chassis, instead still using the plunger frame 'Garden Gate' machines).

Originally, Joe Craig had nominated the veteran Harold Daniell to have the honour, but, as Geoff himself explained, 'was unable to do so due to an unfortunate spill', going on to explain 'I had a great set-to on Manx Nortons (in the 500cc race at Silverstone) until in an overtaking manoeuvre, Harold grounded his megaphone and slid off, cracking a bone in his hand. I had already entered the event with my Manx machine so Joe (Craig) asked me to ride the works model in place of my own 500.'

Geoff pictured during the *Motor Cycling*-sponsored Silverstone Saturday meeting, 22 April 1950.

Debut day for the Featherbed

Blandford, Dorset, on 29 April 1950 was the debut day for the new McCandless-framed Featherbed (so named by Harold Daniell, after testing, because of the comfort compared with the machines it replaced). A full description of the design is contained in a separate boxed section within this chapter.

AJS, like Norton, were giving their latest road-racing 500cc model an airing. Ted Frend was the rider, but unfortunately a misfire developed during practice. In his heat, Frend could finish no higher than seventh and in the race itself retired on the first lap.

This robbed Geoff, riding the new Norton, of serious opposition. However, he still 'proved' the motorcycle by setting a new lap record for the 3.1 mile circuit, and this was set on a day of high winds, in 2 minutes 7.2 seconds, a speed of 88.88mph.

Geoff did not have such an easy ride in the 350cc race, with *The Motor Cycle* report headline reading 'Final of 350cc Event One Of The Most Thrilling Races Ever Held'.

At the beginning of the 350cc race, Geoff 'appeared unable to weave his way through the massed start', and at the end of lap one the leading four were: teammate Johnny Lockett, Cecil Sandford, Ted Frend

Tested extensively over the winter months, the new McCandless Featherbed-framed works model was given its debut (by Geoff) at Blandford Camp, Dorset, on 29 April 1950, in the 500cc race, which Geoff won.

The Featherbed model as raced by the works team during the 1950 season. It was a winner first time out.

and David Whitworth, with Duke lying in seventh. Soon, Frend (AJS) and Bob Foster (Velocette) were engaged in a thrilling tussle at the front of the field. It took Geoff seven of the 10 laps to annex third spot from Sandford, and as the three riders crossed the finishing line at the end of the race a blanket could have covered all of them. Even though the result read Frend, Foster and Duke in that order, Geoff had put in a magnificent performance – and again set a new lap record for the class.

The Scottish Six Days

At Silverstone, Geoff was unable to take part in the final race of the day (the Handicap event). This was because he had to leave early – 'to be in Scotland the next morning to weigh in for the Scottish Six Days Trial'.

Previously, post-war, the SSDT had to be held over a course distance of some 800 miles, but because fuel rationing was now less restricted the total distance for the 1950 event was raised to 1,000 miles. This had enabled the organisers, the Edinburgh Club, to revert to the traditional practice of starting as well as finishing the trial at Edinburgh. So the first day's run would take competitors to Fort William, the centre of the first four days' circuits, and on the fifth and sixth days the course led back to Edinburgh. Not only were there foreign riders (from Czechoslovakia and Austria), but a record number of entries had been received.

Although, when early on Monday morning the trial had got under way, by the time riders reached the first observed section at Stoney Brae 'light rain had set in and had given the rocks a coating of slime' *(The Motor Cycle)*. Heavy rain then set in for some two hours and, as *The Motor Cycle* report stated, 'the ride north-west from Killin to Tyndrum and Glen Coe was a grim fight against windborne wetness. Snow freckled the peaks of the surrounding hills, some of which were shrouded in grey cloud.'

But in typical contrasting Scottish weather, there was a mixture for the competitors, with dry sunny conditions offset by lashing rain on other occasions.

It was not until the fourth day that the name G.E. Duke was mentioned as one of the front men, having conceded a total of 34 marks so far, compared with the leader L.A. Ratcliffe (347cc Matchless) with nine. It was the latter who was to emerge the winner at the end of the six days with a total of 12; meanwhile, Geoff did not add to his tally.

Once again he had proved himself to be an excellent trials rider.

The North West 200

Records were again shattered in the annual North West 200 road race over the Portstewart–Coleraine–Portrush circuit, Northern Ireland. One of the greatest challenges faced by the riders was, as *The Motor Cycle* described, 'tar "bleeding" caused by strong sun over three hot days'.

Artie Bell won the 500cc class – his third successive victory in the event, while Geoff won the 350cc category (all three races being run concurrently as in previous years). He also set up a new 350cc lap record of 7 minutes 58 seconds, a speed of 83.40mph. His record average speed for the race was 82.54mph, which *The Motor Cycle* called 'an easy victory'.

350cc North West 200 – 17 laps – 188 miles

1st	G.E. Duke (Norton)
2nd	A.F. Wheeler (Velocette)
3rd	A.J. Glazebrook (AJS)
4th	R.T. Matthews (Velocette)
5th	J.F. Kentish (AJS)
6th	C.B. Carr (Velocette)

TT practice begins

In an article headed 'Who Will Win the Junior?', *The Motor Cycle* journalist Michael Kirk looked at 'nine likely winners'. This is what he had to say about Geoff Duke: 'Has all it takes. Fearless. A superb stylist. Displays marvellous judgement for one so young. Tomorrow's world champion if he has reasonable luck. Might even hold Bell on equal mounts.' Besides Geoff,

Geoff about to push his factory Norton into life at the start of the 1950 Junior TT; he finished second to teammate Artie Bell.

the other riders picked by Kirk were teammates Bell, Daniell and Lockett, AJS men Les Graham, Bill Doran and Ted Frend, plus the Velocette duo of Bob Foster and Reg Armstrong.

Practice for the 1950 TT began at 4.45am on Thursday 25 May. Geoff was the fastest 350 in this session, going round in 27 minutes 27 seconds (82.49mph). But the biggest talking point was his one-piece leather racing suit.

Then, on Monday morning, 29 May, Geoff, out for the first time on one of the new Featherbed-framed 350s, lapped at 26 minutes 32 seconds (85.34mph), which was one second better than the 26 minutes 33 seconds record lap standing for the Junior race (achieved by Stanley Woods on a Velocette with petrol-benzole fuel in 1938).

But it was the setting of the first post-war 90mph TT lap on Wednesday morning, 31 May, which really grabbed the headlines, when Geoff took his 500cc model round in 25 minutes 5 seconds (90.27mph).

The Junior race

The weather for the 1950 Junior race day was absolutely perfect. Exactly 100 starters (the very maximum) began the race, with Geoff down in 79th position. His teammate and friend Artie Bell was 64th. Later, Geoff commented:

This was a positive disadvantage and unquestionably dangerous as we had to overtake much slower riders, many of whom could provide the

But in the Senior TT, Geoff turned the tables on Artie, with the Ulsterman (seen here), taking the runner-up spot.

Geoff, speeding along the Glencrutchery Road at over 100mph in the 1950 Senior TT. During the race he broke the outright course lap record which had been held by Harold Daniell since 1938

unexpected by suddenly changing line or speed at a crucial moment. I was subsequently instrumental in persuading the ACU to bring in a grading system which put acknowledged top-flight riders into the first 20 places on the starting grid.

As Geoff admits, he dropped the clutch too quickly at the start, and so wasted time pulling back on compression and starting again. So, to his 'astonishment', the signal at the end of the first lap 'indicating my position at Ramsey Hairpin showed me to be in second place – two seconds down on Les Graham's AJS.'

But in the end, Geoff had to be content with the runner-up spot, behind teammate Artie Bell. Not only did Norton finish first, second and third (third position going to Harold Daniell), but the Birmingham marque also took the Manufacturer's Team Prize.

A record-breaking Senior victory

If the Junior race had been exciting in terms of Geoff's performance, the Senior, held four days later on Friday 11 June, was described by *The Motor Cycle* headline which said it all: 'A 92.27mph Senior TT A Record Shattered: Geoff Duke Leads from Start to Finish and Laps at 93.33mph: Nortons are 1, 2, 3 and Win Manufacturer's Team Prize.'

Once again, conditions were ideal. As *The Motor Cycle* stated, 'The roads could not have been better. Record crowds lined all the vantage points, touching their maximum at the Bungalow.'

A serious challenge had been expected from the 1949 500cc world champion Les Graham, and so it proved, the AJS teamster finishing fourth. But as Geoff was later to reveal, it might have been a very different ending. 'At Governor's Bridge (on the last lap) I was on Artie's tail and we crossed the finishing line together. My greatest ambition had been achieved – I had won the Senior TT. When the usual check was made, though, my petrol tank was completely dry!'

Norton took the first three places in the 1950 Senior TT, here the winner Geoff (57), is seen with Artie Bell (41, runner-up) and Johnny Lockett (49, third).

Senior TT – 7 laps – 264.11 miles

1st	G.E. Duke	(Norton)
2nd	A.J. Bell	(Norton)
3rd	J. Lockett	(Norton)
4th	R.L. Graham	(AJS)
5th	H.L. Daniell	(Norton)
6th	H.R. Armstrong	(Velocette)

At the prize giving Geoff said 'It's only when you get one of Joe Craig's five-hundreds that you realise how well the McCandless frame steers. I think Professor [a nickname created by Artie Bell] Craig issued me with a quick one.' While Norton's first, second and third in both Senior and Junior had been achieved only once before, again by Norton in 1933, in 1950 they had gone one better by gaining both team prizes, in addition to breaking the lap and course records for both events.

The problems start

After such fabulous results, the Norton team, including Geoff, were full of confidence for the forthcoming Continental races. However, fate was about to enter the arena… resulting in not only forced retirements from vital racers, but also a career-ending crash for one of the Norton teamsters.

After the TT came the Belgian Grand Prix, held over the recently modified Francorchamps–Malmédy–Stavelot circuit in the Ardennes, close to the German border.

The first of the races counting towards World Championship points that scorching Sunday 2 July 1950 was the 350cc race, which was won by Velocette-mounted Bob Foster, with Artie Bell second and Geoff third. Next came the sidecars, which was duly won by Eric Oliver's Norton from the four-cylinder Gilera of Ercole Frigerio.

As *The Motor Cycle* reported:

The line-up of 40 starters for the 500cc event over 14 laps held dynamic possibilities. Nortons ridden by A.J. Bell, G.E. Duke and J. Lockett; AJSs with R.L. Graham, E.J. Frend and A.R. Foster; H.R. Armstrong and W. Lomas on the big Velocettes; N. Pagani, U. Masetti and C. Bandirola on the 4-cylinder Gileras; A. Artesiani on the new 4-cylinder MV Agusta.

As for the sound these machines made when they left the starting grid, as one commentator said, 'The reverberating boom of the megaphone singles, the light refrain from the twins, the snarling whine from the fours, produced an indescribable racket which insulted the ear-drums at first, but became music as the machines stretched away.' And a titanic battle ensued. Although Carlo Bandirola led, Nello Pagani, Artie Bell and Geoff Duke were close behind, as were Les Graham and Johnny Lockett. Two seconds covered the first six riders at the end of the first lap.

Tragedy

Then, as *The Motor Cycle* so vividly described:

Bandirola in front brought the average above 100mph for the two laps, unaware of the tragedy that occurred a foot or so behind his back wheel. On a corner about a mile from the end of the second lap, he eased slightly to the discomforture of Graham inches away. Graham crash-braked and was thrown; Bell took to the bank to avoid the spinning AJS and was seriously injured. Duke managed, but only just, to miss the debacle and carried on. Graham was unhurt.

This left Geoff second, hemmed in by three Gileras.

Next, Geoff assumed the lead, and *The Motor Cycle* report stated 'Behind him, and being outridden, were Pagani and Masetti.' But the final drama came on lap 12, when Geoff too experienced problems. In Geoff's own words:

There was a loud bang and I felt something hit my backside, followed by 'juddering' from the rear wheel. A large section of the tread had detached itself from the casing of the rear tyre. I toured back to the pits

During the Belgian Grand Prix, in July 1950, Geoff's great friend and Norton teammate Artie Bell was to suffer a career-ending crash.

*to learn that Harold Daniell and Johnny Lockett had both retired with
the same problem.*

As for poor Artie Bell, even with the very best treatment possible, he lost
the use of his right arm and was never to race again. Obviously the Norton
camp were none too happy with Dunlop – their tyre suppliers. But new
improved tyres were promised by the next meeting, the Dutch TT at Assen.

Assen
As Geoff later explained, 'practice at the Dutch, on the old road circuit, was
uneventful'. And again Bob Foster took his Velocette to victory in the 350cc
event, with Geoff finally annexing the runner-up spot after slipstreaming Bill
Lomas on another Velo.

But once again, the 500cc race was to present a return to the tyre
gremlins. As Geoff explained:

*It would prove to be a very short race for me. On only the second lap,
while being 'towed' along by Masetti at 200–300rpm over Norton's
normal maximums in top gear, and having just left a long avenue of
trees lining both sides of the road, there was another ominous 'bang'.
The rear wheel locked, the bike went out of control and literally stood
up on its front wheel!*

Fortunately for Geoff, he was to land on the grass verge at 'the left side
of the road, but the bike went end over end down the road and was a total
write-off.'

No more Dunlops
With the next round of the World Championship series, the Swiss Grand
Prix, a mere two weeks away, Norton had a serious dilemma. What to do
about the serious tyre failures. As Geoff was later to recall, 'There was no
way I intended risking being thrown down the road like that once more and
I vowed never to race again on Dunlop tyres – and I never did.' Short term
the team switched to Pirelli, before signing a contract with the Avon India
Rubber Company of Melksham, Wiltshire. This came after a series of tests
conclusively proved the Avons to be superior to the Dunlops.

The 1950 Swiss GP was held over a 3.73-mile circuit on 23 July in the
suburbs of Geneva. Besides a small, roughly triangular section, the greater
part of the course was made up by riders running down one side of the main
Geneva–Lausanne highway, semi-circling round in the road and coming up

the other side – the road being separated by straw bales. In truth, not only was it an uninteresting venue, but also it was dangerous – even more so in the wet conditions which prevailed.

The Motor Cycle said the road surface was 'Akin to wet ice!' There were even tramlines on one section…

Les Graham went on to win both the 350 and 500cc races. Although Geoff finished third and fourth respectively, he did not enjoy the experience one little bit.

Back in England

On their return to England, as Geoff said, 'Joe Craig set to work to find more power while I went to Blandford to try and restore my lost confidence.'

Victory at Blandford

August Bank Holiday Monday saw Geoff return to his winning ways with victories in both his heat and the final of the 500cc class.

The first of two 500cc heats saw Geoff bring his works Featherbed Norton to the line, together with teammate Johnny Lockett (who on this occasion was riding a Francis Beart Manx model). As one race report said, 'Both rode in sparkling style and Duke broke the lap record, of which he was already the holder, with a time of 2 minutes 7.2 seconds (88.95mph).'

In the final the report stated 'The race was notable for the brilliant riding of Duke, who, though never passed, lapped consistently at record speeds'. Eventually he raised the lap record to over 90mph for the Dorset circuit in the final race of the day, the 16-lap Senior Invitation, which he won from Lockett, Dickie Dale and Peter Romaine (all riding Nortons).

The Ulster

Geoff made a winning debut in the Ulster Grand Prix, held over the 16½-mile Clady circuit. Not only this, but he also set new race and lap records. In addition, he was also a member of the winning manufacturer's team (together with Johnny Lockett and Norton's new signing Dickie Dale). Finally, he was also awarded a special trophy for the fastest rider over 100mph, when he upped the lap record to 101.77mph.

As the races were run consecutively (like the North West 200), Geoff could only ride in one class.

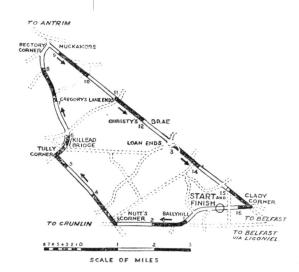

Ulster GP – 15 laps – 247.5 miles

1st   G.E. Duke (Norton)

2nd   R.L. Graham (AJS)

3rd   J.H. Lockett (Norton)

4th   R.H. Dale (Norton)

5th   J.M. West (AJS)

6th   U. Masetti (Gilera)

Next came an interlude between the Grand Prix action, with a visit to Thruxton at the end of August. Although hindered in his 350cc heat by carburettor trouble, he only just missed out, the win going to Cecil Sandford (Velocette). However, in the final the positions were reversed, with Geoff winning by a wide margin. But after winning his heat in the 500cc section, Geoff (and Sandford) were turned away from the Senior final start. It transpired that both had been using 348cc machines, although entered on machines of larger capacity. Instead the winner was S.T. Barnett (Norton).

A double at Monza

By taking double victories at the Grand Prix des Nations at Monza on Sunday 17 September, Geoff was able to illustrate 'what might have been' had not the Norton team been afflicted by the tyre gremlins encountered earlier.

Staged in Monza Park, with a 6.3 kilometre-circuit (almost 4 miles) constructed exclusively for racing and completed only the previous year, the Italian track was a particularly fast venue, helped by one straight section which measured around 1½ miles in length. *The Motor Cycle* commented that:

The outline of the circuit resembles a dog's leg, and the slow corners, which demand bottom or second gear on the average five-hundred, are at the extremities; there are, in fact, two right-hand, right-angle corners at each end and so close together as almost to make wide hairpins. Other deviations from straight ahead are of the top-gear, full-throttle curve type.

Conditions for both races were ideal with wall-to-wall sunshine.

Geoff had gone into the final round of the Championship with what he described as 'a fighting a chance of collecting the 500cc World Championship'. However, it was necessary for the Englishman to win and Gilera's Umberto Masetti to finish no higher than third. But although Geoff did his bit by winning, Masetti, although well beaten on the day, came home runner-up to scoop the title.

In the earlier 350cc event Geoff had come from behind to win, narrowly from Les Graham (AJS) and Harry Hinton (Norton).

350cc Italian GP Monza – 24 laps – 93.9 miles
1st   G.E. Duke (Norton)
2nd   R.L. Graham (AJS)
3rd   H. Hinton (Norton)
4th   R.H. Dale (Norton)
5th   W. Lomas (Velocette)
6th   C. Sandford (Velocette)

500cc Italian GP Monza – 32 laps – 125.2 miles
1st   G.E. Duke (Norton)
2nd   U. Masetti (Gilera)
3rd   A. Artesiani (MV Agusta)
4th   A. Milani (Gilera)
5th   C. Bandirola (Gilera)
6th   R.H. Dale (Norton)

And so Geoff Duke finished runner-up in both the 350 and 500cc World Championships in 1950. And in the 500cc, at least, he was robbed of the title by only one point due to his tyres rather than anything he or his motorcycle had not done. What a truly brilliant, but at the same time unlucky, first Grand Prix season.

Geoff was in record-breaking form at Scarborough on 22–23 September 1950, winning both the 350cc and 500cc finals with record laps in both. Here he is seen at the start of the 500cc event (number 8 on second row).

Geoff about to set off on a lap of honour on his five-hundred Norton after winning the News Chronicle Trophy, Oliver's Mount, Scarborough, 23 September 1950.

Ending the season

After the excitement of Grand Prix action, it was back home to a couple of short-circuit race meetings (Scarborough and Silverstone), plus some trials action later on.

At Scarborough, although he did not win his 350cc heat, Geoff won both the 350 and 500cc finals and in the process set a new lap record of 62.46mph for the tricky Oliver's Mount course.

But at Silverstone, a week later on 30 September, Geoff had a thoroughly miserable day in more ways than one. First, the weather was truly awful with consistent heavy rain, so much so that he withdrew from the meeting. Just how bad things were is evident from *The Motor Cycle's* report:

Rain – cold, all-pervading and almost unceasing – took the glamour from Bemsee's 'all-star' meeting at Silverstone. It continued: *From the riders' point of view, the circuit was at its trickiest – the quantity of rubber and oil which had been left on the curves and corners during the car meeting made the going dicey, and the perpetual drizzle was blinding.*

Shortly after the end of the road-racing season, a dinner party was given by members of the Norton staff in honour of Geoff's achievements that year. During the evening he was presented with the Fred G. Craner (an important figure at Donington Park pre-war, with the Craner Curves still named after him today) Challenge Trophy, offered by the East Midlands Centre to the British rider making the best aggregate performance in the year's classic road races.

At the same time it was revealed that for the 1951 season the Norton team would comprise Geoff, plus Dickie Dale and Johnny Lockett, while Harold Daniell had decided to retire from the sport to concentrate on his South London motorcycle dealership.

More trials action

During the weekend of 20–22 October 1950, Geoff had taken part in the John Douglas Trial. Knowing that this manufacturer-supported event would bring to the Bristol area many star riders, the organisers roped in Geoff as the principle speaker at a special Friday evening function. But no special effort was made to publicise Geoff's visit. As *The Motor Cycle* reported:

This was fortunate, because with some 300 in the audience, the Student's Common Room of the Victoria Rooms, Clifton, was metaphorically bulging. Few motorcyclists have become so popular in

so short a time as Geoff Duke – this, in spite of his pronounced
reticence and unassuming ways. An example of his diffidence arose in
the arrangements for Friday's gathering. Rather than give a talk, Duke
advised the Bristol Club officials that he would prefer simply to
answer questions – from which one gets the impression that he would
not presume to take the liberty of 'lecturing' anyone.

But if Geoff thought he was in for a quiet time, he was to be mistaken!
This question and answer session lasted more than 2½ hours. As for the
questions which kept Geoff so busy, these ranged from physical fitness to
tyre pressures; from ordinary riding on the road to the possibility of a
100mph TT lap; from 'narrow squeaks' when racing to views on
superchargers and alcohol fuel; from rotary valves to pre-select gearboxes
and many more facets of the racing game. The whole exercise was adjudged
a resounding success.

Then, the following morning Geoff was out in action on his works 500T
Norton trials job, finishing with a First Class Award and the loss of only 23
marks.

Towards the end of November came two other events, the Streatham
Trophy Trial (near Liphook, Hampshire) and the British Experts' Trial
(Shropshire). In the former Geoff missed out by a single point on overall
victory.

In the Experts' he rode brilliantly to finish joint fifth.

British Experts' Trial, 25–26 November 1950

1st	W. Nicholson (499cc BSA)	43 marks lost
2nd	G.J. Draper (348cc BSA)	49 marks lost
3rd	B.H.M. Viney (347cc AJS)	57 marks lost
4th	C.M. Ray (497cc Ariel)	60 marks lost
5th	G.E. Duke (490cc Norton)	63 marks lost
	L.A. Ratcliffe (347cc AJS)	

And so 1950 came to a close, a year in which Geoff Duke had gone from
simply being an excellent all-rounder to a superstar and world champion
elect.

Chapter 3

World Champion

The year 1951 began for Geoff Duke in early February when he took part in the first of the new year's national manufacturer-supported events, the Colmore Cup Trial, run in the Cotswolds, with its start and finish at Shipston-on-Stour, Warwickshire.

As *The Motor Cycle*, dated 15 February 1951, reported:

Among the machines with interesting features was W. Nicholson's 499cc BSA with a duplex tubular frame welded at the joints, and G.E. Duke's 490cc Norton – the TT type frame which had appeared in scrambles fitted with a Dominator twin cylinder engine, but which, last Saturday, had a single cylinder power unit.

However, for once Geoff did not feature in the results.

At the end of that month Geoff rode in the 27th Victory Cup Trial (an event he won the previous year). This time BSA's Bill Nicholson took the win, with Geoff fifth. One place behind was a new member of the Norton trials squad, a certain J.V. Smith Junior (Jeff Smith, later to become a double world motocross champion with BSA in the mid-1960s).

Next came the Hurst Cup Trial, where Geoff, although he 'provided a bit of full-bore stuff for the big crowd at the summit', did not feature in the top contenders in the points tally. And things were no better at a muddy Kickham Trial a few days later. While in the Cotswell Cups Trial, Geoff gained a First Class Award for his efforts. But, in truth, his thoughts seemed elsewhere – to the coming road-race season.

As Geoff was later to recall, 'Bearing in mind that I was already 25 years old when I started racing in 1948, I still believe that 1951 was my peak year as a rider.' Geoff also acknowledged the help he received from the gifted Polish engineer Leo Kuzmicki, who had arrived at the Norton factory.

As described in the separate boxed section within this chapter, Leo Kuzmicki was to play a vital role in Geoff's successes during 1951 and 1952 with Norton. And the reasons why the Pole is not more widely known is explained in full in another separate boxed section within this chapter.

Easter Weekend

Geoff took in two race meetings over the Easter Holiday Weekend to get his 1951 season under way; Brough (East Yorkshire) on Saturday 24 March, followed by Thruxton (Hampshire) on Monday 26 March.

At Brough Airfield, after a snowstorm in the morning, the weather brightened, with some sunshine in the afternoon. Riding a pair of standard-production Featherbed Manx Nortons, Geoff was runner-up in both the 350 and 500cc events, behind Mick Featherstone (AJS) and C. Horn (Norton) respectively.

At Thruxton two days later there were 'vast crowds' (*The Motor Cycle*), despite what was described as 'unkind weather'. Although Geoff (again riding the latest production Manx machines) won the all-important 500cc final, he had been beaten in the heat by the up-and-coming Dave Bennett. In his 350cc heat Geoff was third (behind Bill Doran and Robin Sherry – both riding AJS models), while the final was as follows:

350cc Thruxton – 7 laps – 15 miles

1st	W. Doran (AJS)
2nd	G.E. Duke (Norton)
3rd	C.C. Sandford (Velocette)
4th	L.A. Dear (AJS)
5th	J. Lockett (Norton)
6th	G. Monty (AJS)

Then Geoff journeyed to the South of France where he was victorious in both the 350 and 500cc events in the international (but non-Championship) Marseilles Grand Prix. He won the former race by two laps, averaging 66.15mph, while in the latter he finished a lap ahead of Collet (Gilera) and three laps in front of the third man, Behra (Moto Guzzi).

Goodwood and Mettet

Goodwood, in West Sussex, was the next call for Geoff, and here too he scored what *The Motor Cycle* race report dated 19 April 1951 described as

Leo Kuzmicki

Leo Kuzmicki was the man who found the extra power from the ageing Norton dohc singles, during 1951 and 1952, which enabled Geoff Duke to successfully challenge the best in the world and gain three world titles in these two seasons. However, until very recently little had been known of this quiet, unassuming, but brilliant engineer – largely because of what had transpired during the dark days of World War Two. And because of this, very few post-World War Two photographs of the man exist.

Leo Kuzmicki was born into a family of Polish nobility on 25 October 1910. His father, Stanislow, a famous eye specialist and General in the Polish Armed Forces, and mother Maria, a lecturer in music at Warsaw University, were prominent people in Polish society.

Leo was the second of four sons. His schooling was comprehensive to say the least. For example, after gaining a Higher School Certificate in 1931 (the first of his many qualifications), from 1933 until 1938 he attended the University of Lwow, where he studied mechanical engineering. By the outbreak of war in September 1939 he held a position of Research Engineer, specialising in diesel engines, having already acquired a university degree comparable with the British MSc in Mechanical Engineering.

When Germany invaded, Leo was called up for active duty with the Polish Air Force as a flight engineer, having already served as a reservist for two years. Subsequently, following Poland's defeat, he found himself in the arms of a Russian ambush. He was then transported to Moscow, where he was incarcerated and tortured, before being sent to a labour camp within the Arctic Circle. When he realised that death by starvation awaited him and his fellow prisoners, his only option was escape. This he did, walking overland via Tashkent, Samarkand, Krasnowodst and through to the Persian Gulf to Bombay, where he eventually boarded a ship destined for Britain. This ship eventually docked in Liverpool in June 1942. However, besides forcing Leo (and his subsequent wife Nancy) to become very reclusive for fear of the KGB, his marathon journey had taken its toll. Starvation and exhaustion had caused permanent damage to his circulation, which was to eventually cause his death, aged 72, in 1982.

However, all this was very much in the future, when, in 1942, he joined the RAF (as a flight engineer). Then, upon his demob, he became a shareholder and chief designer for the AJW motorcycle firm during the late 1940s.

His next move was to join Norton (in great secrecy because of the KGB), where he, in effect, took over the development of the works racing engines.

At the end of 1953 Leo left Norton to take up the appointment of Chief Engineer (Racing) with Vandervell Products. This company was owned by Tony Vandervell, also a Norton director. At Vanwall (the Vandervell automobile racing arm – note, cars not bikes), Kuzmicki was largely responsible for the design of the Formula 1 engine. Interestingly, this was essentially four Norton top ends on a common (inline) crankcase. By 1958 the dohc motor was putting out 285bhp at 7,400rpm on alcohol fuel. The same year Vanwall became the first-ever team to win the coveted Formula 1 Constructor's Championship.

The next move for Leo Kuzmicki was to Humber, as Senior Development Engineer. Later, when Humber became part of the Rootes Group of Companies, Leo was promoted to Deputy Chief Engineer on the Imp project. Then, in late 1963, he became Chief Engineer responsible for design and development.

In 1965 Leo was put in charge of Group Engineering Co-Ordination. Then, for 1966 and 1967 (Rootes having been taken over by the American Chrysler Corporation), he was appointed Head of Engine and Transmission Design.

In 1975, then aged 65, he became Engineering Manager of the Octel Company which had its engine laboratory at Watling Street, Bletchley, Buckinghamshire. Later still, in 1981, he was brought in as Senior Consultant at Hesketh. One of his tasks, shortly before his death in 1982, was to resolve problems with the new V1000 Hesketh superbike. But before he could undertake this work he became ill. The cause of death was attributed to the starvation he had endured during his time in the Soviet Union, which caused his veins to shrink and his subsequent ill health in later years.

Over the years Geoff Duke has acknowledged just what an impact Leo Kuzmicki made at Norton. For example, when Mick Woollett interviewed Geoff in a *Classic Bike* article in its April 2003 issue (celebrating Geoff's 80th birthday), Mick put the question 'In 1950 you finished second in the 350cc World Championship, beaten by Bob Foster on a Velocette. Yet, in 1951 you won easily. What made the difference?' Geoff's reply was simple: 'A man named Leo Kuzmicki.' Going on to say 'the original 350 of 1950 churned out just 28bhp at 7200rpm, but by the time Kuzmicki had finished with it, the power was up to 36bhp at 8000rpm. It was a 30 percent increase and on top of that it was a lot smoother.'

'Another Duke Double on his Norton machines.' The 2.4-mile Goodwood lap abounded with very fast, sweeping bends, and, as one commentator said, 'therefore is a first-class nursery for the TT'. Geoff also set the fastest lap of the meeting on his 499cc Norton at 89.1mph.

More rider preparation for the forthcoming Grand Prix races came with a visit to the Belgian Mettet circuit, which, together with Floreffe, held around the same time, were popular with the works teams of that time.

Mettet was some 8½ kilometres (5¼ miles) in length. The course itself formed a figure of eight and ran through thickly-wooded country between the rivers of Sambre and Meuse.

For the 1951 meeting held on Sunday 29 April, around 16,000 spectators watched the racing in spite of frequent rain and hail storms. In some sections of the circuit there was even standing water. So when one realises that Geoff Duke broke the outright motorcycle lap record for the course (previously held by Italy's Enrico Lorenzetti on a Moto Guzzi v-twin), raising the speed from 95.5 to 96.52mph, it was, as more than one commentator said, 'a remarkable feat'.

Geoff at speed along the Promenade at Portstewart, during his record-breaking race victory at the Irish North West 200, May 1951.

Geoff covered the 20 laps (105 miles) in 1 hour 6 minutes 59.30 seconds, a speed of 94.61mph, beating the runner-up Mick Featherstone (AJS twin) by over a minute and a half. Bill Doran on another AJS was third, with Dickie Dale (Norton) fourth, a lap behind the winner!

In the 350cc event Geoff could only manage a third, behind the winner Doran (AJS) and runner-up Les Graham (Velocette).

Record breaking in Ulster

There was more success for Geoff in the Irish North West 200. Yet again the St Helens lad was in top form, not only winning the 500cc race, but also setting a new lap record for the Ulster course in 7 minutes 12 seconds, a speed of 92.27mph, the record which had previously been held by Artie Bell.

A crowd estimated to have been 'well over 35,000' *(The Motor Cycle)* saw what was described as 'a class display of riding' by Geoff Duke, who was in such excellent form that he almost lapped the third man, teammate Dickie Dale! Johnny Lockett on another Norton was runner-up.

Although Geoff was a non-finisher in the 350cc race (held two days earlier on Thursday 10 May), it was notable as it was the first race for the new three-fifty Norton engine, which was the work of Polish engineer Leo Kuzmicki. Geoff's retirement in the race (due to magneto problems which affected the spark plug gap) could not hide the huge improvement over the 1950 engine. The centre of the new power unit was its flat-topped piston, which used the 'squish' principle to maximise power, rather than the previous massively-domed piston assembly. As Geoff himself recalled, 'The net result was a phenomenal 30 percent increase in power, from 28bhp at 7200rpm to 36bhp at 8000rpm.' One has also to take into account that this was achieved on a very low octane rating, which makes this increase even more impressive. And yet another positive feature of the Kuzmicki engine was its greatly improved tractability (torque).

The final meeting prior to the start of the World Championship series came at Blandford on Whit Monday 14 May, a mere two days after the end of the North West 200 races. Here Geoff only rode his three-fifty Norton, as only one five-hundred model was available and this was allocated to Johnny Lockett. The three 350cc heats were won by Dickie Dale, Cecil Sandford and Geoff.

The 350cc final, held over 10 laps of the 3.14 mile course, saw Dale and Sandford build up a 100-yard lead at the end of the first lap. Then Geoff set about reducing the gap. Within two more laps he was right up with them. There then followed a cat-and-mouse situation, before Duke finally established a clear lead over Dale. Thereafter, Geoff remained at the front of the field to win at an average speed of 84.64mph.

By now Geoff was becoming a true superstar and was extremely popular with press and public alike.

Heavy rain in Switzerland

The Swiss Grand Prix, held over the tree-lined 4.5-mile Bremgarten circuit in Berne, was in fact the second round of the 1951 World Championship series; the first Spanish round in Barcelona had not staged a 350cc class, so the Norton team had declined to compete.

But, all-in-all, what with the truly awful weather and ill-fortune, it must have seemed that coming to Switzerland over Saturday 26 and Sunday 27 May had been a wasted journey.

In the 350cc event there were two official entries, Geoff Duke plus the Swiss rider Georges Cordey. At the start of the race Les Graham, riding a KTT Velocette, led, and then Geoff got ahead, but Graham shot past as Duke slowed across the finishing line where oil had been spilled. The new Norton was 'outstandingly' faster than the previous year's model, and so Geoff zoomed past Graham on the straight during lap four. As *The Motor Cycle* report said, 'He was lapping at around 81mph – by no means a record-breaking speed but absolutely superb on wet roads.' Cordey was a safe third, before being put out of the race through magneto trouble, and just as Geoff seemingly established an unassailable lead, he too was struck down with magneto failure.

In Northern Ireland it had been thought, wrongly, that the KLG plug's excessive gap had been the sole problem and a switch made to Lodge plugs. However, after the Swiss debacle the Norton engineers discovered that it was the magneto which was causing the plug to arch and so widen…

The 500cc race was staged on Sunday, but conditions were no better – even more rain fell relentlessly from a canopy of unbroken cloud. Even so, the crowds were massive. On paper the 500cc class was far more competitive, with factory-mounted riders from not only Norton but Gilera, Moto Guzzi, MV Agusta and AJS taking part.

Again, the Norton team comprised Duke and Cordey, the other main contenders being Fergus Anderson (Guzzi), Les Graham (MV), Nello Pagani (Gilera) and Reg Armstrong (AJS). As in the 350cc race the previous day, Geoff led (and also set the fastest lap at 89.4mph) before both he and Cordey were again struck down with faulty magnetos!

With TT practice having already started, Norton had some serious worries. But after flying from Berne to the Isle of Man (with a stop in Brussels) aboard a twin-engined Douglas DC3, a cure was found for the magneto gremlins, simply by switching to the newly-developed rotating-magnet instrument Lucas had on the stocks.

TT practice

Geoff said that 'My 350cc engine was incredibly smooth and free-revving, and this combination, along with perfect weather conditions, almost produced a disaster on my first practice lap.' This is how he described the incident:

It happened as I approached the long, rock-faced right-hand sweep before Laurel Bank. I was so exhilarated by the occasion that I failed to realise, until almost too late, that I was approaching this deceptive bend at a speed more akin to that of the previous year's 500. I had no option but to lay my machine over to the point where both wheels began to break away and, still on the overrun, negotiate the following left-hander totally off line.

Practice for the 1951 TT races 'could not have opened much more quietly – or much more dismally'. The first official practice session was held on Thursday morning at 4.30am prior to the Swiss Grand Prix. It was already raining at Kirkmichael and Ramsey when practice started, and the rain quickly spread to the remainder of the island. To make matters worse, there was a strong wind blowing across the mountain. In the circumstances, the Norton team did not miss much!

The Australian Harry Hinton on his 348cc Norton during the Junior TT, 5 June 1951. The race distance was seven laps (264.133 miles).

Arriving on the Sunday evening, Geoff was in action in the next practice session, on Monday evening 28 May, when he took his Junior mount round fastest in 25 minutes 29 seconds, a speed of 88.85mph, which surpassed Artie Bell's record of 25 minutes 56 seconds with ease.

Later in the week Geoff also beat his existing Senior lap record (on Thursday 31 May), circulating in 24 minutes 13 seconds, a speed of 93.52mph.

Norton first, second and third in Junior race

Riding the Kuzmicki 348cc model, Geoff broke the lap record from a standing start in 25 minutes 14 seconds (89.75mph). His second, third and fifth laps all exceeded 90mph, with the second lap the fastest at 91.38mph (24 minutes 47 seconds). Thereafter he slowed, knowing the race was in his

Geoff won the 1951 Junior TT on his Leo Kuzmicki-tuned works Norton. He is seen here after the race, having broken the lap record from a standing start in 25 minutes 14 seconds (89.75mph).

pocket, but still finished the race with an average speed of 89.90mph – a superb showing. Norton riders also took second and third positions, Johnny Lockett and Jack Brett respectively. There were 59 finishers, and Norton won the Manufacturer's team prize (Duke, Lockett and Brett).

Junior TT – 7 laps – 264.11 miles

1st	G.E. Duke (Norton)
2nd	J. Lockett (Norton)
3rd	J. Brett (Norton)
4th	M. Featherstone (AJS)
5th	W.A. Lomas (Velocette)
6th	A.R. Foster (Velocette)

A repeat performance

On Friday 9 June 1951 Geoff won his second Senior TT. As in the Junior four days earlier, all records were again shattered. And as with the Junior, the Senior race was staged in perfect weather before a record crowd – and except for the runner-up (Bill Doran, AJS) all of the first 12 finishers were Norton mounted!

Brett had taken over the works Norton at the last minute when Dickie Dale was unfit to ride. Geoff was also part of the winning Birmingham Club team (with Albert Moule and E.R. Evans).

Yorkshireman Jack Brett was part of the winning Norton Manufacturer's team. Brett finished third, with Geoff Duke first and Johnny Lockett runner-up.

Senior TT – 7 laps – 264.11 miles

1st   G.E. Duke (Norton)
2nd   W. Doran (AJS)
3rd   W.A.C. McCandless (Norton)
4th   T. McEwan (Norton)
5th   M. Barrington (Norton)
6th   A.L. Parry (Norton)

At the official prize giving for the Senior race on Friday evening at the Villa Marina, double-winner Geoff said he 'could not find words to describe adequately his feelings, no more than he could find words to describe the terrific machines he had been riding.' He added, 'it was fantastic, in fact it frightened me to death. But I should like to commiserate with Les Graham on his bad luck.' This referred to the latter's retirement on the four-cylinder MV Agusta. Geoff also thanked 'Doc Darbishire for the usual rapid pit work' and his mechanics.

On 8 June 1951 Geoff, then 25 years of age, became the fourth man to score a Junior/Senior TT double when he won the Senior race at record speed and record lap at 95.22mph – the first over 95mph.

1951 Senior TT, Geoff walks back to the paddock after winning the race on his works Norton. With him is race official Norman Brown.

Geoff (1) about to pass Tommy McEwan (85) during the 1951 Senior TT.

Johnny Lockett. He provided reliable support to Geoff Duke in the Norton team until the end of the 1951 season.

Johnny Lockett

Johnny Lockett was a teammate of Geoff Duke's in the Norton factory racing team. Born in 1915, Johnny had begun his motorcycling career when aged 17 and still at the Merchant Taylors School. As Harry Louis said in an article on Lockett in the 26 February 1948 issue of *The Motor Cycle*, 'His introduction was abrupt and bordering on the disastrous.' A school friend had a Francis-Barnett two-stroke, which Johnny borrowed to ride round a tennis court. And, as Louis continued, 'The first lap was successful, but second time round he smote some tough bushes and bent the forks.' But the fuse had been lit, resulting in the purchase of a 1930 172cc AKD ohv model. Later, this was exchanged for an old long-stroke Sunbeam, which in turn gave way for a 1928 ohv Humber.

Then, in 1933 Johnny Lockett joined the ranks of competitive motorcycling. Having enlisted with the Streatham Club, he entered the club's Half-Crown Trial. Thereafter, he competed in the South Eastern Centre trials regularly, the Humber making way for a 1927 Velocette KSS – his first overhead camshaft model.

With a party of club members, Johnny spent his 1935 vacation in the Isle of Man to spectate at the annual Manx Grand Prix. He took with him his first brand new motorcycle, another KSS Velocette. And, in his own words, 'put in innumerable laps of the TT course that I nearly wore the Velo out in the fortnight'. Those laps aroused his interest in racing, and so, before the 1936 season had started, there was a racing three-fifty Norton in the Lockett garage.

A 350cc Norton trials bike was also acquired at the same time, because Johnny 'enjoyed all forms of motorcycle sport' and believed that racing, trials and scrambles were 'complementary'.

With the racing Norton, he competed at Brooklands, Donington Park and the Junior Manx Grand Prix, finishing fifth in the latter at 69.3mph.

The following year, 1937, he had a three-fifty 'springer' Norton and was third in the Junior MGP and ninth in the Senior race on the same machine – the first 350 to finish.

Then, through his association with Brooklands, he met Francis Beart.

The two formed a successful partnership for the 1938 and 1939 seasons. Highlights included runner-up in the 1938 Senior Manx GP (at 84.09mph), and, in 1939, the Brooklands five-lap Mountain record in the 750cc class and the one-lap Campbell circuit record. Numerous successes at Donington included the eight-lap 350cc record. This, and the Brooklands records, were to remain unbeaten. Another notable achievement was a Brooklands Gold Star for a lap of 101.85mph on 1 April 1939, with the Beart 350cc Norton. He also made his TT debut that year, but ran out of fuel in the Junior race to push in for 16th position, while in the Senior he retired on the fifth lap with engine trouble, while lying in a creditable eighth.

The war saw Johnny with the unglamorous work of an Aircraft Inspector, and the only motorcycle was that provided for Home Guard training.

During the immediate post-war period, Johnny rode Steve Lancefield's machines at grass track, airfield racing, and the legendary Shelsley Walsh Hill climb. The combination of Lockett and Lancefield proved the springboard to Norton signing the former for the 1948 season, even though, for a considerable part of 1947, he was suffering from a spine damaged in a car crash. But later that year, riding a factory Norton for the first time, he won the 350cc Ulster Grand Prix.

In the first year of the World Championship series (1949), Johnny finished fourth in the 350cc title rankings. But his best year was 1951, when he was runner-up (again in the 350cc category), behind Geoff Duke, in the latter's Norton double (350/500cc) Championship year.

Johnny Lockett was not what could be described as a 'legend' in the same way as Duke, Surtees or Hailwood, but more of a reliable back-up man in the Norton team – a job he performed until his works contract was not renewed for 1952; he then called it a day, but still had some brilliant memories to look back on.

Johnny Lockett in action on a works Norton during the 1951 North West 200 in Northern Ireland.

Geoff with his girlfriend (later wife), Pat Reid, and his mother and father after his 1951 Senior TT victory. Norton's managing director Gilbert Smith (with glasses and hat) is to Geoff's right.

Getting engaged and more GP action

Shortly after his TT success Geoff became engaged to Patricia Reid, the attractive 20-year-old youngest daughter of the Reverend R.H. Reid, who was chairman of the Manx Grand Prix committee. Then the Norton team, together with Geoff, were off to Continental Europe for more Grand Prix action.

British riders and machinery dominated all three races at the 1951 Belgian Grand Prix, with not only Geoff Duke scoring a highly impressive 350/500cc double, but fellow Norton teamster Eric Oliver winning the sidecar event. When one considers that both Geoff (500cc) and Eric won their races with a four-cylinder Gilera in the runner-up position – and that this was at Europe's fastest circuit – the extent of their triumphs becomes even more apparent.

The meeting was also notable in the history of the famous 8.8 mile Francorchamps – Malmedy – Stavelot circuit because only the year before, the 500cc race had been won at an average speed of over 100mph for the first time. Yet now, in 1951, Geoff had exceeded the magic three-figure speed on his 350cc machine! His average for the 96.4 miles was 100.52mph, as *The Motor Cycle* reported, 'Not unexpectedly Geoff Duke (Norton) also came home first in the 500cc event at an average speed of 106.66mph.' In this latter event he also established a lap speed of 107.8mph – which was at that time the highest ever achieved in a classic road circuit. Just by studying the results of the 500cc race, it is evident that Geoff's was an outstanding performance. And behind the scenes the input by engineering genius Leo Kuzmicki is evident too, as by now he was beginning to wave his magic on not just the 350cc engine, but the 500cc power unit too.

500cc Belgian GP – 14 laps – 122.7 miles
1st   G.E. Duke (Norton)
2nd   A. Milani (Gilera)
3rd   S. Geminiani (Moto Guzzi)
4th   H.R. Armstrong (AJS)
5th   N. Pagani (Gilera)
6th   J. Lockett (Norton)
7th   J. Brett (Norton)
8th   E. Lorenzetti (Moto Guzzi)
9th   U. Masetti (Gilera)

All but the Norton's were either twin or four-cylinder machines. Not only this, but with Geoff's teammates (Lockett and Brett) down in sixth and seventh places, in reality our hero was the lone foil against the multi-cylinder opposition.

It was here, at the Belgian Grand Prix, that Joe Craig, as Geoff later described, 'paid me a great compliment'. Essentially he told his star rider 'that during his many years' involvement in road racing, in his opinion only

The 1951 350cc Belgian Grand Prix was notable as with the Kuzmicki engine Geoff was able to average 100.52mph for the 96.4-mile race – only a year before had seen the first 100mph average on a 500cc machine!

two riders had been "naturals" – Tim Hunt, who had ridden Nortons during the early 1930s, and me!' When one considers the other riders who had ridden for Craig – such as Jimmy Guthrie, Stanley Woods and Harold Daniell to name but three – this was a compliment indeed.

His proudest moment

In his autobiography, Geoff said:

Looking back, the 1951 500cc Belgian Grand Prix, then the world's fastest road race, must go down in my book as the hardest race of my career. As I stood on the winner's rostrum, listening to our national anthem, it was also my proudest moment.

But it was down to earth with a bump only six days later, when Geoff crashed at well over 100mph during the 350cc race at the Dutch TT, while leading. As he was to admit:

With the help of the following wind, my 350 was really flying on the approach to the flat-out S-bend after the start. Too late, I realised at near 500cc speed that I should have peeled off earlier into the 'S' – I was then forced to bank over at a much greater angle than usual to keep on the racing line. The result was that the front tyre suddenly lost all grip and down I went.

Luckily, although his motorcycle had been extensively damaged, Geoff was able to 'walk back to the paddock for medical attention'. Not only this, but later in the day he was fit enough to win the 500cc race, from Alfredo Milani (Gilera) and Enrico Lorenzetti (Moto Guzzi). And to secure the victory after such a setback was surely the mark of a true champion.

Honours divided in France

Almost 20 years had elapsed since a road race with FIM classic status had been held in France. As *The Motor Cycle* report dated 19 July 1951 commented, 'The quiescant period was brought to an end last Sunday when the French Grand Prix took place over the 5½-mile Albi circuit.'

Successes were divided between Italy and Great Britain. In the 500cc event Alfredo Milani (Gilera) was victorious, and his compatriot Bruno Ruffo (Moto Guzzi) won the 250cc race. But Norton bikes won both the 350cc (Geoff Duke) and Sidecar (Eric Oliver).

The 350cc class was staged in the morning, with clouds of spray from

Joe Craig

Born in the town of Ballymena near Belfast, Northern Ireland, on 11 January 1898, Joe Craig is considered by many to have been the greatest racing team manager that has ever been seen in the history of motorcycle sport. And when he died in a car accident in Austria during March 1957, he was 59 years of age and his name synonymous with road racing, and particularly with Norton, since 1925.

Joe Craig took his first steps towards fame when he began an apprenticeship in a local Ulster garage dealing almost exclusively with cars. Soon after this he purchased his first motorcycle, a side-valve Norton, with which he competed regularly in hill climbs. This bike was followed by an overhead-valve Model 18, with which he took part in the 1923 Ulster Grand Prix. He won, albeit helped by the retirement of the two leading contenders, but the following year he repeated the performance – attracting the attention of the Norton factory.

But it was to be Craig's technical abilities and management expertise, rather than his riding skills, which brought him his great career successes.

Right from the start of his racing, technical development of the machine meant a great deal more to him than the mere pleasure of riding. One can but imagine, therefore, the thrill and excitement that Joe Craig must have experienced when the very first factory machine, for whose preparation he was responsible, won the Grand Prix of Europe in Barcelona at the end of 1929, ridden by Tim Hunt. From that time (except for the war years), the softly-spoken Irishman with the prominent nose, jutting chin and stooped shoulders, dominated European racing as no one else – not as a glamorous ace rider or even a brilliant designer, but as a tuner, development engineer and team boss. There is no doubt that the vast majority of the greats in racing who came under his wing, such as Stanley Woods, Jimmy Guthrie, Harold Daniell, Freddie Frith, Artie Bell, Ray Amm, John Surtees and Geoff Duke himself, all benefitted from Joe Craig's vast experience.

Motorcycle racing was, quite simply, Joe Craig's entire life. He displayed a dedicated purpose that very, very few men could have achieved – and do not forget, this was over a time span of many years, not days or even months!

If anything, the advancement of years – his fame already established – only seemed to intensify his purpose. He firmly believed that to do a job correctly, that task had to receive top priority and all his personal concentration. In other words, he was not someone who found delegation easy.

There is also no doubt that the best riders received his best attention and that he did not suffer fools gladly.

The following is what Geoff Duke said in *The Motor Cycle* dated 14 March 1957, following Joe Craig's death: 'It was tragic to hear about the

Norton's race supremo for almost a quarter of a century, Ulsterman Joe Craig with one of his beloved Norton Singles, spring 1951.

With Crommie
McCandless, Dickie Dale,
Joe Craig and Johnny
Lockett.

loss of a great friend just as I returned from South Africa (see Chapter
Five). In 1948 Joe Craig was responsible for my start at Norton's, which led
ultimately to my life's ambition – a career in racing. Joe was a man with a
great knowledge of his chosen career. He possessed in full measure that
great attribute which is so rare and yet so essential a characteristic of the
successful development engineer – he had an open mind. His help,
understanding and truly fantastic wealth of experience, which he so
willingly conveyed to me on so many occasions, I have always considered
contributed greatly to my own racing success.'

rain-soaked roads being an additional hazard for the riders to contend with
at the start. But by the second lap Geoff had established a significant lead –
by some 15 seconds after the end of the third lap. The rain had stopped, but
the roads were still water covered, and with speeds now beginning to rise,
Duke was already lapping the tail-enders. But in spite of his commanding
position, Geoff went faster and faster lap by lap. The roads were now
beginning to dry. One commentator questioned if he could exceed a 90mph
lap, and in what *The Motor Cycle* described as 'that searing last lap', Geoff
made the best time of the race, with a lap of 3 minutes 38 seconds
(91.28mph). Not only this, but with a race average speed of 87.97mph he
just exceeded Les Graham's speed the previous year, in the non-
Championship meeting when the roads were dry.

350cc French GP – 17 laps – 94 miles
1st   G.E. Duke (Norton)
2nd   J. Brett (Norton)
3rd   W. Doran (AJS)

4th   J. Lockett (Norton)
5th   H.R. Armstrong (AJS)
6th   R.W. Coleman (AJS)

Geoff could 'only' manage a fifth in the 500cc race, his cause not being helped by low-grade fuel which was given to all competitors. As Geoff was to recall, this 'took the edge off performance, but the twin and four-cylinder machines of AJS, Gilera and Guzzi were virtually unaffected.'

500cc French GP – 23 laps – 127 miles
1st   A. Milani (Gilera)
2nd   W. Doran (AJS)
3rd   N. Pagani (Gilera)
4th   U. Masetti (Gilera)
5th   G.E. Duke (Norton)
6th   J. Brett (Norton)

Press reaction

Maybe because the British press had become used to Geoff Duke putting in race-winning performances wherever he went, *The Motor Cycle's* Occasional Comments Column (by Ixion), entitled simply 'Geoff', carried the following in its 9 August issue:

During the past few weeks Geoff Duke has stepped off that superhuman pedestal on which he had resided. Incredibly, in two consecutive meetings on the Continent he did not figure as the winner. In one (the 350cc Dutch Grand Prix), to quote his own phrase, he 'just fell off'! In the other, the 500cc French GP, possibly owing to the official fuel muddle, he was outpaced by four – yes, four – assorted rivals. The interest and dismay among members of the general public created by brief reports of these mishaps in the daily papers were an enormous tribute to his popularity, and add to the pride two-wheeled Britons take in his feats. On the other hand, I think he has encountered – not for the first time – that disappointment which is the common fate of more ordinary fellows. We can confidently expect more records from him in the near future, and we are glad that he is not so greedy as to monopolise all the available victories.

A wet Thruxton

August Bank Holiday, Monday 6 August, saw Geoff back racing in England, at Thruxton, the scene of the ACU's big international road races, where there were massive crowds braving what were generally described as appalling conditions with never-ending heavy rain. As *The Motor Cycle* said, 'riding conditions were vile'.

In the 15-lap 350cc final there was a battle royal between Geoff and AJS teamster Bill Doran, and after challenging hard for most of the race, Doran got by with two laps to spare, a position he retained until the flag. The AJS rider also put in the fastest lap.

But the Norton man got his revenge in both races, in which he rode his larger machine, the 1000cc, at the Festival of Britain Invitation event.

On both occasions Geoff was hotly pursued by a certain youngster riding a Vincent Gray Flash. His name? John Surtees! And it was here, at Thruxton, on that horribly wet day in August 1951, that the Surtees name first came to the fore. On the day he was the only man to give Duke a run for his money in the two larger-capacity races. On both occasions John had to finally give best to the more experienced rider, but at the prize-giving ceremony Geoff Duke praised 'the remarkable riding of young John Surtees who made me ride so fast'.

Yet more rain

There was yet more rain when Geoff returned to Grand Prix action in Ulster later that month. But this did not cramp the Norton star's winning ways, as he took victories in both the 350 and 500cc races.

Held over the 16½-mile Clady-road circuit, this was the first year in which the Ulster was held over two days. Previously all classes had been run concurrently. However, this traditional arrangement was not possible under the 1951 FIM ruling for World Championship meetings, whereby the programme had to be such that a rider could take part in at least one race in each of the groups (a) 125, 250, and 350cc solo and (b) 500cc solo and 500cc sidecar.

In consequence, the 125, 250 and 350cc classes were staged on Thursday evening, 16 August, with the 500cc solo (there was no sidecar race) held on the Saturday, 18 August.

The meeting marked the debut of the Australian Ken Kavanagh on a factory Norton, and it was the newcomer to the team who finished runner-up to Geoff in both races.

But more importantly for this book, 'the irrepressible Duke' *(The Motor Cycle)* had become the first man to be a double world champion in one year – and also the first to score three doubles (the Isle of Man, Belgian and Ulster) in one season's classic events.

350cc Ulster GP – 13 laps – 214.5 miles

1st   G.E. Duke (Norton)
2nd   K. Kavanagh (Norton)
3rd   J. Lockett (Norton)
4th   H.R. Armstrong (AJS)
5th   W. Doran (AJS)
6th   J. Brett (Norton)

500cc Ulster GP – 15 laps – 247.5 miles

1st   G.E. Duke (Norton)
2nd   K. Kavanagh (Norton)
3rd   U. Masetti (Gilera)
4th   A. Milani (Gilera)
5th   J. Lockett (Norton)
6th   W. Doran (AJS)

Another double

It was yet another victorious double victory for Geoff on Sunday 26 August in the German Grand Prix, staged at the picture-postcard Solitude circuit near Stuttgart, in front of over 400,000 spectators.

The 7.1 mile, largely tree-lined circuit was host to what, up to that time, was probably a record for a sporting event held anywhere in the world.

The start of the 350cc German GP at Solitude on 26 August 1951, which Geoff (60) won. Note the masses of spectators right next to the track side. What would our current health and safety regime think of this?

Geoff with his new Norton teammate Ken Kavanagh, the pair finished first and second respectively on their Norton's in the 350cc Italian GP at Monza, 9 September 1951.

This vast gathering reflected the fact that not only was motorcycle racing supremely popular in Germany (as it had been in pre-war days), but that the country had just been re-admitted to the FIM and could therefore stage a World Championship status event for the very first time.

The 350cc race was again dominated by British machines, with Norton taking the first three places. In this event Geoff also established a new class record lap in 5 minutes 11.5 seconds, a speed of 82.34mph. But Ken Kavanagh crashed on one of the tricky S-bends just over 5 miles from the start and was thus an early retirement.

However, this had not damped the Australian rider's spirit as it was Kavanagh, rather than Duke, who set the fastest lap (an absolute record for the track) in the later 500cc race. Even so, it was Mr Duke who emerged as the victor once again.

Besides the Nortons, BMW put out works entries in the hands of the old master of German road racing and 1939 Senior TT winner Georg Meier (then 44 years of age) and the young Walter Zeller.

At the end of this race (the last of the day), vast crowds besieged the starting area to get, as *The Motor Cycle* described, 'a glimpse of the winners and their beloved Georg Meier'.

Thereafter, for hours the whole Solitude circuit was jammed with people and vehicles – and at nightfall streams of motorcycles, cars, vans and buses, their lights ablaze, were still threading their way like, as one commentator vividly described it, 'enormous illuminated caterpillars' from the circuit in every direction which roads led!

350cc German GP – 12 laps – 85.5 miles
1st	G.E. Duke (Norton)
2nd	J. Lockett (Norton)
3rd	J. Brett (Norton)
4th	W. Petch (AJS)
5th	J. Kläger (AJS)
6th	A. Goffin (Norton)

500cc German GP – 12 laps – 85.5 miles
1st	G.E. Duke (Norton)
2nd	K. Kavanagh (Norton)
3rd	J. Brett (Norton)
4th	J. Lockett (Norton)
5th	G. Meier (BMW)
6th	W. Zeller (BMW)

And had not Kavanagh crashed his machine in the 350cc race, Norton would, undoubtedly, have had a clean sweep of both races, this proving how fast *and* reliable the machines had become since Leo Kuzmicki's participation in their development that year.

Grand Prix des Nations

Next in the classic calendar came the Grand Prix des Nations at Monza in Italy on Sunday 9 September; this meeting was also the last of the ones counting towards Championship points for 1951.

When race day dawned, it broke bright and clear with no signs that it would be anything other than the usual 'Monza scorcher' *(The Motor Cycle)*, and nor was it.

The 6.3km (4 mile) Monza Autodrome circuit was very much about speed and yet more speed as the main requirement to victory, and although Geoff won the 350cc event (from his Norton teammates Kavanagh and Brett), the 500cc race was an entirely different matter. With a host of local four-cylinder entries from both Gilera and MV Agusta, plus the Moto Guzzi v-twins, Norton's task was always going to be difficult to say the least. And so it proved.

Actually, Kavanagh was leading Geoff until his final drive chain broke, but had still been outpaced by the quickest Gileras.

Geoff ultimately came home fourth behind a trio of Gileras, ridden by Milani, Masetti and Pagani. Actually, as Geoff was later to admit, Alfredo Milani, although originally regarded primarily as a sidecar man, was definitely Italy's best large-capacity solo rider at the time. Besides winning the race, Alfredo also set the fastest lap (at 107.18mph).

350cc Italian GP – 24 laps – 93.9 miles

1st	G.E. Duke (Norton)
2nd	K. Kavanagh (Norton)
3rd	J. Brett (Norton)
4th	W. Doran (AJS)
5th	H.R. Armstrong (AJS)
6th	R. Coleman (AJS)

500cc Italian GP – 32 laps – 125.2 miles

1st	A. Milani (Gilera)
2nd	U. Masetti (Gilera)
3rd	N. Pagani (Gilera)
4th	G.E. Duke (Norton)

5th   B. Ruffo (Moto Guzzi)
6th   W. Doran (AJS)

Getting married

Next stop for Geoff in 1951 was getting married. This is how *The Motor Cycle* reported the event in its 20 September 1951 issue:

> *World's 350cc and 500cc Road-racing champion, Geoffrey Ernest Duke, who is 28, was married last Friday, to 20-year-old Miss Patricia Ann Reid, second daughter of the Rev. N. Reid M.A., chairman of the Manx Motor Cycle and Automobile Clubs. Held at St. George's Church, Douglas, Isle of Man, the ceremony was performed by the bride's father, assisted by the Rev. Canon E.H. Stenning M.A., president of the Manx MCC. Best man was Dr Steve Darbishire, who was third in the Senior Manx GP of 1935 and came second to Freddie Frith in the Junior Manx of that year. The bride was given away by her brother, Mr Guy Reid.*

And what a wedding it turned out to be, the church was 'packed beyond its capacity of 900, and more than 1,000 people thronged all the available space outside', and just to seal a perfect day the sun shone. After the reception at the Fort Anne Hotel, the newly-wed Mr and Mrs Duke flew to Speke, Liverpool, where Geoff's car was waiting. For the honeymoon the pair motored first to Paris and then on to Switzerland.

Back to 'business'

Next it was back to the business of racing, with Geoff's first meeting on his return coming at the BMCRC's Silverstone races. *The Motor Cycle* reported that it 'proved a thrilling climax to a thrilling racing season'. And that 'not a single enthusiast set off on his return journey disappointed' – such was the standard of racing that day. It was once again 'The Phenomenal Duke (Nortons)' who 'Dominated Major Events' *(The Motor Cycle)*.

In both the two main 17-lap (50 mile) 350 and 500cc events, quite simply Geoff dominated the proceedings to such an extent that typical press comments of the day included examples such as 'Duke fast disappeared into the blue and by half-distance he was lapping everyone but the first seven or eight in a field of over 40!' Geoff raised the circuit lap record to 92.92mph.

Perhaps most amazingly, for the newly-crowned double-world champion it was then back to some dirt-bike events, including the Inter-Centre Team Championship Trial in late October.

Showtime honours

Among the many Earls Court, London, Motorcycle show functions, were two in honour of Geoff and his magnificent achievement of becoming double world champion for 1951.

The first on the Tuesday evening of the Show in mid-November was given by Nortons and held at the Park Lane (London) Hotel. In charge of the proceedings was C.A. Vandervell (Cav or Sparks as he was affectionately known due to his other business connections as head of a leading engineering/electrical firm). As chairman of the Norton board of directors, Mr Vandervell presented Geoff, together with Eric Oliver (the 1951 Sidecar champion) and team manager Joe Craig, with a leather suitcase inscribed with their initials.

The second occasion was staged by the Lucas company – one of Nortons main trade sponsors – and was held the following evening at the Mayfair hotel.

1952 begins

1952 began with news in early January that Geoff was to enter the retail motorcycle business, with a dealership opening in early April, in his home town of St Helens. The business was to be known as Geoff Duke Ltd, with premises at Greenfield Garage, Greenfield Road.

Then, in the 13 March 1952 issue of *The Motor Cycle*, came more news entitled 'Duke's Plans'. The story is repeated below:

Rumour has been rife recently concerning Geoff Duke's future plans. Here is the true position. In the first place, it may be taken as official that he has no intention of quitting the motorcycle racing game in the foreseeable future. He is, however, interested in driving sports cars and this year Aston Martin are keen to have him race their cars in meetings which do not clash with motorcycle races. Geoff has agreed to this, provided Astons can arrange that he uses certain equipment of the same make as he does on motorcycles. This is not a question of finance, incidentally, but a personal fad of Geoff's. Should this matter be satisfactorily arranged, then Geoff may be seen driving sports cars this year; the first occasion will probably be the British Empire Trophy meeting on the IOM, which will take place on May 29 – the day practice begins for the TT races. As regards his motorcycle business in St Helens, – the official opening between the Swiss GP and the TT – Geoff will spend all his time there between races. This said, I hope that I have heard for the last time the story that Duke is giving up motorcycle racing!

A January 1952 advertisement promoting 'The Unapproachable Norton Upholder of the British Motor Cycle Supremacy throughout the World'. An image of Geoff Duke was used to force home the message.

On 9 April 1952 Geoff was presented with the annual Sportsman of the Year Trophy at the Savoy Hotel in London... imagine a motorcyclist winning today!

Awards

Also in early March Geoff was honoured by the City of Birmingham. In company with several Norton executives and staff, together with seven members of the Manx Motor Cycle club who had flown over from the Isle of Man, he was received by the Lord Mayor in his chambers at the Council House. Prior to attending the ceremony, the Manx officials were met at Elmdon Airfield and thereafter shown round the Norton works by the company's managing director, Gilbert Smith. Afterwards, a luncheon was given in their honour at the Regency club.

Then, on Wednesday 9 April came the climax of the Sportsman of the

Year ballot organised by *The Sporting Record* newspaper, when Geoff Duke was presented with the trophy at the Savoy Hotel, London. First begun back in 1946, worldwide response had been generated by the 1951 ballot and Lord Aberdare, who made the presentation, said 'there could be no doubt that the final result was a fair expression of public opinion'.

It is interesting to realise that the award is still carried on to this present day, albeit for many years by BBC Television, and it illustrates the heights to which Geoff's popularity had risen.

'A Springtime Silverstone'

'A Springtime Silverstone' was *The Motor Cycle's* headline for its report of the rival *Motor Cycling's* annual meeting, held on Saturday 19 April, which got Geoff's 1952 road-racing season under way. And what a way to begin, with his domination of both the 350 and 500cc races on his Nortons. For once, perfect weather favoured the Northamptonshire speed venue. It is estimated over 50,000 spectators attended.

Besides his clear-cut victories, Geoff also set the fastest laps in both his races; 88.5mph in the 350cc and 92.10mph on his bigger model. The word invincible was widely used by the commentary team for Duke's performance that sunny, spring day.

After Saturday's Silverstone meeting, Geoff flew to the South of France to compete in the following day's San Remo international road races. He won the 500cc class (his only outing) on his Norton at an average speed of some 60mph, from the Gilera riders Nello Pagani and O. Valdinosi. Geoff started last from the grid, but had gained the lead by the fourth of the 55 laps. Although challenged repeatedly by both riders, Duke eventually won by 20 seconds.

Armstrong joins the team

By the time the Irish Leinster 100 meeting was held at the beginning of May, Norton had their latest works machinery. But Geoff Duke was a non-starter, the official explanation given at the time being that 'he was unable to make the journey to Ireland'. However, former AJS rider Reg Armstrong (an Irishman himself) was having his first appearance on factory Nortons and won both the 350 and 500c races, with teammate Ken Kavanagh runner-up on both occasions. Joe Craig was there to oversee the team.

Then, on Saturday 10 May, Geoff appeared in a somewhat different role, when at the *Daily Express*

Spring 1952, the works Norton team. Left to right: Geoff, Ken Kavanagh, Reg Armstrong and Len Parry. Note the 16-inch rear wheel on the five-hundred Norton (soon axed).

On Saturday 10 May 1952 Geoff appeared in a different role, when at the International Trophy Car meeting at Silverstone he acted as pacemaker to world-record cyclist José Meiffret. Mounted on a standard Model 7 Dominator twin with a massive shield, he paced Meiffret, whose bicycle could achieve over 100mph.

International Trophy Car meeting at Silverstone he acted as pacemaker to the world-record cyclist José Meiffret. Mounted on a standard Norton 77 Dominator twin fitted with a massive shield, he paced Meiffret, whose bicycle featured the 275in gear with which the latter had set up his world-record speed of 109mph.

At that time it also became apparent why Geoff had not been in Ireland, instead he had scored yet another victory, this time at the Italian Codogno circuit, where he had won on his 500cc Norton in the 40-lap, 97-mile-long race. At the finish he was ahead by a mile from the second man, Nello Pagani (Gilera). Duke won at an average speed of 131.787kmh (82mph), in a time of 1 hour 10 minutes 0.8 seconds.

The first Grand Prix of the year

The first Grand Prix of the year counting towards Championship points was the Swiss, held over the tricky 4.5-mile Bremgarten circuit at Berne.

In contrast to the Swiss GP weekend of the previous year, the weather was described by *The Motor Cycle's* race report dated 22 May 1952 as 'magnificent'.

This meeting was also unique because it saw Geoff in action both on bikes (Nortons) and cars (Aston Martin). As Geoff himself said in his autobiography:

> *It was the only Grand Prix where they held car and motorcycle races at the same event, and in previous years, after finishing my motorcycle practising on the Norton, I would always go to the S-bend at the top of the hill to watch Fangio – the absolute maestro. So when Aston Martin asked me if I would like to drive at Berne, I was delighted. I was also pleased that the car was a DB2 because it handled like a motorcycle – it went where it was pointed and stayed in line.*

As a matter of interest, Geoff was to finish fourth – behind three Mercedes.

As for the motorcycle part of the meeting, for the second year running this was to act as a test session prior to the all-important TT, and, as in 1951, was to reveal a technical problem (the new camshaft which allowed the exhaust valve head to break off on some engines).

Although Geoff somewhat easily won the 350cc race, it was an entirely different matter in the 500cc event, as he was later to relate:

Car Racing

In his 1988 autobiography Geoff revealed that on the day he was presented with the Sportsman of the Year trophy in 1951, at the Savoy Hotel in London, Lord Brabazon had asked him if he had ever thought of racing on four wheels. Geoff had answered that he had not, but that 'I enjoy driving fast cars.' Lord Brabazon then suggested that if Geoff was interested he 'could arrange a test for me by Aston Martin'. And so, subsequently, Geoff was contacted by John Wyler, Aston Martin's racing manager.

It was Lord Brabazon who suggested that Geoff should take up car racing.

Later, in his book *Racing With the David Brown Aston Martins*, John Wyler was to comment 'I know that my opinion of Duke's abilities as a driver differs from that of most contemporary observers, and the generally accepted judgement is that he was a very great motorcyclist who failed to make the transition to cars. I maintain that I had more opportunity to evaluate him than anybody else and I am convinced that he had great potential.' John Wyler continued, 'Temperamentally, he had difficulty in settling down in the team and certainly the established drivers did nothing to make it easier for him. Not unnaturally, they resented the fact that he got more publicity than they did. But I will always regard Geoff Duke's early retirement as a loss to motor racing.'

The above is also the main reason why, in the end, Geoff took the decision to stick with two wheels, rather than four. But during his time with Aston Martin he not only put on some excellent performances, but also managed to race on both two and four wheels (Norton and Aston Martin, respectively) at the 1952 Swiss Grand Prix, staged over the Bremgarten (Berne) course.

Geoff also competed, during the same year, in the Isle of Man, both with bikes and cars (the latter event being the Empire Trophy Race).

But, unlike John Surtees, Geoff Duke's four-wheel racing was mainly confined to sport car events, rather than the transition to Formula 1. Also, the time scale was much shorter, with Geoff's car career lasting little more than 12 months before he quit, having realised how much he enjoyed the bikes after riding a standard three-fifty Manx Norton at Silverstone in spring 1953. He then immediately (as fully documented in Chapters 3 and 4) took the decision to sign for Gilera, thus ending his four-wheel connection.

However, several months after his retirement from motorcycle racing Geoff received an offer from Graham Warner of the West London (Chiswick) Chequered Flag dealership to drive one of the company's Formula Junior cars in 1960. Unfortunately, this rear-engined vehicle was very much in the development stage, and, as Geoff was to recall later, 'the opportunities to drive were few and far between'. Then, at the end of that year, Graham Warner advised Geoff that his company was unable to continue in the sport.

Finally, in mid-1961 came a call 'out of the blue' from Fred Tuck, a former speedway rider and owner of a Formula 1 Cooper car, with the offer of two drives – at the Nürburgring in Germany and Karlskoga in Sweden. Geoff was genuinely enthusiastic about driving at the former, but far less so about the latter venue, which he considered 'a short, bumpy and uninteresting circuit'.

But the promised outing at the Nürburgring did not take place, as Geoff was to write in his autobiography: 'My total lack of enthusiasm for Karlskoga should have prompted me to refuse. But I did not want to let Fred down so, reluctantly, I agreed to race.'

This turned out to be a bad decision, as not only was the car vastly over-geared for the circuit, but the gearbox eventually locked during the race – causing the most serious injuries Geoff had experienced during his entire racing career on either two or four wheels, including 'ribs torn from the sternum, a collapsed left lung, damage to my heart muscles, broken collarbone, cracked pelvis and a burst blood vessel that produced a "balloon" on my left hip.'

The whole experience was 'the most physically shattering experience of my life'. Geoff realised just how serious things had been, and, as he says, 'I got the message…'

Geoff with Stirling Moss, 14 April 1952 – Geoff was driving an Aston Martin.

The 500cc race was a much more comprehensive event than the 350cc,
with three works Nortons (myself, Armstrong and Bennett), three
AJSs (Doran, Coleman and Brett), three Gileras (Alfredo Milani,
Masetti and Liberati), and two MV Agustas (Graham and Bandirola),
plus 14 others to make up a field of 25.

Even so, Geoff and the Norton led until passing the finishing line at the
end of the 19th lap, 'his engine ceased to fire and clanked like worn-out
farm machinery' *(The Motor Cycle)* ...the exhaust valve had broken! Then,
sadly, on the 27th circuit the promising career of newcomer Dave Bennett

The first Grand Prix of the 1952 season counting towards Championship points was the Swiss, held over the tricky 4.5-mile Bremgarten circuit at Berne. This meeting was also unique because it saw Geoff in action both on bikes (Nortons – he is shown here after winning the 350cc event) and cars (Aston Martin).

came to a sudden halt, when he was fatally injured after crashing his machine.

The Isle of Man

Next stop was the Isle of Man and the annual TT series. Once again, Geoff was late in starting practice, but when he did (on Monday 2 June) he posted the fastest Junior Lap in 25 minutes 56 seconds, a speed of 87.31mph. Then on Thursday evening, 5 June, he took his Senior mount round in 23 minutes 59 seconds (94.40mph) from a standing start! This being only 12 seconds slower than his record lap the previous year; most impressive.

Starting with the number-one plate in both Junior and Senior races, Geoff had a clear road before him. In the Junior he responded by leading from start to finish – and setting the fastest lap of the race in 24 minutes 53 seconds (91mph).

Junior TT – 7 laps – 264.11 miles
1st	G.E. Duke (Norton)
2nd	H.R. Armstrong (Norton)
3rd	R. Coleman (AJS)
4th	W.A. Lomas (AJS)
5th	S. Lawton (AJS)
6th	G. Brown (AJS)

At the end of the race, although he said he had 'a trouble-free run on my machine', he also commented that he had been bothered from the end of the first lap 'with cramp' in his right leg.

Victory in the Senior (four days later on Friday 13 June) would have

Geoff's winning three-fifty Norton he used in the 1952 Junior TT. He led from start to finish and also set the fastest lap of the race in 24 minutes 53 seconds (91mph).

Line up of works Nortons in the team's garage at the 1952 Isle of Man TT.

given Geoff a Senior hat-trick – something which even the great Stanley Woods had not achieved. But as Geoff was later to recall, 'something told me that I would not pull it off – and after my hunch proved correct, Steve Darbishire told me that he, too, had had the same premonition.'

And so to the race. With the exhaust valve issue solved, Geoff should have been alright, but first a misfire and later clutch gremlins were to cause his retirement. The ultimate cause of the retirement was that:

some bright spark in the drawing office at Bracebridge Street had decided that (the normal works component) was not good enough and had specified that the bearing cage (of the clutch), a standard fitting on standard road machines, should also be fitted to the Manx racers!

Victory in the Senior would have given Geoff a Senior hat-trick – something which even the great Stanley Woods had not achieved. But it was not to be, Geoff instead retiring early on, with Irishman Reg Armstrong (seen here) on another Norton taking the victory instead.

1952 Senior TT, Les Graham (MV, 17) leads the eventual winner, Norton-mounted Reg Armstrong, at Parliament Square, Ramsey.

Needless to say, this 'improvement' was dropped after this one demonstration of its possibilities.

The Senior TT was won by Reg Armstrong, whose primary chain broke as he crossed the finishing line… talk about Irish luck!

Beaten narrowly by Masetti (Gilera) in Holland and Belgium

Following the TT came the traditional Dutch and Belgian rounds in the World Championship series. In both Geoff was narrowly beaten by Umberto Masetti's four-cylinder Gilera.

The Norton team now comprised Kavanagh, Armstrong, Ray Amm and Geoff, but for the first time, regardless of who was riding, the Gilera was sufficiently fast that it could still win – certainly with a good rider aboard. There is no doubt that Geoff also realised this, as subsequent events were to prove.

It was little consolation that he was still able to win on the smaller Norton, as it was the 'Blue Riband' 500cc class where the true glory lay, and

Following the TT came the traditional Dutch and Belgian rounds in the World Championship series. In both 500cc races Geoff was to suffer defeats to Gilera's Umberto Masetti. Then came a fateful day, at the non-Championship Schotten meeting in Germany, where Geoff suffered a serious accident, which put him out of action for the remainder of the season.

Before his accident, Geoff had been involved in the development of an overhead cam Norton scrambles machine. But ultimately this was to prove unsuccessful, even though a similar private effort ridden by Les Archer did go on to win the European title in 1956.

Geoff was not one to fool himself otherwise. Additionally, in three of the four races, the new team member, Southern Rhodesian Ray Amm, had managed to stay with Geoff, albeit on all three occasions the Norton team leader had come out on top, but there was no doubt that a new star had been born.

A fateful day at Schotten

Then came a most fateful day in Geoff Duke's racing career; when competing in a non-Championship event at the international Schotten circuit in Germany on his works three-fifty Norton, he suffered a serious accident. As he was to comment later, 'I can honestly state that my crash at Schotten was the only occasion during my entire racing career where an accident was due to my error.' And he continued, 'it was certainly the one and only time I ever allowed my concentration to lapse', Geoff having slowed after having a comfortable lead from Ray Amm.

There then followed some 13 weeks in plaster below his right knee, during which time he said, in his 1988 book *In Pursuit of Perfection* (Osprey), 'I suffered a great deal of pain which required pain-killing drugs and sleeping pills.'

Just prior to his Schotten accident Geoff had been awarded the famous Seagrave Trophy for 1951. First presented in 1930, the trophy was set-up to preserve the memory of the late Sir Henry Seagrave and was awarded to the British subject 'who accomplishes the most outstanding demonstration of the possibilities of transport by land, air or water'. The winning of the

Without Geoff, Norton relied on Armstrong, Kavanagh and new signing Ray Amm for the remainder of the 1952 season. The trio are seen here at the Italian Grand Prix at Monza in September of that year.

Seagrave Trophy was yet another accolade for Duke's magnificent achievements in 1951, and, as we know, 1952, even though he was to emerge as 350cc champion, could not match this by some considerable distance.

No more racing that year

At the end of August it was officially announced by Norton that 'Geoff Duke will not be able to race again this season'. The Norton press release went on to say 'His injuries will keep him out of the saddle for six to eight weeks, by which time the international calendar will be finished', the last of the classic road races being the Spanish Grand Prix, due to be held in Barcelona on 5 October 1952.

Then, towards the end of October came news that his ankle injury had been slower to mend than was anticipated. In a letter to Harry Louis of *The Motor Cycle*, Geoff said 'After seeing the X-ray negatives from Germany, the specialist treating me isn't at all surprised.' Geoff went on to reveal that he still received hospital treatment each day, although he could now walk without assistance. Geoff ended by saying that he hoped to be able to ride a motorcycle again by the end of the year. As for his future plans, 'as yet I've made nothing definite regarding next year's racing'.

So what of the future?

As *The Motor Cycle* commented in its 13 November 1952 issue, 'his plans for 1953 are vague. It is not certain that he will be physically fit and he has signed no contracts. It is known that he had had tempting offers to ride foreign machines. But he is intensely pro-national and it is doubtful whether he will accept.'

Geoff was now 29, married and living in Southport, Lancashire, and a partner in the motorcycle business bearing his name in St Helens, his home town. *The Motor Cycle* commented:

> *In spite of his enormous list of successes and the popularity which goes with it, Geoff remains a particularly modest young man. He has learned much in the past few years and his opinions on racing matters, on machines and circuits are well worth listening to. He displays an aptitude for clear, constructive thought, unusual in one of his years.*

It should also be remembered that at that time Geoff was involved with not only motorcycle racing, but cars too.

During the closed season 1952–53 no one, let alone Geoff himself, knew what the now three-times world champion would be doing during the following season. As had previously been mentioned, he had already received offers to race foreign motorcycles, and there was the Aston Martin car racing. But Geoff was keen to remain with Norton, but only if the long-promised four-cylinder project was to be part of their plans that coming year.

So Geoff, during a visit from Gilbert Smith of Nortons, questioned the factory boss, after the latter had asked if the former would resume riding for the team in 1953. But Mr Smith admitted that there was 'no possibility' of the four being ready for racing that year.

So as Geoff said in his autobiography, 'I told him that I would have happily been involved in the development, albeit slow, of an engine with a winning future...but not with the single which, as far as I was concerned, only had a past.'

By the end of 1952 Norton were able to advertise no less that 30 TT victories. However, as Geoff had already realised, success was getting ever harder.

Winner of 30 T.T. Races

world champions

THE UNAPPROACHABLE

Norton

THE WORLD'S BEST ROAD HOLDER

NORTON MOTORS LTD · BRACEBRIDGE ST · BIRMINGHAM 6

That, and another later meeting when Geoff visited Gilbert Smith while he was confined to bed at his home, convinced Geoff that his future lay elsewhere...maybe simply cars. However, after riding a three-fifty standard production Manx model at Silverstone (a full works machine having been promised) in April 1953 (organised by Graham Walker), Geoff realised just how much he enjoyed racing bikes – and not so much cars.

And so the stage was set for the next dramatic chapter in the Geoff Duke story.

Chapter 4

Gilera 1953–1954

Geoff Duke had had two approaches from the Italian Gilera company. The first came at the end of 1950, when their team manager Piero Taruffi had written Geoff a letter asking him if he would be interested in racing their four-cylinder 500cc machine. The second was towards the end of 1952, when the Englishman was recovering from his Schotten injuries. This letter contact had been made by Austin Munks, a personal friend of Giuseppe Gilera and a well-known racing sponsor and entrant (Austin was a close associate of the author's great friend the late Sam Coupland; both Austin and Sam were near neighbours in South Lincolnshire).

Exchanging Norton for Gilera

As explained in the previous chapter, Geoff had realised that the Norton single was no longer the equal of the Italian four-cylinder models, in particular the Gilera. But at the time of the second Gilera approach, he was still undecided as to what he would do regarding racing; would it be bikes or cars?

What finally decided it for him was the joint events of the behaviour of Norton's managing director Gilbert Smith, in which a story was published in the *Birmingham Mail* to the effect that Geoff had 'pleaded to be brought into the Norton team again', and the realisation after driving an Aston Martin at Silverstone that 'I was not enjoying the cars, that I still loved motorcycle racing and maybe it was better for a British rider to win on a foreign bike rather than to have no British interest at all.'

The above events all happened within hours, and

Geoff with Austin Munks (pictured here in the middle), the Lincolnshire-based racing entrant/sponsor, who was largely responsible for Geoff joining the Italian Gilera team in the spring of 1953.

Giuseppe Gilera, pictured
at the Belgian GP, Spa
Francorchamps, 8 July
1956.

Giuseppe Gilera

Born in a small village near Milan on 21 December 1887, Giuseppe Gilera, and his younger brother Luigi, did more than most to transform the face of motorcycle racing. For it was the company founded in 1911, rather than any other factory, who introduced the across-the-frame, four-cylinder to Grand Prix racing. Others, such as MV Agusta, Benelli and Honda, took up the layout, but it was Gilera who got in first.

Others may have noticed the possibilities of the machine raced by the Rome-based Rondine squad during the mid-1930s, but Giuseppe Gilera was the one who took the opportunity by purchasing the design rights.

The Rondine became the Gilera in 1936, and, after almost three years of development, became the champion of Europe in 1939. Quite simply, provided it kept going, the 500cc liquid-cooled supercharged Gilera had a turn of speed which nothing else on two wheels could catch, in the months leading up to the outbreak of World War Two.

Giuseppe Gilera was also a talent scout and gifted engineer. For starters, he not only coped when Ing. Remor left for MV Agusta at the end of 1949, but also helped to develop Remor's air-cooled, normally aspirated four into World-Championship material. In this he was greatly helped by the procurement of the services of Geoff Duke, whom he finally signed early in 1953 (after making his original advances as early as 1950).

Geoff was later to recall 'He was a fabulous man, a real gentleman and most generous, not just a boardroom figurehead. You couldn't fault him on a single thing.'

Duke quit Norton to sign for Gilera, and in his first year, 1953, he won the 500cc World Title – the first of his three consecutive individual World crowns for the Arcore factory.

And it was Geoff Duke who was largely responsible for Gilera signing Bob McIntyre, who was to give Giuseppe Gilera not only the marques crowning glory of the first official 100mph lap of the legendary 37.73-mile Isle of Man circuit, and the Junior-Senior double in the 1957 Golden Jubilee Tourist Trophy, but also the one-hour world speed record (achieved at Monza in November 1957).

But sadly, for Giuseppe Gilera himself, his later years were to be filled with great disappointment. Firstly, his beloved and only son, Ferruccio (then only 26 years old), died of a heart attack while on a business trip to the Argentinian Gilera subsidiary in October 1956. Then, during the 1960s he was forced to fight an uphill battle in a declining motorcycle market to keep the company he had created afloat. It proved to be a feat that, ultimately, even he was unable to achieve, with Gilera being taken over in 1969 by the Piaggio organisation.

Only a few short months later, on 21 November 1971, Giuseppe Gilera passed away. He was 83 years old.

A wagon and trailor about to leave the Gilera works at Arcore with a shipment of series production motorcycles during the early 1950s.

The 1953 four-cylinder Gilera with which Geoff went on to win the 500cc World Championship that year. Details included dohc, magneto ignition, duplex frame, a quartet of Dell Orto carburettors and extended exhaust pipes rather than meggaphones.

while Geoff was driving back to his home he stopped in Wellington, Shropshire, telephoned Austin Munks and 'asked him if he thought Gilera would still be interested in me riding for them'.

Even though it was only some three weeks before TT practice was due to start, Austin told Geoff that he was 'sure Gilera would be interested and promised to phone them straight away and get back to me the following morning'. And this is exactly what transpired, as Geoff was to recall many years later, 'Sure enough he rang me to say they were delighted and that I'd be hearing from them that day. A telegram arrived within hours asking me to fly out immediately to try the bikes.' As for Austin Munks, Giuseppe Gilera was so pleased that he brought Geoff to his company, that he subsequently presented a gift of a new Gilera 150 Sport motorcycle, which Austin was to keep as a prized possession until his death many years later.

The New Years Honours List

Earlier in 1953 Geoff's name had appeared in the New Year's Honours List, when he was awarded the OBE (Order of the British Empire). The honour had been conferred 'for services to British motorcycle racing'. Geoff thus became only the second man in post-war years to be recognised in this way, as in 1950 the OBE had been given to Freddie Frith.

Testing at Monza

In mid-May Geoff flew to Italy to tie up the Gilera agreement and carry out what was described as 'preliminary testing' on the four-cylinder Gilera, at the Monza Autodrome on the outskirts of Milan. He lapped consistently in far from ideal conditions in 2 minutes 13 seconds. As *The Motor Cycle* commented: 'Pundits say this is a first-class "training" time; it compares with the lap record of 2m 10.6s.'

Although Geoff was very impressed with the engine, there were other aspects with which he was less happy. He once described the early Gilera's handling in the following terms: 'almost unmanageable'. Another concerned gear selection problems. For these Geoff suggested a cure, which at first was rather reluctantly taken on by the Gilera engineering team, but when they found it worked, Geoff was never again to experience a reluctance on their part to help. In fact, as Geoff was to say in *In Pursuit of Perfection*:

> *Piero Taruffi was, in my opinion, the most outstanding combination of team manager and engineer I have ever had the good fortune to know. Here was a man, immediately friendly and appreciative, with whom one could discuss – and argue – the relative pros and cons of a machine, knowing that when the final decision was reached, action would be taken.*

Teammates

As far as fellow riders, at the time Gilera had several on contract, including not only Geoff, but Reg Armstrong, Dickie Dale, and the Milani brothers Alfredo and Albino.

As for his TT entries, originally these (made by Geoff Duke Ltd) were for both the Junior and Senior races, and as *The Motor Cycle* reported in its 28 May 1953 issue:

Geoff (third from left) with Gilera team manager Piero Taruffi (to Geoffs right), Reg Armstrong, Dickie Dale, Sam Coupland (Austin Munks Friend) and Geoff's wife Pat. Giovanni Fumagalli is working on the machine. The setting is the 1953 Isle of Man TT practice.

Hailing from Southern Ireland, Reg Armstrong was unique in that he was a teammate of Geoff Duke's at both Norton (1952) and Gilera (1953-1956).

Reg Armstrong

Hailing from Southern Ireland, Reg Armstrong was unique in that he was a teammate of Geoff Duke's at both Norton (1952) and Gilera (1953–56).

In all, Reg raced for 11 years, eight of which were as a works rider, for AJS, Norton, NSU and Gilera. During this time he won seven classic races in addition to numerous more minor ones. Yet he suffered very few crashes, of which only two are worth a mention, causing minor damage to the machine and rider, and even then one of these was caused by mechanical failure. This latter event came at the very first motorcycle meeting at the Silverstone circuit (in 1949). Reg was leading the 350cc race, on a works AJS, when the rivets securing the rear brake torque arm shattered, thus locking the wheel and causing the crash. The second occurred some four years later in the Spanish GP on a four-cylinder Gilera. In teeming rain which marred the 1953 event, the power of the four was more a hindrance than an asset around the sinuous Montjuich Park circuit and off he came, bruising his pelvis. Thus, Reg Armstrong built up a reputation as not only a fast rider, but a safe one too. Someone with whom it could be relied on would finish a race. And this helps explain why four leading factories wanted his services.

Although Reg never won a World Championship title, he was none the less runner-up four times (behind Geoff Duke three times – Norton 350cc 1952, Gilera 500cc 1953, Gilera 1955), plus NSU 250cc 1953.

Other Championship positions included: third 1949 AJS (350cc); sixth 1950 Velocette (350cc); third 1952 Norton (500cc); fourth 1954 Gilera (500cc); fifth 1956 Gilera (500cc).

In an interview conducted by Vic Willoughby in *The Motor Cycle*, dated 11 April 1957, following his retirement from the sport, Reg Armstrong revealed that he never had to ride to orders in the Gilera team to which he said he had 'a strong sense of loyalty'. Like the factory, Reg said, he considered the rider with the best chance of winning a Championship should be helped, not hindered, by his colleagues. He went on to say that he would like to see more riders put their duty to the factory first, if necessary at the expense of personal ambitions.

As for his fellow riders, he considered 'Duke is unquestionably the greatest on any grand prix circuit.'

Reg Armstrong (and of course Geoff Duke) was one of the 17 riders suspended following incidents in the 1957 Dutch TT (see Chapter 5). Interestingly, in the April 1957 interview, Armstrong considered that: 'Some responsibility for the present troubled state of the racing world is laid at the door of the FIM.' Not because Reg was one of the 17 suspended riders, but because the ruling body, he considered, 'pays insufficient heed to the problems of manufacturers and riders, and is inclined to be dictatorial'. In fact, he went as far as saying 'some of its (the FIM) officers are not strangers to rudeness'. And Reg would have liked to see the constitution of the Federation modified 'to include some responsible ex-competition men of recent experience – men in close touch with current difficulties'.

Reg retired from racing at the age of 28 in November 1956, this was because of the demands surrounding his thriving motorcycle business in Dublin; however, he was not to be lost to the racing scene. In fact, he instead used his experience and contacts to help a variety of other riders – including Geoff Duke.

Later still he became the Southern Ireland distributor for the Japanese Honda concern and in 1962 Honda racing-team manager, and was instrumental in Bob McIntyre joining the squad.

Over 100,00 spectators crowded around the seven-kilometre Hedemora circuit to witness the Swedish GP on Saturday and Sunday 17–18 July 1954. Reg set the fastest lap (in the 500cc event) at 102.52mph.

a good deal of controversy had arisen over Geoff's entry in the Junior race. He is nominated on an AJS, but the chances are that he will not in fact start. The machine at his disposal is a standard production 7R.

And with the arrival of his works Gilera commitments, that is precisely what happened; he only practiced and raced in the Senior on the Italian four.

The Italian machines, a total of eight, arrived in the island on Wednesday 27 May, and the following day Geoff did three standing-start laps using a different Gilera each time but with the number plates transferred. One of these laps (88.62mph) was the best time of the morning practice session. *The Motor Cycle* reported:

Observation at Hillberry suggested Graham on the MV as the fastest man on the bend even though the rear suspension was pitching a good deal. Duke appeared a shade slower, but displayed all his usual impeccable style.

But on Friday 29 May, not only were weather conditions almost perfect but Geoff had obviously got up to speed on his new machine, setting not only the fastest lap in the evening session, but his speed of 93.89mph was only 1mph slower than the fastest lap in the previous year's Senior race, and less than 1½mph slower than Duke's own lap record for the course (which stood at 95.22mph).

At number 67, Geoff Duke was faced with the problem of having to cut through many slower riders, whereas his teammate Reg Armstrong was number 28. But his main challenger Ray Amm (Norton), at 61, was hardly any better placed.

To set the scene for the 1953 TT race week, which was sunny every day, comes the following newspaper extract from the period: 'Each morning, short sleeves and light cotton dresses proved that holiday makers were confident of the day continuing fine.'

At 5.45pm on Thursday 11 June a large crowd at the weigh-in for the next day's Senior TT were there mainly to see Geoff with his Gilera. As *The Motor Cycle* reported, 'The walk along the front of the stands was

27 June 1953 Dutch TT, Assen. Gilera team riders, left to right: Geoff, Giuseppe Colnago, Alfredo Milani and Umberto Masetti.

Gilera Four Cylinder

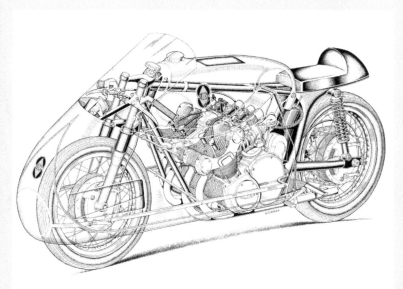

The 1955-type Gilera four. This superb drawing was commisioned by Gilera from the artist Gianni Cavara.

The Gilera four-cylinder first hit the headlines in April 1937, when Piero Taruffi broke the 1-hour speed record previously held by Norton and Jimmy Guthrie at 114mph. Taruffi raised this to 121.33mph over a 28-mile course, comprising a section of the Bergamo-Brescia autostrada. The motorcycle the Italian was piloting was a fully enclosed, liquid-cooled, four-cylinder model developed from the earlier Rondine design, itself conceived from the air-cooled four of the mid-1920s. As for Gilera itself, the marque had been founded by Giuseppe Gilera in 1911 (see separate boxed section within this chapter).

Signor Gilera had been shrewd enough to realise the Rondine's potential, with the basic design being steadily improved through an intensive racing and records programme until 1939. Gilera was on course to achieve supremacy in the all-important 500cc Grand Prix class. Twice during that year, rider Dorino Serafini achieved magnificent victories – beating BMW on its home ground in the German Grand Prix and winning the Ulster Grand Prix at record speed.

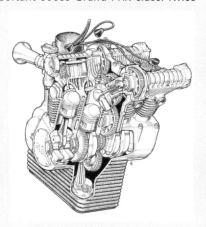

Cutaway drawing of the famous four-cylinder power plant

When racing resumed again after World War Two, the use of supercharging had been banned, so Gilera returned with new air-cooled fours designed by Ing. Piero Remor. Then, in late 1949 Remor quit to join rivals MV Agusta. However, Remor's exit left his former assistants at Gilera,

Franco Passoni and Sandro Columbo, to carry out a redesign, which meant that in effect Gilera stayed ahead of MV, thanks to a lighter, more powerful engine during much of the 1950s.

Gilera's first world title arrived in 1950 (the second year of the FIM official Championship series) when Umberto Masetti took the crown. From then on success followed success, particularly after Englishman Geoff Duke joined the Arcore factory in the spring of 1953. Duke brought with him the ideas of a new chassis which greatly improved the handling.

In eight seasons from 1950, Gilera riders Masetti, Duke and finally Libero Liberati won the 500cc Championship no less than six times, winning 31 races in the process. It was on a Gilera, too, that Bob McIntyre scored a historic Junior and Senior TT double in 1957 and became the first man to lap the legendary 37.73-mile Mountain Course at over 100mph. In addition, there were also the performances of the sidecar ace Erole Frigero, who was consistently successful, but is today almost totally unknown. For several years Frigero was second only to the great Eric Oliver (Norton) in the World Sidecar Championship.

The four-cylinder 500 Gilera, which ran from 1948, displaced 496.7cc (52 x 58mm) and was joined by a smaller 350 version in 1956. This latter engine displaced 349.7cc (46 x 52.6mm). As developed by Geoff Duke, both sported five-speed gearboxes; telescopic front forks; duplex, steel cradle frames and twin shock, swinging arm rear suspension.

When Gilera retired from the sport it did so on a crest of a wave, with a series of record-breaking achievements at Monza in November 1957, crowned by Bob McIntyre's incredible 141.37 miles in a single hour on one of the 350cc four-cylinder models; the Monza surface for the speed bowl was in such poor condition at this time that riding the 500cc version was considered too dangerous.

Although Gilera made a number of much publicised comebacks during the next decade, notably with Scuderia Duke in 1963, and the diminutive Argentian Benedicto Calderella a year later, the Arcore company was never to recapture its former dominance of the sport.

Libero Liberati at speed on the streamlined Gilera four at the *Circuito di Napoli*, 19 March 1955.

interrupted every yard or so by stops to satisfy the irresistible demands of amateur photographers, a rough count made 150 cameras. When Geoff had passed through, crowds melted away in a matter of minutes. Who said Duke's popularity was on the wane?'

The race

And so came Geoff's first-ever race on the Gilera four, in no lesser event than the most demanding of all races, the Senior TT, scheduled to be run over seven laps of the legendary 37.73-mile Mountain circuit, a total of 264.11 miles.

The lap record was broken four times in all, thrice by Geoff on his Gilera with times of 23 minutes 30 seconds (96.38mph) on his first lap, 23 minutes 22 seconds (96.93mph) on his second lap, and 23 minutes 18 seconds (97.20mph) on his third lap. But the final holder emerged as Norton-mounted Ray Amm, who, on the third lap, cut the Gilera time by three seconds to 23 minutes 15 seconds (97.41mph).

At the end of lap three Geoff led Amm by a full minute on corrected time. But shortly afterwards, as he accelerated out of the Quarter Bridge turn, he was cast off his motorcycle. As *The Motor Cycle* so aptly put it, 'he was not a penny the worse personally, but the Gilera would motor no more today.'

This incident not only robbed Duke of a certain victory, but put in train a volley of press comments and readers letters on the subject of his unfortunate get-off.

Probably the definitive view was expressed by an 'eye witness' and was published in the 27 August 1953 issue of *The Motor Cycle*, written by reader W.S. Radcliffe of Liverpool. It is worth repeating in full as it explains exactly what happened – and gave an accurate unbiased account of that awful moment:

Ever since the event, we have been reading controversial statements week by week re Geoff Duke's spill in the Senior TT. I had the good fortune to be able to spend my day at Quarter Bridge for the Senior, and I watched Geoff right through the corner each time he came round. I am not going to suggest what it was that caused the spill, but I would like to tell you what I saw with my own eyes. Duke had gone through, and had straightened up when it happened. Judging by his exhaust note, he had the clutch home and was turning it on, when the back wheel just went away under him towards the verge. He stayed with the machine a bit, but couldn't hold it, and I have the most vivid recollection of the maestro going over the top like a cat, kicking the machine away as he went, and landing on all fours to roll in the grass. It was a great mercy that it didn't happen 20 yards further on, where he would have landed head-on into a solid wall; I estimate he was doing at least 50mph at the time. The man deserves congratulations, not only for his memorable ride, but for his split-second, faultless reaction when danger threatened.

As Geoff himself recalled later:

Accelerating hard out of the slow right-hander at Quarter Bridge, I drifted a little wider than normal and my rear wheel hit a patch of molten tar which had oozed from beneath some newly-laid granite chippings. The Gilera went into a full-lock slide and, unaccustomed to a light flywheel, I snapped shut the throttle and the engine stopped. The rear tyre bit, the machine jerked upright and went into a lock-to-lock wobble before we hit the deck. Unharmed, I rushed to pick up the machine, only to discover petrol pouring out from the shaped platform at the bottom of the tank, on which the rider rested his arms while lying prone. The rough road surface had ground through the metal and there was no way that I could get back into the race.

So, with only one race, that was Geoff's TT exploits over for another 12 months. And sadly, Les Graham had lost his life when crashing the MV four at the bottom of the fearsome Bray Hill at the start of lap two.

The Championship chase

If the Isle of Man TT was over, the chase for the Championship title was certainly not. The next road race came just over two weeks later at the Dutch TT, held over the 10.2-mile Van Drenthe road circuit near Assen on Saturday 27 June. This meeting saw race and lap records smashed in all classes (125, 250, 350, 500cc – there being no sidecar event).

And the 500cc race was *the* event, with the field of 40 representing the very cream of European racing talent, and as *The Motor Cycle* reported: 'The fastest machines in practice had been a block of four Gileras', these being piloted by G.E. Duke, A. Milani, G. Colnago and U. Masetti, in that order. Ranged against them were the new inline four-cylinder Moto Guzzis (ridden by F.K. Anderson and E. Lorenzetti) and the fuel injected BMW flat twin of Walter Zeller, while Great Britain was represented by the Norton and AJS teams. The MV Agustas and works Horex entries had not arrived.

As a typical race report commented: 'No one could challenge the meteoric Duke. His performance re-established him as the champion of champions.' There is no doubt that the 1953 Dutch TT signalled to the world that Geoff

Duke had returned to top form – and was a serious challenger on the Gilera. Surprisingly, Ray Amm (Norton) had set the fastest lap – a new record – but run out of fuel while well behind Duke.

500cc Dutch TT – 16 laps – 163.84 miles

1st	G.E. Duke	(Gilera)
2nd	H.R. Armstrong	(Gilera)
3rd	K. Kavanagh	(Norton)
4th	G. Colnago	(Gilera)
5th	J. Brett	(Norton)
6th	W. Doran	(AJS)
7th	W. Zeller	(BMW)

A retirement in Belgium

After his victorious ride in Holland, Geoff was the favourite to repeat the performance eight days later in Belgium. But after dominating the race and establishing a new course-lap record of 112.33mph, and with three circuits of the 15-lap 131.5 mile race to run, Geoff hit mechanical problems. The press at the time said he had ridden too hard and blown his engine. Actually, this was completely inaccurate. What actually occurred was that a nipple for one throttle control cable had been insecurely soldered on and had pulled off – thus preventing one carb slide from opening!

The next round of the Championship was, of all places, due to be staged at Schotten, the very circuit where Geoff had had his serious accident the previous year. However, the AJS, Norton, Gilera and Moto Guzzi teams decided that they would not take part, after inspecting the course prior to the start of official practice. Besides being very narrow in places and tree-lined, it was also exceedingly slippery in some places. In the end, the FIM decided that only the 125 and 250cc races would count towards Championship points.

2 August 1953 and Geoff celebrates winning the 500cc French GP at Rouen; Gilera team manager Piero Taruffi holds the microphone.

The French GP

The French Grand Prix was not staged at Albi in 1953, but instead on the three-mile Rouen-Les Essarts course. Held in excellent weather conditions, some of the pressure was relieved for Geoff when Norton's number-one rider Ray Amm crashed in the preceding 350cc race, putting himself out of action. But instead the competition came from within the Gilera squad itself, in the shape of Reg Armstrong.

There were no fewer than seven Gilera fours on the grid for

Ray Amm, seen here with his wife Jill, replaced Geoff Duke as Norton's number-one rider after he joined rivals Gilera.

Ray Amm

Ray (William Raymond) Amm succeeded Geoff Duke as head of the Norton team when the latter switched to Gilera in the spring of 1953. Born in Salisbury, Southern Rhodesia (now Zimbabwe), in 1927, Ray first raced in grass-track events in his homeland and later in South African road events, such as the Port Elizabeth 200. By profession Ray was a draughtsman, although just prior to him leaving for Europe in 1951 he had entered into partnership with his brother in the motorcycle business.

Back in December 1949, Ray had married Jill, who subsequently accompanied him throughout his travels and who was a familiar figure in the race paddocks of the world in her own right.

First arriving in the United Kingdom for the TT races in 1951, he was soon noted for his fast and aggressive riding style, with *The Motor Cycle* describing him as 'probably one of the most courageous (some would say foolhardy) riders ever to appear in racing circles'.

At first, Ray was a private entrant, riding standard production Manx Norton machines, but he was soon noticed by the Norton team boss Joe Craig, resulting in the offer of works bikes for both the Junior and Senior races after an excellent showing in practice week for the 1952 TT. After retiring in the Junior race when lying fourth, he finished third in the Senior race behind Geoff Duke and Les Graham riding Norton and MV Agusta machines respectively.

He was then to remain with Norton until the Birmingham company's retirement from full-blown factory support at the end of 1954.

As well as many international victories, Ray is best remembered for achieving the TT double in 1953 and his controversial victory in the 1954 Senior race. He also set a new outright lap record for the legendary 37.73-mile Mountain Circuit in 1953 of 97.41mph.

When his beloved Norton factory quit, Ray finally signed for a foreign marque, MV Agusta, who had, with other factories, been trying to gain his signature for some considerable time.

His first race for his new team came at the international Shell Gold Cup at Imola, Italy, in April 1955. He was riding a fully streamlined four-cylinder model when he crashed in the 350cc event, suffering a fractured skull, and died 20 minutes after reaching hospital. Strangely, the accident is generally agreed to have been caused due to Ray using old tyres from a privately-owned Norton.

With his passing went one of the world's greatest triers – in later years some would say he tried too hard on occasions. But the fact remains that Ray Amm was the man who succeeded the legendary Geoff Duke and did the task well – no mean feat.

Ray Amm flat on the tank during his record-breaking victory in the 1953 Junior TT.

the 40-lap, 126.68-mile 500cc race. And it was Armstrong who seized the initiative at the start, with Duke trailing well behind to such an extent that it was not until the eighth lap that he finally took the lead, a position he then held to the end, even though teammate Armstrong speeded up, setting the fastest lap of the race on lap 36.

500cc French GP – 40 laps – 126.68 miles
1st   G.E. Duke (Gilera)
2nd   H.R. Armstrong (Gilera)
3rd   A. Milani (Gilera)
4th   K. Kavanagh (Norton)
5th   G. Colnago (Gilera)
6th   J. Brett (Norton)

Duke v Kavanagh in Ulster

Next round in the Championship trail was the Ulster Grand Prix, run for the first time over the 7½-mile Dundrod road circuit. *The Motor Cycle* described it in the following terms:

> *The 30ft-wide road twists in a seemingly endless sequence of fast second- and third-gear bends from start to finish. The longest straight, where the road passes the pits and grandstands, measures little more than a quarter of a mile, one bottom-gear hairpin is included a mile from the finish, and frequent undulations add to the riders' problems.*

For the first half of the 500cc race, held on Saturday afternoon, 15 August, Geoff increased his lead over the second man, Kavanagh, by around four seconds a lap. And thus, when the Gilera teamleader pulled in to his pit to refuel at the end of the 19th lap, he had a comfortable minute+ lead. However, shortly before his stop Geoff had begun to suffer clutch trouble (later to be revealed as a broken plate) and experienced trouble restarting, which meant Kavanagh had gone through before the Gilera got under way again. This was to remain the position for the rest of the race, with Geoff's old Norton teammate taking the victory. As for Geoff himself, he felt 'fortunate' to have finished second. This result, in which both Geoff and Ken shared the fastest lap of 91.74mph, left the Championship table reading: Reg Armstrong 23, Geoff Duke 22 and Ken Kavanagh 18.

500cc Ulster GP – 30 laps – 222.27 miles
1st   K. Kavanagh (Norton)

2nd   G.E. Duke (Gilera)

3rd   J. Brett (Norton)

4th   H.R. Armstrong (Gilera)

5th   D.K. Farrant (AJS)

6th   K.H. Mudford (Norton)

The Swiss Grand Prix

A week later, the GP circus was in Berne for the Swiss round. As Geoff himself recalled later, 'the 4.5-mile Bremgarten circuit was one of the best in Europe and certainly a riders' course'.

No less than a quarter of the 24-strong entry race were riding Gilera four-cylinder machines, plus three works BMWs, two works Nortons and a single Horex twin.

During practice the Gileras had largely dominated the proceedings, so that four of the five front row grid positions were occupied by the Arcore models (Geoff, plus Armstrong, Colnago and Alfredo Milani) plus the lone Norton of Ken Kavanagh.

Alfredo Milani overtook the quick-starting Geoff to take the lead on the climb from the lowest part of the circuit, and headed the field at the end of lap one.

Soon the lap record of 96.68mph, established the previous year by Jack Brett, was eclipsed. Milani returned 97.64mph on his second lap, Duke 98.06 on his third and then 98.4 on his sixth. This latter circuit brought Geoff very close to the Italian leader, and two laps later the Englishman was in the lead himself – a position he was to hold until the flag. However, as Geoff was to admit later, 'try as I might, I could only edge away from him. It was in this race that I realised just how good a rider Alfredo Milani was.'

The eight points gained by Geoff in Switzerland with the victory brought him to the top of the World Championship table, with 30 points to Armstrong's 27.

500cc Swiss GP – 28 laps – 127 miles

1st   G.E. Duke (Gilera)

2nd   A. Milani (Gilera)

3rd   H.R. Armstrong (Gilera)

4th   G. Colnago (Gilera)

5th   R.W. Coleman (AJS)

6th   D.K. Farrant (AJS)

7th   R.H. Dale (Gilera)

8th   W. Zeller (BMW)

Geoff during the Italian Grand Prix at Monza on the 5 September 1953 which he won.

9th   N. Pagani (Gilera)
10th   H. Baltisberger (BMW)

World champion again

Individual World Championship titles in four classes – including the Blue Riband 500cc – were decided at the Grand Prix des Nations on Sunday 5 September.

Practice held during the week preceding the race was fraught with confusion and, indeed, it appeared for a while that the 500cc race would not take place at all! The problem arose as a result of the organisers' decision not to pay starting money to the factory-backed riders of Moto Guzzi, MV Agusta and Gilera. Such money, they said, had to be paid by the manufacturers. Though the latter did not object to this, the riders themselves did – on a point of principal. They said that they would not ride unless starting money was paid by the Federazione Motociclistica Italiana. The riders' feeling was that if they acted otherwise, they would establish a precedent of which other organisers might later take advantage.

Numerous private owners who had been guaranteed starting money lined up with the factory riders concerned.

Although eventually this problem was resolved, the incident was to have serious consequences a couple of years later, which was to have a major effect on Geoff's racing career (see Chapter Five). During practice at Monza, Alfredo Milani came off his Gilera at the Lesmo Curve. But even so, with 29 starters the 500cc race was destined to be the biggest grid of the day. It is also worth noting that between practising and the race, Geoff's Gilera engine was discovered to have a serious problem and chief mechanic Giovanni Fumagalli built a new engine the night prior to the race.

Three Gileras shared the front row of the start with three MV Agustas, BMW, Moto Guzzi and Norton sharing the next three rows. But, as one commentator pointed out, 'Inexplicably, Geoff Duke was, or should have been, in the third row. But the starter's flag was dropped when some of the Gileras were still at their pit.' But Geoff, quick-witted as only a true professional can be, pushed off from where he was standing and streaked through the pack. Reg Armstrong and Nello Pagani were less fortunate and were severely baulked, losing time which manifestly could never be recovered.

Carlo Bandirola (MV Agusta) led for just as long as it took Geoff to catch the Italian, and thereafter proceeded to dominate the race in his 'most polished, courageous and brilliant style' (*The Motor Cycle*). The only man to even seriously challenge Geoff was teammate Dickie Dale, but from lap seven Duke simply turned up the wick and disappeared over the horizon; even so Dale was credited with the fastest lap. Actually, the big difference between Geoff Duke and the many other talented riders ranged against him was that he could circulate at race-winning speeds for the entire race distance, whereas the others could put in an impressive, but often short-lived, spurt to record a super-quick lap, but not be able to do it on a consistent basis. As an illustration of this, Geoff's

The Avon Tyre Company produced its 1953 year book, featuring Geoff's successes, which included victories in the Dutch, French, Swiss and Italian GPs.

After Monza Geoff travelled to Scarborough, for the International Gold Cup meeting over the famous North Yorkshire seaside venue. He won both his heat and final – and set a new course lap record.

winning time and speed at Monza in 1953 was 1 hour 10 minutes 18.3 seconds, 107.12mph, against runner-up Dale's figures of 1 hour 11 minutes 10 seconds, 105.51mph.

500cc Italian GP – 32 laps – 125.19 miles

1st	G.E. Duke (Gilera)
2nd	R.H. Dale (Gilera)
3rd	L. Liberati (Gilera)
4th	H.R. Armstrong (Gilera)
5th	C.C. Sandford (MV Agusta)
6th	H.P. Müller (MV Agusta)
7th	N. Pagani (Gilera)
8th	B. Franisci (MV Agusta)
9th	P. Monneret (Gilera)

The result of the 500cc Italian GP certainly reinforced Geoff's view – and the reason he finally left Norton – that the British singles time at the top was effectively over everywhere except, possibly, the Isle of Man.

Back to the short circuits

Having regained his 500cc crown, Geoff then returned to England and the short circuits – namely Oliver's Mount, Scarborough, for the international road races on Friday 18 and Saturday 19 September. And, strangely, this was to be a repeat of the Monza result with Geoff victorious and Dickie Dale runner-up.

As *The Motor Cycle* reported in its 24 September 1953 issue:

For several hours before noon on Saturday sluggish convoys of coaches, cars and motorcycles converged on Oliver's Mount. The sun was warm and Geoff Duke was to augment the star riders who had raced the previous day. More than 30,000 people poured on to the circuit area to enjoy the spectacle.

Having easily won his heat, in the 500cc final Geoff was not only ranged against his Gilera teammate but also the factory Norton entries of Ken Kavanagh, Jack Brett and the up-and-coming John Surtees.

Dale scorched off the line to lead the race and it took Duke a few miles to overhaul Dale around the tight, tricky Yorkshire seaside circuit, but on lap four, along the top straight, Geoff finally took the lead, Surtees having fallen off. This left Geoff leading Dale and Kavanagh. Thereafter, the newly-crowned world champion relentlessly moved further ahead as every lap unfolded. Kavanagh and Brett both retired with clutch trouble, while Geoff set the fastest lap at 63.93mph.

For the 1954 season Gilera, at various times, used either top half, or as seen here, more fully enclosed streamlining.

500cc Scarborough – 16 laps – 43.2 miles

1st   G.E. Duke (Gilera)
2nd   R.H. Dale (Gilera)
3rd   D. Parkinson (Norton)
4th   B. Freestone (Norton)
5th   S.T. Barnett (Norton)

End of season

Both Ray Amm and Geoff Duke were billed as the star riders for the annual Hutchinson 100 meeting at Silverstone on Saturday 25 September, but both were destined to be non-starters. Amm was not quite fit after his shoulder injuries sustained in the 350cc French GP, while Geoff had his machine slide from under him during practice. This resulted in a somewhat bent Gilera and slight facial abrasions to the rider. It was generally agreed that car racing had 'polished' (*The Motor Cycle*) the road surface to such an extent that tyre adhesion on the fast bends was at a premium. Duke's crash also ruled him a non-starter at the final Grand Prix of the year, the Spanish at Barcelona the following weekend.

And so Geoff Duke's 1953 season, his first with Gilera, came to an end in something of an anti-climax.

In late October it was officially announced that Geoff was to ride Gileras again, when he renewed his contract during a visit to their works at Arcore near Milan.

A new year and a son is born
At 10.20pm on Thursday 31 December 1953, Geoff's wife Pat presented him with an 8¼lb baby boy, later christened Peter and so Mr and Mrs Duke were able to start a new year as parents for the first time.

Major redesign
During the closed season of 1953–1954, the Gilera engineering team headed by Ing. Francesco Passoni carried out what Geoff described as a 'major redesign' and included 'some simple modifications that I had suggested'.

The majority of the work was centred on the engine. The stroke was increased from 58 to 58.8mm, giving a new displacement of 499.50cc (previously 52x58mm – 496.692cc). The sump was modified to allow the engine to be located lower in the frame, yet at the same time ground clearance was increased by tucking the exhaust pipes closer to the engine. The valve angle was widened from 80 to 90 degrees (later 100 degrees); the valve diameter was also changed. It is worth noting that the exhaust valves, which were sodium cooled, were 15 percent smaller in diameter than the inlet ones. All eight valves were supported by helical springs enclosed by cylindrical tappets that were in direct contact with the camshafts.

Passoni also experimented with various crankshaft types: a forged one-piece item, necessitating the use of split big ends and split edges for the big-end rollers, a built-up version in several pieces that were pressed together, and a built-up type assembled by the Hirth process. Some of these cranks were built by Gilera itself, while others were manufactured in Germany.

Eventually it was determined that built-up cranks were best, having a life of between 50 and 100 hours under racing conditions. A total of no less than six main bearings supported the crankshaft, and the whole engine assembly benefitted from the employment of both bearings and bushes of more than adequate dimensions for their particular task. The gearbox was later given a fifth ratio, mainly in the interests of providing a lower first gear, thus restricting the use of the clutch.

Passoni also carried out experiments with battery/coil ignition, but ultimately it was found that the latest type of Lucas rotating-magnet magneto was superior. The factory claimed a power output of 64bhp at 10,500rpm for the 1954 Gilera engine.

Other changes

Changes to the cycle parts were of equal importance and included shortening the frame, narrowing the rear forks and fitting a streamlined cowling.

The modifications suggested by Geoff himself included a reduction in handlebar diameter from 1 inch to ⅞ inch, a quick action twistgrip, and by reducing the overall width between the carburettors (by machining the inlet ports at an angle) the width of the rear of the fuel tank was reduced considerably. Geoff's modifications meant that the bike was now easier and more comfortable to ride, while Passoni's gave improved performance and handling.

In his autobiography Geoff said that what Passoni achieved 'during the winter of 1953–54 was almost beyond belief, and the end product was quite the most exciting machine it has ever been my good fortune to ride'.

A first outing at Silverstone

A first outing for the newly-revised Gilera came on Saturday 10 April 1954 at Silverstone, Northamptonshire. This was the first national-status road race to be held in Britain that year and large crowds enjoyed some excellent racing.

Geoff had only one outing, this being the 500cc BMCRC Championship event, held over 17 laps, which he won from Ray Amm (Norton) and Derek Farrant (AJS).

It was to be a month before the Gilera star was back in action, at the North West 200 in Ulster on 15 May. But after leading the race comfortably – and setting a new lap record of 97.37mph – he retired after examining his machine at the road side, this allowing his teammate Reg Armstrong through to victory. He also retired in the French GP.

Early for TT practice

This year Geoff was on the island early for the start of TT practice, with a Gilera four waiting for him to ride in the very first session, on the morning of 2 June, when he went round in 25 minutes 12 seconds (89.9mph), compared with Bob McIntyre in 24 minutes 48 seconds (91.3mph) – the Scot riding a works AJS Porcupine twin.

However, the following morning Duke led with a lap of 24 minutes 30 seconds (92.5mph), followed by Ray Amm (Norton) in 25 minutes 10 seconds (90mph).

By the evening of Monday 7 June Geoff had speeded up with a lap in 23 minutes 36 seconds (96mph).

A four-lap Senior TT debacle

And so to the race itself. For the most part the practice period had been blessed by good weather, but not race day, and owing to poor visibility was twice postponed. Even when things did get under way the visibility was poor. The truth is, the race should *not* have been started at all, but it was, and allowed to run for four laps when by the second circuit the conditions were truly appalling. So why was it continued? The answer – so that it could count towards World Championship points. Not one rider was happy with what took place that day, certainly not Geoff Duke himself.

There is absolutely no shadow of doubt that the officials got it seriously wrong. As there was no warning that the race was to end after lap four,

The 1954 Senior TT winner Ray Amm (Norton). His victory was controversial to say the least, as the race was stopped prematurely after only four of the scheduled seven laps had been completed, just after Geoff's Gilera had been refuelled.

Geoff had refuelled at the end of lap three, whereas his main challenger, Norton-mounted Ray Amm, had not stopped because the Norton did not need to take on fuel for the expected seven-lap distance.

The officials' decision was 'harshly criticised by many of the spectators and by most of the riders, for by then (when the race came to an end) the conditions had notably improved' (*The Motor Cycle*).

Actually, visibility had been at its worst on the second lap, and almost instantly after the race came to an end the mists and rain disappeared and the sun shone for the rest of the day!

As soon as the decision to stop the race was known, Gilera team manager Piero Taruffi made a formal protest on behalf of the Italian company.

The stewards then sat for two hours and at the end of this time stated that, in accordance with rule 21 of the supplementary regulations, the results of the race would stand and protests were quashed.

Senior TT – 4 laps – 150.92 miles

1st   W.R. Amm (Norton)
2nd   G.E. Duke (Gilera)
3rd   J. Brett (Norton)
4th   H.R. Armstrong (Gilera)
5th   R. Allison (Norton)
6th   G. Laing (Norton)
7th   R.H. Dale (MV Agusta)

Finally, it is worth repeating what *The Motor Cycle* reported in its 24 June 1954 issue regarding the prize presentations on the evening of the controversial race:

The atmosphere was electric at the Senior prize presentation, which was held last Friday evening in the Villa Marina gardens. It was estimated that 10,000 people were present, and it was evident that the majority had gone not in order to cheer the winners but to hear the explanation of the day's happenings.

And the mood was very much against the officials, with many shouting from the audience 'You shouldn't have run it.'

When it was Geoff Duke's turn to speak, there was 'tumultuous applause' (*The Motor Cycle*). After the usual congratulations to the winner Ray Amm, Geoff concluded by expressing the view 'that enormous harm has been done to the TT by the stewards' decisions'.

A trio of five-hundred four-cylinder Gileras pictured in the paddock at the 1954 French GP, held that year at Rheims. Geoff was to retire with what *The MotorCycle* described as 'expensive noises' coming from his engine.

After the TT came the Ulster GP at the end of June, but Moto Guzzi, MV Agusta and Gilera did not take part. And as Ray Amm again took a victory, he now led the Championship table with two victories and Geoff had yet to open his 1954 defence of his title.

Victories in Belgium and Holland

But it was not long before Geoff was able to restore the balance in his favour, with wins in both Belgium and Holland within only six days.

First came the ultra-fast Belgian Grand Prix at Spa Francorchamps in the Ardennes region, near the German border. The 500cc race saw a field of 28 represented by eight makes of machine and the cream of riders from 11 nations.

Besides the usual Gilera team members were Pierre Monneret of France and Luis Martin of Belgium – the former riding in the place of Alfredo Milani who had crashed and sustained serious leg injuries while giving the machines a pre-race test session at Monza a few days earlier.

As the traffic lights' starting signal flashed red, then amber and finally green, the field stretched away with Rod Coleman (AJS) clearly in the lead at Eau Rouge. At Burnenville the New Zealander still led; another New Zealander, Leo Simpson (AJS), was second, Ken Kavanagh (Moto Guzzi) third, with Geoff fourth. But by the time the competitors reached La Source hairpin towards the end of that first lap, Duke had moved into the lead, a position the Gilera star was to retain until the end.

500cc Belgian GP – 15 laps – 131.5 miles

1st	G.E. Duke (Gilera)
2nd	K.T. Kavanagh (Moto Guzzi)
3rd	L. Martin (Gilera)
4th	R. McIntyre (AJS)
5th	K. Campbell (Norton)
6th	G. Murphy (Matchless)

In taking a second victory within six days, Geoff Duke smashed both the race and lap records for the Dutch TT, held over the 10.2-mile Van Drenthe circuit in the north of the country near Assen. Actually, at that time many considered the Dutch circuit to be less of a riders' course than any other in Europe. The reason was that the lap comprised six long straights, three or four medium-high speed bends, and perhaps eight or nine slow corners on which riding ability counted for little. However, it was a fast course and one which put the brakes under a severe test, and although Geoff won, he found that he experienced serious brake fade from his front stopper. So much so that amazingly the Gilera works produced a new, 1½ inch larger drum in the period between the Dutch and German GPs, the latter only two weeks later!

But getting back to the race itself, watched by over 100,000 spectators, there was a huge amount of competition with MVs, Gileras, Moto Guzzis, Nortons, BMWs, AJSs and Matchlesses vying for honours.

Again, as in Belgium, Coleman led on his AJS twin from the start, but at Hooghalen halfway around the first lap Duke led from Fergus Anderson (Moto Guzzi) and Ray Amm (Norton). Behind them came Dale and Bandirola (MVs), Coleman, McIntyre and Simpson (AJSs), Armstrong (Gilera), Montanari (Moto Guzzi) and H. Veer (on a third works Gilera). Pagani on another four-cylinder MV led the first of the private owners, the Australian Maurice Quincey (Norton). Meanwhile, the Moto Guzzi of Ken Kavanagh had been troubled with suspension and braking problems, and retired after another lap.

Duke simply continued to pile up his lead, and it was obvious that only misfortune could rob him of another victory. Such was the speed of the race that the first six men home all finished at a higher average speed than the winning race speed in the previous year's event. Geoff averaged 104.24mph, with a new lap record of 105.42mph.

For the 1954 Dutch TT, Gilera drafted in the local rider H. Drikus Veer. The Dutchman is seen here at the event in the Assen paddock that year. He came home eighth in the 500cc race.

Dutch TT – 16 laps – 163.84 miles

1st	G.E. Duke (Gilera)
2nd	F.K. Anderson (Moto Guzzi)
3rd	C. Bandirola (MV Agusta)
4th	R.W. Coleman (AJS)
5th	R.H. Dale (MV Agusta)
6th	R. McIntyre (AJS)
7th	N. Pagani (MV Agusta)
8th	H. Veer (Gilera)

Half-million crowd at German GP

Two weeks later, no less than half a million spectators crowded around the 7.1-mile Solitude circuit to watch some truly magnificent racing, in which race and lap records were pulverised in all classes.

Unlike the Dutch and Belgian circuits, the Solitude venue, with its twists and turns and undulating nature, was certainly not a speed bowl. Its tortuous curves demanded considerable study, concentration and a high standard of riding ability, and, for these reasons, the circuit was popular with both competitors and spectators alike.

In contrast to the Isle of Man, at Solitude the riders' concerns were listened to and acted upon immediately. For example, after complaints regarding the treacherous nature of sections of the road surface where the sun's heat had melted the tar and an extensive oil deposit during the Saturday practice had added to the hazards, straight away Jack Brett, Rod Coleman and Geoff, representing Norton, AJS and Gilera respectively, were invited to tour the circuit and point out to the organisers any particular problem areas. Chippings were then immediately rolled into the surface at these points, and as an additional safety measure, the programme was re-arranged so that the Sidecar race took place after the solo races had been run.

At the start of Sunday's 500cc race, as the field peeled off into the Glamseck turns for the first time, Ray Amm (Norton) nosed his way to the front, and by the end of the lap he led Geoff; Bob McIntyre (AJS) lay third just ahead of Fergus Anderson (Moto Guzzi). Dickie Dale (MV Agusta), his right hand damaged in a practice spill, occupied fifth spot, with Reg Armstrong on the second Gilera sixth.

After another lap Duke had closed up on Amm, while Anderson and Armstrong had passed McIntyre. Dale had dropped to seventh, just behind his teammate Carlo Bandirola.

As The Motor Cycle dated 29 July 1954 reported, 'Riding with superb smoothness, Duke swept past Amm and immediately proceeded to draw away. Such was the pace that already Anderson, though still in third position, had lost considerable ground.'

Geoff then eased the pace and maintained a steady gap of approximately a quarter of a mile over Amm. Meanwhile, Kavanagh had moved up several places to take sixth behind his teammate Anderson. At half-distance the leading sextet was: Duke, Amm, Armstrong, Anderson, Kavanagh and McIntyre.

Then, two laps later, Amm, with a record lap of 90.42mph, re-passed Geoff. But the Norton man's advantage was short-lived, for the positions were again reversed after a few miles.

There then took place probably Geoff's closest battle of the entire 1954 season, with neither rider giving or taking an inch. Then, finally, a couple of laps from the finish, Geoff put in a tremendous effort, during which he raised the lap record to 91.6mph and finally secured victory.

500cc German GP – 18 laps – 128 miles

1st	G.E. Duke (Gilera)
2nd	W.R. Amm (Norton)
3rd	H.R. Armstrong (Gilera)
4th	K.T. Kavanagh (Moto Guzzi)
5th	F.K. Anderson (Moto Guzzi)
6th	J. Brett (Norton)
7th	R. McIntyre (AJS)
8th	R.W. Coleman (AJS)

Although the braking had been improved, the additional weight of the larger drum had caused an adverse effect on the handling. So, after speaking with team boss Piero Taruffi, it was agreed that Geoff would visit the Girling competition department in Birmingham upon his return to Britain.

Girling had already been actively involved in the manufacture of racing disc brakes for cars, but, as Geoff was later to recall, 'at that time, to the best of my knowledge, nobody had then considered the merits of fitting a disc brake to a motorcycle'.

And after a meeting with Girling staff, Geoff was advised that the idea was possible, but, as development was expected to be costly, a decision whether to proceed was needed from boardroom level.

So Geoff returned to his Southport home to await an answer. Three weeks later a letter arrived from Girling, simply stating 'After careful consideration, it is with regret that the directors are unable to offer their assistance, as in their opinion, there is no commercial future for disc brakes on motorcycles.' Of course, as we know now, this was to be a short-sighted decision...

Senigallia and Silverstone

As an interlude between the Grand Prix scene, Geoff took in a couple of non-Championship meetings at Senigallia and Silverstone.

After creating a lap record at 102mph at Senigallia, Italy, on Sunday 1 August 1954, Duke was forced to retire and the race victory went to Carlo Bandirola (MV Agusta), who averaged 96mph. Second place was taken by Nello Pagani, also MV-mounted. The Swiss Norton rider Luigi Taveri was third.

Conditions were very different when back in Britain six days later for the international Hutchinson 100 meeting at Silverstone on Saturday 7 August – the Northamptonshire circuit was flooded with heavy rain. But even so, Geoff managed to win both his 500cc races – these having distances of five laps and 10 laps. He was also awarded the George Reynolds Trophy for the fastest lap of the meeting in 1 minute 55 seconds (91.39mph).

Because of the extreme weather conditions, the stewards had cut the length of the 500cc Championship from 20 laps to 10. Ironically, almost in a replay of the Isle of Man Senior TT, this race was run in bright sunshine, though the track was still awash. And as chronicled in my book *John Surtees: Motorcycle Maestro (Breedon),* Surtees was in great form, gaining around 5 seconds a lap on the Gilera world champion, until, at the halfway stage, stripped bevel gears on his Norton single robbed him of certain victory. As it was, Geoff Duke won the race from R.D. Keeler (Norton) with John Hartle on another Norton third.

Wet roads for the Swiss GP

And it was wet roads which greeted competitors for the Swiss GP at Berne. However, the 500cc race, held on 22 August 1954, still managed to be a superb affair, with full works teams not only from Gilera, but Moto Guzzi, AJS and Norton.

Earlier, Moto Guzzi had finished first and second in the 350cc event (Anderson and Kavanagh). And at the start of the 500cc it was Kavanagh who seized the advantage, building up a full 10-second lead over teammate Anderson by the end of the lap, who was in second position a long way ahead of Amm, third; Duke was fourth, Armstrong fifth and Coleman sixth.

As the race progressed, with Anderson first, then Bob McIntyre and finally Kavanagh, all hit trouble (mainly caused through an ingress of water into their machines). After Kavanagh stopped, Amm led Duke by some 50 yards. Behind the two leaders the order was Armstrong, Brett, Coleman, Farrant and Pierre Monneret (on the third Gilera). But Monneret (some distance behind Coleman) was lapped by both Amm and Duke on the 16th circuit.

Spectators had, by then, begun to consider that the combination of Amm-Norton could beat Duke-Gilera. However, on the 21st lap, with seven remaining, Geoff turned in what one commentator described as a 'ferocious' lap at a fraction under 97mph. And, as *The Motor Cycle* race report dated 26 August 1954 commented, 'Such speed and style on wet roads took the breath away. His charge carried the Gilera world champion almost into Amm's slipstream and he kept the crowds "on tenterhooks" by staying there for another three laps of the 4.5-mile Bremgarten circuit.'

With three laps remaining, Geoff and the Gilera proved that, even on a riders' circuit such as Berne, speed and the ability to use it still told. He streaked past Amm, under the very noses of the massed crowds in the stands, and headed fast into the middle distance… there was simply nothing Amm could do about it.

The Motor Cycle report ended 'Duke, it transpired, had merely been biding his time, confident that he had the speed to win. Seldom in post-war years has there been a finer illustration of planned riding.'

Swiss GP – 28 laps – 127 miles

1st	G.E. Duke (Gilera)
2nd	W.R. Amm (Norton)
3rd	H.R. Armstrong (Gilera)
4th	J. Brett (Norton)
5th	R.W. Coleman (AJS)
6th	D.K. Farrant (AJS)
7th	P. Monneret (Gilera)

Talking to Mrs Topham
In early September Geoff, together with other well-known riders, met Mrs Topham, the owner of the new Aintree circuit near Liverpool, and vetted the course, which was due to stage its first motorcycle meeting later that month.

Clinching the World title
Then it was off to Italy for the Italian Grand Prix at Monza, the 500cc race being staged on Sunday 12 September.

Geoff is seen here with Mrs Muriel Topham, the owner of the Aintree course near Liverpool in 1954, prior to the first motorcycle race meeting at the venue later, at the end of September that year.

Taking the flag after a winning ride in the 500cc Italian Grand Prix at Monza on Sunday 12 September 1954. Note the new, fully-enclosed dustbin streamlining shell.

This turned out to be a notable event, as the eighth classic of 1954 can historically be regarded as the occasion at which streamlining became finally accepted as essential equipment for road-racing motorcycles.

As *The Motor Cycle* stated:

More than that; almost all the fairings bore so close a resemblance to that evolved by Moto Guzzi earlier in the year that it would not be unkind to the many brains which have been exercised on streamlining problems to say that the famous Moto Guzzi Mandello wind tunnel has been of service to them all.

During unofficial practice the previous week and the official practising on Saturday 11 September, it had become obvious that speeds in all classes were markedly up on those of previous years, and that a major reason for this was the reduced 'windage' which streamlining had provided.

An example of the sporting attitude enjoyed at the time is to relate that a practice spill, caused by a patch of oil on the Vedano curve, had jeopardised Rod Coleman's chances of starting in the 350cc race. His AJS caught fire and looked very much the worse for wear after the fire squad had done its job with foam extinguishers. But not all was lost, because the full resources of the rival Moto Guzzi factory were employed to refurbish the AJS for the race.

Race of the giants
The largest field of the meeting lined up for the start of the 500cc race. And what a scene it was, with fully-faired machines from all the factories except AJS.

Geoff Duke was the established firm favourite to take the victory. Nevertheless, the Italians were always anxious to win on their home ground, and they also enjoyed the advantages of knowing Monza more intimately than visiting riders did. So the scene was set for a memorable race.

And in such a star-studded field, Geoff proceeded to make everyone, except his teammate Umberto Masetti, 'appear crawlers' (*The Motor Cycle*).

After a superb 112.4mph on the 10th lap, he led the race by a commanding distance, having already frequently pulverised the previous record which had stood at around 108mph. His race-winning average speed was 111.45mph, with an ultimate fastest, record-breaking lap of 113.03mph. And he had become world champion yet again.

500cc Italian GP – 32 laps – 125.19 miles

1st	G.E. Duke (Gilera)
2nd	U. Masetti (Gilera)
3rd	C. Bandirola (MV Agusta)
4th	R.H. Dale (MV Agusta)
5th	H.R. Armstrong (Gilera)
6th	K.T. Kavanagh (Moto Guzzi)
7th	W.R. Amm (Norton)
8th	W.A. Lomas (MV Agusta)
9th	F.K. Anderson (Moto Guzzi)
10th	L. Taveri (MV Agusta)
11th	J. Brett (Norton)
12th	N. Pagani (MV Agusta)
13th	W. Zeller (BMW)
14th	T. Forconi (Gilera)

Scarborough international races
Geoff had long been a supporter of the Oliver's Mount Scarborough International Gold Cup meeting, and so it was in 1954, when he again showed his mastery by beating the likes of John Surtees, Bob McIntyre and Dickie Dale to win the main 500cc race at the Yorkshire venue.

Giuseppe Gilera
congratulates Geoff after his
record-breaking victory in
the 1954 500cc Italian GP.

At the beginning of the race Bob McIntyre, riding an AJS twin, led until the third lap, when Geoff took charge and established a new circuit lap record. John Surtees, who had earlier won the 350cc race, was soon harrying McIntyre, and then, on the sixth lap, he passed the Scot and set after the world champion. This threat was met by yet another record lap to the credit of the Gilera rider, who zoomed round at 66.94mph.

Behind the leading trio, Dickie Dale hurled his four-cylinder MV Agusta after McIntyre, while John Hartle and F.M. Fox battled for fifth place. Further back, Pierre Monneret (AJS) and Reg Armstrong (Gilera) scrapped just as furiously. Then, the French champion lost second gear and had to retire, leaving Armstrong in seventh. The order did not change. McIntyre and Dale stormed home in third and fourth places, with Hartle, Fox and Armstrong in fifth, sixth and seventh places respectively.

As one newspaper report of the day said, 'It had been a fine meeting, well organised from every angle, with large, enthusiastic crowds, fine dry weather, and hard fought racing.' What else could one wish for?

Aintree

The first-ever motorcycle race meeting to be held at Aintree took place on Saturday 25 September 1954, organised by the North Western Centre of the ACU and sponsored by the *Daily Telegraph*.

Among the entries for the 500cc race were Reg Armstrong and Geoff Duke (Gileras), Ray Amm and Jack Brett (Nortons), Rod Coleman, Bob McIntyre and Derek Farrant (AJSs), and Dickie Dale (MV Agusta).

The Aintree circuit measured three miles to the lap and ran side-by-side with the world-famous Grand National race course. Completed in May that year, at a cost reported to have been £100,000 (current equivalent £4 million), there was stand accommodation for 20,000 spectators, while the total capacity of the circuit was said to be 200,000 people.

The meeting was held in dry but windy conditions. After the lunch break, riders took their places for the 20-lap, 60-mile 1000cc race. The expected and much publicised duel between Geoff and Ray Amm did not take place, as the latter had broken his collarbone in a crash on his works Norton in the 350cc event. Even so, there were the likes of Coleman, Brett, McIntyre and Surtees to do battle with the Gileras of Duke and Armstrong. And, it turned out, the Italian fours were not destined to have things all their own way.

As the starter's flag fell, John Surtees (Norton) made a tremendous start, and went away 'like a shot from a gun' (*The Motor Cycle*). Although both Armstrong and Geoff had passed Surtees by the end of the second lap, this was far from the end of the matter. On lap three the order remained, but on the fourth circuit Geoff pushed ahead of Armstrong into the lead, shaking off Surtees in the process. The Norton rider then promptly slipstreamed Armstrong's Gilera. At Beechers Bend, Surtees pulled out and passed Armstrong to take second place, and he began to draw slowly away from the Irishman from then on.

Meanwhile, Geoff had been keeping a wary eye on the happenings astern, and placed himself with a respectable distance to the good at the front with the fastest lap of the race at 81.57mph. At half distance, Geoff led by 12 seconds from Surtees, himself six seconds ahead of Armstrong. So swiftly had the top three men been circulating, that over half a minute separated Armstrong from the fourth man, Rod Coleman (AJS). By the end of the race, Geoff had once again shown his complete mastery; quite simply, no one could match the combination of him and the Gilera at that time.

1000cc Aintree – 20 laps – 60 miles

1st	G.E. Duke (Gilera)
2nd	J. Surtees (Norton)
3rd	H.R. Armstrong (Gilera)
4th	R.W. Coleman (AJS)
5th	P.H. Carter (Norton)
6th	R. McIntyre (AJS)

A November 1954 Avon Tyres advertisement after Geoff's 'wonderful' season that year.

Congratulations to Geoff Duke on a wonderful Season—and on winning the 1954 500 c.c. World Road Racing Championship

GEOFF DUKE WRITES
I cannot find enough superlatives to describe the wonderful stability, wheel grip, safety and wearing qualities of the Avon tyres—not to mention the excellent service. Do as I do, ride on Avon.

AVON
to-day's leading tyres

And so another season came to an end, and one in which Geoff Duke had shown that he was back to the glittering form which he had displayed in 1951 when he was double world champion.

Although he did not know it at the time, and even though he was still to put in some excellent performances and again taste success as world champion, 1954 was to be, in the author's opinion, the high point of Geoff's Gilera career.

Chapter 5

Gilera 1955–1957

Geoff Duke began 1955 with a racing tour of Australia, which covered 36,000 miles in 10 weeks, during which time he won 10 Australian races riding a works four-cylinder Gilera five-hundred (he actually had two machines at his disposal).

An earlier visit down under, when he was contracted to the British Norton factory in 1952, did not take place due to his unfortunate accident at Schotten that year (see Chapter Three).

The journey to and from Australia involved 24,000 miles, and while he was in the country Geoff covered another 12,000 miles travelling from one circuit to another. As one commentator put it at the time:

the size of Australia is not often appreciated in other parts of the world. In fact, the area of the continent, the island of Tasmania included, is nearly three million square miles – or over 30 times the area of Britain.

During his stay, Geoff visited all six states and, in truth, had very little spare time. Besides the actual racing he was accorded civil receptions, introduced to governors, appeared on commercial radio and gave several talks and film shows. In fact, it would be fair to say that he acted not just as an ambassador for the Gilera company, but for the entire motorcycling movement.

Geoff had originally planned to leave for Australia in time to compete at the Mildura races

Geoff at the Australian Mount Druitt circuit on 13 February 1955, receiving the victory laurels after winning the Blue Mountains Grand Prix on his five-hundred Gilera.

Gilera's renowned mechanic Giovanni Fumagalli, who often worked on Geoff's machines during his time as a Gilera works rider.

on Boxing Day 1954, but, as Geoff recalled later, 'we were unable to make reservations for my machines and mechanic (Giovanni Fumagelli) on the ship leaving Genoa in time to make the race'.

As it was, the machines arrived on 2 January 1955 in Freemantle, the port of disembarkation for Perth, where Geoff was due to contest his first race in Australia.

As for Mr Duke himself, he travelled by plane via Rome, Cairo, Karachi, Singapore, Colombo, Darwin and Sydney, thereafter transferring to a local airline for the final leg of his journey to Perth, some 2,500 miles further on. As Geoff commented:

My arrival in Sydney gave me my first insight into Australian enthusiasm and hospitality when I was greeted by a host of trade people, plus my old friend Harry Hinton, looking not a day older than he did in 1950 and now fully recovered from his crash in the 1951 Junior TT.

As for the races themselves, he raced at the following:
Mooliabeenie circuit, near Perth
Gawler Airstrip, Adelaide
Bandiana, near Melbourne
Mount Driutt, near Sydney
Fisherman's Bend, Melbourne
Tasmanian TT, Longford, near Launceston
Geoff also took in scrambles (riding a borrowed BSA 250), while every meeting in which he competed attracted record crowds of spectators.

Some of the surfaces encountered left a lot to be desired – for example, as *The Motor Cycle* described:

At Gawler Airstrip, there was about an inch of chippings on the straight and some of the corners were loose. Along the straight, the Gilera was suffering from wheel-spin in top gear and snaking badly.

Returning to Europe

Upon his return to Europe, he left Britain for Italy on Monday 21 March 1955 to 'make up the leeway' with the Gilera factory.

Geoff's first race on his return was at Imola, on Monday 11 April. But it was not to be a successful outing as, on the 22nd lap of the 50-lap (157-mile)

Shell Gold Cup race, the current world champion fell off his five-hundred Gilera; the machine was damaged, but Geoff escaped unhurt. Instead, victory went to teammate Libero Liberati, who won averaging 88mph.

Victory at Silverstone

Although no one could match John Surtees's speed in the 350cc Championship race at the *Motor Cycling* sponsored BMCRC Silverstone Saturday meeting on 23 April, John's best efforts were insufficient to hold Geoff at bay in the 500cc Championship event. Though the Norton rider made his usual electrifying start to take an early lead, Duke's Gilera screamed by on the fifth lap, after which Surtees had no option but to give ground. When the world champion got into his stride, his style was as impeccable as ever and he raised the lap record to 94.84mph. Third place eventually went, deservedly, to Bob McIntyre, riding a Joe Potts Norton.

A debut in Spain

1955 was the first year in which Geoff Duke competed in the annual Spanish Grand Prix, held over the sinuous 2.35-mile circuit in the beautiful Montjuich Park, Barcelona. Sunday 1 May thus saw Geoff on the start line for the 53-lap, 124.76-mile long 500cc event, and the race was dominated by Italian multi-cylinder machines. Of the eight still circulating at the finish, the first seven were Gilera and MV Agusta fours, the last a private Norton ridden by a local Spanish rider.

Prior to the start, the highlight of the race was expected to be a battle royal between Geoff and Carlo Bandirola (MV Agusta). Although visiting the circuit for the first time, the Englishman had put up the fastest practice time, while Bandirola was something of a specialist for this twisting, undulating course.

So real disappointment was felt when Geoff, after leading for the first two laps, was then slowed by a misfire and retired at the pits after only six laps. Ultimately, it was Reg Armstrong who won on another Gilera, from Bandirola's MV, with Umberto Masetti third on another MV. The fastest lap was put in by Ken Kavanagh (Moto Guzzi) before he retired.

Victory at Hockenheim

After Spain came a visit to the German Hockenheim circuit, where, on Sunday 8 May, Geoff scored a runaway win in the 500cc event, completing the 20 laps (96.6 miles) at an average speed of no less than 122.6mph. The Gilera star also established a new lap record of 123.83mph. Ken Kavanagh (Moto Guzzi), who had earlier won the 350cc race, was runner-up.

The 1955 French Grand Prix was staged over the 5.18-mile circuit at Rheims on Sunday 15 May. And with both AJS and Norton having decided to only enter standard production models after the end of 1954, Italian machinery dominated all three classes. Indeed, in the two larger classes it was a three-way battle between Moto Guzzi, MV Agusta and Gilera, while the 125cc category was dominated by MV Agusta and FB Mondial (there being no 250cc class at this meeting).

The Rheims circuit placed the premium on only two aspects of machine performance, namely sheer maximum speed and a sufficient degree of reliability to sustain that speed for the duration of the race. Roughly triangular in shape, the French circuit included a two-mile downhill straight begun and ended by bottom-gear corners, a one-and-a-half-mile uphill straight on which was situated the start and finish, and a third leg incorporating a few sweeping bends negotiated in top and third (or fourth) gears by the riders of the quickest motorcycles.

The combination of Geoff Duke and the Gilera four proved invincible in the 500cc event. In winning by a margin of more than two minutes he lapped all riders behind the third man, teammate Reg Armstrong. Impressively, Geoff's first flying lap bettered the previous record by two seconds! And continuing to lap consistently at around the 115mph figure, the world champion gained an average of three seconds per lap on his nearest rival, the Frenchman Pierre Monneret (Gilera). From an early stage of the race, the private owners were so completely outclassed that interest was focused only on the works entries.

Rain interrupted speeds if not positions from the 11th lap and also seemed to herald a number of retirements, including the MVs of Bandirola and Pagani, plus Monneret's Gilera which went sick and eventually struggled in 10th and last, having completed 22 laps.

500cc French GP – 30 laps – 115.5 miles
1st	G.E. Duke (Gilera)
2nd	L. Liberati (Gilera)
3rd	H.R. Armstrong (Gilera)
4th	T. Forconi (MV Agusta)
5th	J. Collot (Norton)
6th	F. Dauwe (Norton)

Next came the annual North West 200 in Ulster. The highlight was Geoff's bid to be the first to register a 100mph lap on the triangular 11-mile circuit linking the towns of Portstewart, Coleraine and Portrush. And the

J.J. Wood with his Geoff Duke entered BSA Gold Star during the 1955 North West 200; he won the 350cc class.

Gilera rider came within a second of achieving this long-sought-after record lap, with a circuit of 6 minutes 39 seconds – a speed of 99.98mph. His race-winning average of 97.60mph in the 500cc event was a record.

500cc North West 200 – 18 laps – 198 miles

1st   G.E. Duke (Gilera)
2nd   H.R. Armstrong (Gilera)
3rd   J. Brett (Norton)
4th   M.E. Low (BSA)
5th   M.P. Roche (Norton)
6th   A.R. Sutherland (BSA)

TT practice

When Geoff made his first appearance during 1955 TT practice on Thursday morning 26 May, he completed two laps on what was described as a 'hack' Gilera four. And although he commented to feeling 'like a novice' after a year's absence from the circuit, he nonetheless put in what was easily the fastest lap of the morning at 92.82mph – nearly 4½mph faster than the next best speed, recorded by Maurice Quincey of Australia on a Norton.

On Monday morning 30 May he put in only one lap, which included a standing start and coasting finish; his speed of 96.45mph was the highest of the morning by nearly 1mph and he was only 14 seconds outside the Senior lap record. The following day, Geoff completed one lap on each of two Gileras. The first machine featured the old-type steering-head fairing, while the second was equipped with the latest comprehensive 'dustbin-type' streamlining, as used in the French Grand Prix the previous month. Geoff's second lap (97.14mph) was 35 seconds better than his first and was only four seconds outside the lap record, in spite of his starting with a dead engine and coasting over the line at the finish.

For the race, both Geoff and Reg Armstrong decided to use machines fitted with the older type fairing surrounding the steering head and riders' arms. They had decided to use these in preference to the more comprehensively streamlined models featuring additional pannier-type fuel tanks. Though the latter streamlining gave the machine a higher speed, they were more affected by strong side winds and also had the additional complication of fuel pumps.

Another controversy

A year previously, the 1954 Senior TT had caused great controversy by being stopped after only four of the seven laps had been completed. As Geoff Duke had only just taken on fuel, many, including Geoff himself, considered he had been robbed of a certain victory.

Then, on Friday 10 June 1955, for almost three-quarters of an hour, the world thought the Isle of Man Mountain Course had been lapped at 100mph. Though he had not been extended by the opposition, Geoff, on his third lap of the Senior TT, recorded a time of 22 minutes 39 seconds. Heralded by the exclamation 'Here it is!', the commentator said 'Duke has lapped at 100 miles an hour!' Cheers were roared by the vast crowds thronging every vantage point around the 37.73-mile circuit. As one journal of the day reported, 'Boys threw their hats aloft. Pressmen screeched into telephones. The radio spread the news far and wide.'

However, more cautious souls were soon concluding that the official lap-speed chart in the TT programme must be *wrong*. The timekeeper got to work – and later the clerk of the course issued the following statement: 'The chief time-keeper reports that the time recorded to Geoff Duke on his third lap is 22m 39s which equals a speed of 99.97mph.' Forty-one minutes had elapsed since the magic 100mph announcement.

As *The Motor Cycle* race report in its 16 June 1955 issue commented:

As if impelled by a predetermined signal, everybody began shouting at the same time. Compounded of disappointment, amazement and, to some extent, fury, the anti-climax oppressed the senses to the exclusion of all else. Duke, the idol, had been robbed of a deserved honour by half a second. The fact that the Senior Tourist Trophy was as good as on his sideboard seemed mouldy recompense.

But the excellence of his victory should not be obscured by the drama which unfolded afterwards. Because from a standing start, Geoff had smashed the existing lap record of 23 minutes 15 seconds with a time of 23 minutes 1 seconds (98.37mph), had got well below 23 minutes on his second circuit, almost achieved the 100mph lap on his third, and was then an outstanding 1¾ minutes ahead of second-place man Reg Armstrong.

Thereafter, the opposition effectively well out of it, Duke had eased the pace slightly (but not his concentration!) to win at an average speed of 97.93mph.

Senior TT – 7 laps – 264.11 miles

1st   G.E. Duke (Gilera)
2nd   H.R. Armstrong (Gilera)
3rd   K.T. Kavanagh (Moto Guzzi)
4th   J. Brett (Norton)
5th   R. McIntyre (Norton)
6th   D. Ennett (Matchless)
7th   W.A. Lomas (Moto Guzzi)

For the technically-minded reader, I have included a list of components used by both Duke's and Armstrong's Gilera machines in the 1955 TT:

Hepolite piston rings

Dell'Orto carburettors

KLG spark plugs

Lucas magneto

Avon tyres

Ferodo brake and clutch linings

Regina chains

Bowdenex control cables

Smiths rev counters

Girling rear shock absorbers

BP fuel

Castrol oil

Nürburgring

The 1955 German Grand Prix was staged over the 14.165-mile Nürburgring (last used for this event in 1931) – the most difficult of all circuits in the eyes of Geoff himself.

Laid out in 1927, the circuit had a combination of magnificent setting and the concentration of hazards, making it unique. The track wound and

Geoff taking part in the 500cc German GP at the Nürburgring on 26 June 1955. He viewed the course the most difficult of all, the Isle of Man included, but he still won!

dipped in a confusing sequence of blind bends, and undulated over the beautifully-wooded slopes of the Eifel Mountains. During the lap, the road fell and climbed almost 1,000 feet!

The task of the rider in attempting to memorise the circuit's 174 bends was made more acute by the similarity in appearance of the majority of its curves. It was indispensable for a rider to perfect his technique in blending the exit from one curve into the entry of its successor, and thus achieve a smooth and fluent style.

Besides the usual Italian opposition, BMW had not only entered Walter Zeller, but also the young English rider John Surtees.

But making one of his best-ever starts, Geoff Duke 'flashed ahead of his rivals like a shot from a gun', and at the end of the lap led Zeller (who obviously had the advantage of circuit knowledge) by 15 seconds. This lead remained pretty constant for the next five laps, after which the Gilera world champion really began to turn up the heat and thereafter increased his lead over the German by some three seconds a lap.

For the first two and a half laps, Carlo Bandirola (MV Agusta) held third, but was then passed by Reg Armstrong. However, Geoff's teammate was soon forced to retire with engine trouble. Surtees was showing up well on his BMW debut, but was to be forced out later with a serious misfire.

So fast were Duke and Zeller lapping that the latter was some 1½ minutes in front of Bandirola at half distance.

German GP – 9 laps – 127.49 miles

1st	G.E. Duke (Gilera)
2nd	W. Zeller (BMW)
3rd	C. Bandirola (MV Agusta)
4th	U. Masetti (MV Agusta)
5th	G. Colnago (Gilera)
6th	J.J. Ahearn (Norton)

The Belgian Grand Prix

Exactly seven days later, the Belgian Grand Prix was held over the 8.77-mile Spa Francorchamps circuit.

Considerable interest had been aroused by the entry of the new Moto Guzzi V8. This was due to have been ridden by Ken Kavanagh, but suspected big-end cage failure in practice made it a non-starter in the race held on Sunday 3 July.

In stark contrast to his lightning start at the Nürburgring, Geoff's clutch dragged and the rear wheel locked. This meant that he was one of the last riders to get under way. But, equal to the challenge, he rode 'his fantastic best' (*The Motor Cycle*) and began to tear through the pack; by the end of lap one he had climbed to fifth.

The initial leader Reg Armstrong suffered problems and had to call at his pit, this letting MV's Carlo Bandirola into the lead, followed by Gilera's Colnago. These two swapped places, before, after circulating at a phenomenal speed of 114.5mph on his third lap, Geoff swept into the lead. Bandirola then held third place on the leading MV, but he was ousted by Pierre Monneret during the next lap. Gilera machines now filled the first three positions.

Geoff drew comfortably away from Colnago and thereafter eased the pace, to retain a steady 10-second lead just after half distance. Then, with a loud noise, Geoff's Gilera came to a halt on the approach to Stavelot (with failed timing gears).

However, Gilera still finished first, second and third – Colnago winning from Monneret and the Belgian Luis Martin.

The Dutch Incident

Next came what was thereafter referred to as 'The Dutch Incident', when, at the Dutch TT at Assen on Saturday 16 July 1955, an event took

The Gilera's of Alfredo Milani (40) and Giuseppe Colnago (38) lead Moto Guzzi's Ken Kavanagh (4) at Circuito di Senigallia, 31 July 1955, with Milani emerging as the winner. Of the four Milani brothers, Alfredo was considered the best and an excellent rider by Geoff Duke.

place which was to have a major impact on Geoff's racing career – a negative one at that.

The problem arose because of dissatisfaction among private riders concerning start money, or the lack of it. This caused a riders' strike, when 12 of them pulled into the pits after the first lap of the 350cc race.

And the reason why Geoff Duke and Reg Armstrong (plus the Italian members of the Gilera team) gave their support could be traced back to the 1953 Italian Grand Prix (see Chapter Four), when the organisers had refused to pay starting money to British riders of Italian works machines.

In truth, the whole affair was very unfortunate and was to result in a lengthy ban, which meant Geoff (and Reg Armstrong) were to miss much of the 1956 season.

As for the 1955 500cc Dutch TT itself, after what *The Motor Cycle* described as 'a mediocre getaway' Geoff worked his way through the field, and by the end of the sixth lap he had overtaken his teammate Reg Armstrong and the lone MV Agusta four of Umberto Masetti.

At the end, three Gileras (the other ridden by the Dutchman H. Veer) and the lone MV had taken the first four places.

500cc Dutch TT – 27 laps – 129.26 miles

1st	G.E. Duke (Gilera)
2nd	H.R. Armstrong (Gilera)
3rd	U. Masetti (MV Agusta)
4th	H. Veer (Gilera)
5th	R.N. Brown (Matchless)
6th	E.M. Grant (Norton)

Gilera team bikes at Monza in September 1955. Geoff's five-hundred (2) can be clearly seen.

John Surtees (extreme left of picture) with Count Domenico Agusta, MV teammate Umberto Masetti and Mario Agusta, Monza 1957.

John Surtees

Born in the pretty village of Tatsfield on the Kent–Surrey border, a couple of miles south of Biggin Hill Airfield, on 11 February 1934, John Surtees succeeded Geoff Duke as 500cc world champion.

John's first motorcycle race came as a 14-year-old when his father Jack recruited his services as a passenger. The pairing actually won the event but were subsequently disqualified because of John's age. His first solo victory came at age 17, at the tree-lined Aberdare Park circuit in South Wales. He was riding a 499cc Vincent Gray Flash single, which the young Surtees had constructed while serving his apprenticeship at the company's Stevenage works.

Except for a 1953 TT practice accident while riding an EMC 125, John would have been a Norton teamster that year. As it was, Norton retired from fielding full Grand Prix 'Specials' at the end of 1954. However, John, together with John Hartle and Jack Brett, were signed to race works development Manx models for the 1955 season; he responded by having an excellent season, the highlight of which was winning the British Championship title.

Then he signed for the Italian MV Agusta concern to race its four-cylinder models during the 1956 season. In doing this, John was following in the footsteps of Geoff Duke (although Duke had gone from Norton to Gilera). John made his MV debut at Crystal Palace near his South London home in April 1956 in winning style. Then he went on to win the 500cc World Championship title – despite suffering a fall in Germany at the Solitude circuit. Even though he had broken his right arm, which effectively kept him out of racing until the following year, John had already amassed enough points to carry off the title.

Although he could only finish third behind the Gilera pairing of Libero

Born on 11 February 1934, John Surtees is shown here on his way to victory in the 1956 Isle of Man TT riding his works 500 MV. Later that year he was crowned world champion for the first time.

Liberati and Bob McIntyre in the 1957 500cc title race, he had the honour of giving MV its first ever victory with the smaller 350 four at the Belgian Grand Prix in July 1956.

Then came the golden trio of double 350cc and 500cc World Championship title years, when John won just about everything in 1958, 1959 and 1960. Having nothing else to prove in the two-wheel world, Surtees moved to four wheels, first as a driver for Ken Tyrrell, then as a member of the Lotus F1 team. In 1962 came a switch to a Lola, plus drives in a Ferrari 250 GTO in sports car events.

Next came a move into the full Ferrari team, competing in the 1963 and 1964 Formula 1 series. And in the latter year he won the world title and thus became the only man ever to achieve the feat of taking the premier Championship crowns on both two and four wheels.

After Ferrari came a spell with Honda, whom he joined for the 1967 season, and finally BRM in 1969. Then he founded his own team, drivers of which included Mike Hailwood. Team Surtees was disbanded towards the end of the 1970s, its F1 'position' being acquired by Frank Williams.

Hedemora

Although not counting towards the 1955 World Championship, Geoff took part in the Swedish Grand Prix at the tricky 4.34-mile Hedemora circuit, held over the weekend of Saturday 23 and Sunday 24 July.

Although the 350cc race on Saturday was held in wet conditions, things were much improved for Geoff's 500cc outing the following day.

Riding his Gilera with the steering-head fairing only, as in the Senior TT a few weeks before, Geoff took the lead from the start, giving none of his rivals a chance to catch him.

As a newspaper reported:

The polished, graceful style of the world's champion was greatly admired by the crowd of 100,000 which had flocked to the circuit. So effortless appeared Duke's progress that it was difficult to realise that he was lapping at over 102mph.

His main challenge came from the Norton-factory entered trio of John Surtees, John Hartle and Jack Brett. But even Surtees could not match the flying Duke on that summers day in Sweden.

500cc Swedish GP – 30 laps – 130.2 miles

1st	G.E. Duke (Gilera)
2nd	J. Surtees (Norton)
3rd	J. Brett (Norton)
4th	J. Hartle (Norton)

Both Geoff and teammate Reg Armstrong did not take part in the Ulster Grand Prix that year (held on 11–13 August), the organisers being unable to meet the terms of the Gilera stars. So their next outing did not come until the Italian GP at Monza on Sunday 4 September.

The general feeling was that Geoff had only to ride a steady, intelligent race in order to secure victory.

Only Gilera and MV had entered factory teams, after the new Moto Guzzi V8 was again sidelined with mechanical problems at the last minute. In the 35-lap, 125.8-mile race, Geoff was third away at the start, and by lap five he was out in front on his own. Meanwhile, Reg Armstrong and Masetti (MV) fought a terrific duel which lasted the entire race distance.

But with 10 laps left, the engine on Geoff's Gilera began to lose power,

Paddock scene at Monza, September 1955 with Gilera machines in the foreground.

During the 1955 500cc Italian GP Geoff was to suffer from lack of engine revolutions and suspension gremlins, just why is explained in the text. Even so, he still finished third.

and with two laps to go Masetti overtook Geoff on the straight past the grandstands. By now, Duke's machine had lost over 1000rpm and Armstrong followed Masetti through. As Geoff later commented, 'At the finish, Masetti was the victor over Armstrong, while I came third.'

Although the individual and manufacturer's World Championship titles were already secure, Giuseppe Gilera was not happy with the results at Monza. On stripping the Gilera engines, only one spring per valve was intact! It was later discovered that the cause was faulty materials. In addition, Geoff had experienced an out-of-balance front wheel – and the front tyre was unevenly worn and completely lacking of tread in one place!

At first, the tyre manufacturer, Avon, was blamed. However, the following morning, with the broken valve springs replaced, new tyres fitted and a distance piece on each fork stanchion to increase the spring load, Geoff reeled off the full race length of 35 laps around Monza – with complete engine reliability and perfectly-even tyre wear. This not only cleared both Avon and Gilera, but the race department at the Arcore factory 'could now turn to redesigning the streamlined shell, an alteration in weight distribution, and producing alternative fork springs'.

A quartet of British short circuit meetings
With the World Championship done and dusted, Geoff then took in a quartet of British short-circuit meetings at Scarborough, Aintree, Silverstone and Brands Hatch, in that order.

At Scarborough on 16–17 September, Geoff was to admit that he was surprised just how competitive John Surtees was, the young Norton rider providing what one commentator described as 'epic cut and thrust in the 500cc final'.

Surtees had earlier won the 350cc final, and his heat in the 500cc class. But the 500cc final was the first occasion when the two men competed directly against each other at the North Yorkshire venue that year – and what a titanic battle it proved to be. Geoff was so hard pressed that he had to break the course lap record (with a speed of 69.29mph) on the very last lap to ensure victory. The Gilera world champion came home the winner by a mere second at an average speed of 67.94mph, in what many consider one of the very greatest races ever seen at the Oliver's Mount track.

Honours were again even at Aintree on 25 September, where Surtees won the 350 and Geoff the 500cc races. In the final race of the day, the 30-lap handicap, Surtees (348cc Norton) won from Geoff (499cc Gilera), with Sammy Miller (248cc NSU) third, John Hartle (348cc Norton) fourth, and Bob McIntyre (348cc AJS) fifth.

Bob McIntyre

Robert Macgregor (Bob) McIntyre was born on 28 November 1928 in Scotstoun, a suburb of Glasgow. His father had worked as a riveter, building ships on the shores of the River Clyde.

Bob's first job was in a large motor garage near his home, and his first motorcycle a 16H Norton of 1931 vintage. After completing his national service, the young McIntyre returned home and purchased an Ariel Red Hunter, and it was upon this bike that Bob began his competitive career at a scramble event at Auchterarder, near Perth.

After competing in off-road events for some months and getting hooked on motorcycles, Bob found a job with Glasgow dealers Valenti Brothers. His work involved servicing and repairing touring bikes – the firm having little connection with the sport at that time.

After watching his first road race at Beveridge Park, Kirkcaldy, Bob borrowed a friend's 350 BSA Gold Star and entered his first race at Ballado. Riding pillion to the airfield circuit on the bike, they then removed the silencer and lights. His rivals were mounted on pukka racing bikes, including KTT Velocettes, AJS 7Rs and Manx Nortons, but the track was covered in loose gravel and Bob's scrambling experience came to the fore. The result was three wins in four races – and the only reason Bob did not win that one too was because he fell off!

At that time, 1950–51, there was very little trade support for racing in Scotland. However, in 1952 Bob was asked to ride for Troon, Ayrshire dealers Cooper Brothers in the Junior Clubman's TT in the Isle of Man, on a ZB32 Gold Star. As Bob was later to recall, 'that race made me'. He finished runner-up behind the winner Eric Houseley and set the fastest lap (a new class record) at 80.09mph. Not only this, but a couple of days later he finished second in the Senior Clubman's on the same bike.

That September he returned to the island, this time to ride an AJS 7R

in the Junior Manx Grand Prix. Bob not only won, but, again riding the same machine, finished runner-up in the Senior!

From then on he mixed it with the big boys and after a spell working for London-based AMC (Associated Motor Cycles – the makers of AJS and Matchless) began a highly-successful spell with tuner Joe Potts in Bellshill, Glasgow. Besides a famous 250cc Manx, Bob also rode 350 and 500cc Norton Singles for the Potts stable, as did his close friend Alastair King.

By the end of 1956, the McIntyre reputation had become international. The result was that when Geoff Duke was injured at the beginning of 1957, Bob effectively replaced him as Gilera's team leader. The Scot proved his worth by scoring a famous double TT victory in the Jubilee races that year. He also broke the one-hour speed record (on a 350cc Gilera) at Monza later that year, after Gilera quit GP racing. In fact, when Mike Hailwood finally bettered Bob's hour record at Daytona in February 1964, it caused considerable controversy – even Mike saying that Bob's achievement in setting up his record on the bumpy Monza speed bowl in the autumn of 1957 had been 'an incredible feat of endurance and guts'.

Later, Bob rode works bikes for the likes of Bianchi and Honda, but it was on the British short circuits that he continued to make his mark. But it is his time with Gilera for which Bob is now best remembered – and his close association with Geoff Duke, both on and off the track.

Then came that fateful day at Oulton Park in August 1962, when, riding his Joe Potts-tuned 499cc Norton, he crashed heavily in torrential rain, receiving serious injuries from which he was to die nine days later.

The Motor Cycle dated 23 August 1962 carried the following tribute: 'though we mourn, we can be proud that the sport he graced and those who were privileged to enjoy his friendship are richer for his impact'. It continued: 'a life of adventure was as compulsive to Bob as flying is to a bird. Challenge and conquest were food and drink to his spirit.'

Then came the two final meetings, Silverstone on Saturday 1 October and Brands Hatch on Sunday 2 October. At the former, there were two five-lap 500cc races; Surtees won the first, with Geoff taking the second, before they met in the 20-lap 500cc Championship event – which Surtees won from Duke, with both riders sharing the fastest lap of the meeting in 1 minute 49.2 seconds, a speed of 96.28rpm.

Finally, the following day a record crowd of 60,000 at the 1.24-mile Brands Hatch circuit, Kent, saw a major upset, when not only did Surtees head the Gilera world champion home, but Alan Trow (Norton) did so as well.

An involuntary spectator

For much of the first half of 1956 Geoff Duke was what he described as 'an involuntary spectator', as the authorities had ratified a ban on his racing in international events until 1 July that year.

It is interesting to note that in December 1955, after Geoff had visited Milan to receive a presentation from Gilera, in recognition of his third consecutive 500cc World Championship title, he had then flown to Amsterdam. According to the Reuter news agency, the purpose of this was to seek a partial remission of the six-month suspension of his licence imposed to take effect from 1 January 1956. However, upon his return to Britain he was quoted as saying: 'There is no truth in reports that I am trying to have the suspension cut. The international committee's decision is without appeal, and there would be no point in even discussing it.'

Geoff went on to confirm that he had been offered a place in the Gilera team to ride when the suspension was lifted, but so far had made no decision to accept. He added that if he did not ride in 1956 it was 'probable' that he would give up racing altogether. From these statements one can clearly see that the ban had deeply upset him.

Even though, eventually, the FIM relented (in April 1956) and allowed Geoff and the other riders who were suspended to enter some non-Championship races during the period of the international ban, his taking part in the ones counting towards World-Championship points was not relaxed, and so – for the first time in several years – Geoff found himself with time on his hands.

One section of interest was that he became involved in the construction of a fully-streamlined 350cc Velocette KTT-engined special, and the support of J.J. Wood and D. Wright on modified BSA Gold Star machines. Another was that he had moved from his Southport home to become a resident in the Isle of Man – a situation which remains to the present day.

The Velocette three-fifty special, which Geoff Duke was due to ride in the 1956 North West 200, but lack of vital engine spares saw the world champion have to declare himself a non-starter.

April 1956 was a pretty busy month for Geoff: he was now able to plan ahead and get organised for his international return on 1 July, with entries for the North West 200 and short-circuit events at Aintree and Oulton Park, the latter two over the Whitsun weekend. Gilera had made a gift of a 175cc off-road model, while on Sunday 22 April the multi-world champion opened (jointly with Lord Brabazon) the new motorcycle and car museum at Beaulieu in Hampshire.

While Geoff rode the famous 1912 Norton 'Old Miracle', Lord Montague of Beaulieu and Lord Brabazon drove the 1908 Austin racing car with which the latter had won the French Grand Prix.

Back to business
It was then very much back to business. Unfortunately, his first scheduled ride at the North West 200 did not come off. The 348cc Velocette (later campaigned by Jackie Wood) did not even appear in practice, due to a vital spare part which was not forthcoming in time from the mainland. Instead, Geoff explained over the loudspeakers just prior to the start that he had made 'strong efforts' to secure the said component by air, but, unfortunately had failed, and so he was regrettably a non-starter.

Instead, Geoff was forced to wait slightly longer for his return.

Back to winning ways
And when he did return, it was back to winning ways and more lap records.

First, at Aintree on Saturday 19 May, 'The Maestro in Tip Top Form During First Outing This Year' was the headline in *The Motor Cycle* dated 24 May 1956, after Geoff won both his races and equalled the outright lap record for the famous Lancashire circuit.

The machine which Gilera had provided for their world champion was fitted with a top half-only fairing and a 1956-type engine 'capable of 11,000rpm' (*The Motor Cycle*). But, as *The Motor Cycle* stated, 'there appeared little need to use its full power, for, at the halfway stage (in the 500cc event), he had built up a lead of more than half a minute over the second man'.

Then, later in the day came the 30-lap Aintree 90 solo handicap, in which Geoff equalled the lap record of 83.85mph.

Aintree 90 Handicap – 30 laps – 90 miles

1st   G.E. Duke (499cc Gilera)
2nd   S.H. Miller (247cc NSU)
3rd   F.M. Fox (499cc Norton)
4th   M.P. O'Rourke (203cc MV Agusta)
5th   P.H. Carter (499cc Norton)
6th   R. Anderson (499cc Norton)

Then, continuing the same form, two days later Geoff was at Oulton Park on Whit Monday 21 May, where he gave an 'impeccable display' (*Motor Cycling*) to win the main event and establish a new course record.

With a star-studded entry, Geoff had won his heat before 32 riders assembled on the grid for the start of the 19-lap Senior Championship final (which also included the Britannia Vase Trophy). When the flag dropped, Duke's Gilera, positioned on the second row, could be heard above everyone else bursting into life. And he already held a 30-yard lead on every other bike as the field approached the first corner! The only man to be anywhere near the flying Gilera rider was Bob McIntyre (Norton).

After these two meetings, Geoff, together with Reg Armstrong, travelled to Italy for testing at Monza, prior to their debut in the 1956 Grand Prix season at Spa Francorchamps, the home of the Belgian GP.

Still The Master!

'Still The Master!' That was the headline in the 12 July 1956 issue of *The Motor Cycle*. It was in response to the tremendous performance which Geoff had put in to not only breaking the lap record for the 8.77-mile Belgian circuit, but also his overall performance.

Banned from international-status events for the first six months of 1956, Geoff's first outing came on the British short circuits, at Aintree and (seen here) Oulton Park, on 19 and 21 May respectively. The FIM ban stemmed from Geoff's support of privateers at the Dutch TT the previous year.

Unfortunately, with only two laps of the 15-lap, 131.6-mile race left, and with a lead of over a minute on second-place man John Surtees (MV Agusta), Geoff's Gilera engine cried enough when a piston shattered. And with his retirement, Duke surrendered the last vestige of hope in retaining the 500cc World Championship, while Surtees virtually clinched his grip on the title by achieving his third successive classic victory in the 500cc category.

With John Surtees having been signed by Count Domenico Agusta for 1956 – and Geoff Duke out of action for half the year – it had been MV, not Gilera, who had been in the title hunt, Surtees having already won in the Isle of Man, Holland and now Belgium. And after the retirement of not only Geoff, but also the likes of Bill Lomas (Moto Guzzi V8) and Reg Armstrong (Gilera), it had been BMW-mounted Walter Zeller who had finished runner-up to Surtees at Spa Francorchamps.

Before his Gilera had gone sick, it had been pulling the highest top gear ever, and the five ratios were so close that bottom had been a shade high for the La Source hairpin, while the change from fourth to top at 10,000rpm resulted in a drop of only 400–500rpm. On the swoop towards the notorious Burnenville bend, the Gilera had been travelling at almost 160mph. Also, it is interesting to note that for 1956 the Gilera development team had replaced the previous straight-pipe exhausts for megaphone, fitted a revised and more streamlined shell (hence the higher gearing), and provided protruding air scoops to assist both engine and front brake cooling.

In Sweden
Following the Belgium came the non-Championship, but very popular, Swedish Grand Prix at Hedemora.

Not only were lap records broken in all three classes (125, 350 and 500cc), but there was a strong entry and huge crowds (over 85,000 on the combined two days 14–15 July). It was also the first race for the legendary Ducati Desmo single – and a winning debut too for Gianni Degli Antoni in the 125cc event.

Besides the works Gilera fours of Duke and Armstrong, the 500cc field included other factory-backed riders on Norton, AJS and Matchless models. But there were many retirements, including Armstrong (gearbox), Alan Trow (crash), John Storr (engine) and Dick Thomson (crash – broken collarbone).

500cc Swedish GP – 30 laps – 135.30 miles
1st   G.E. Duke (Gilera)
2nd   K. Campbell (Norton)
3rd   J. Hartle (Norton)

4th   J. Brett (Norton)
5th   O. Nygren (Matchless)
6th   R.T. Matthews (Norton)

Retirements and accidents in Germany

Next came the German GP over the 7.1-mile Solitude circuit. To begin with, John Surtees (MV Agusta) sustained a broken arm (which was to sideline the young Londoner for the rest of the year) in the 350cc race. Then, in the 500cc race, there were a succession of sensational retirements, including Geoff (with magneto failure). So, teammate Reg Armstrong went on to score a brilliant win from Umberto Masetti (MV Agusta), with Frenchman Pierre Monneret on another Gilera third.

Both Geoff and teammate Reg Armstrong (who had recieved the same six-month ban) were able to return to the GP scene from 1 July 1956. Reg is shown here after victory in the German GP at Solitude, after Geoff was forced to retire with magneto problems.

The Les Graham Trophy

Les Graham, the former AJS, Benelli, MV Agusta and Velocette rider, and a personal friend of Geoff Duke's, had been tragically killed in the 1953 Senior TT. And it was perhaps fitting that the first outing of this new trophy in his memory should have had Geoff Duke among its entry list. This came at Oulton Park, Cheshire, on Saturday 4 August 1956.

As *The Motor Cycle* reported, 'the day's activity started at the unearthly hour of 6.30am when machines were examined. Practising was from 8 until 11.30am'. This was because there had been no less than 267 entries.

Two 30-strong 1000cc heats (six laps) saw victories for Geoff and Bob McIntyre (Norton). But, in the eight-lap final, McIntyre was involved in a collision which, although it did not cause anyone to fall, broke one of his footrests. So it was Terry Shepherd and Bob Anderson who came home second and third before Geoff and his four-cylinder Gilera.

The last race of the day was the 12-lap handicap for the Les Graham Trophy, and it proved a particularly exciting finale, with Geoff missing out on victory by a mere two seconds after 33 miles. During this, Geoff broke his own circuit lap record with a speed of 85.69mph. Mrs Edna Graham presented awards to conclude what *The Motor Cycle* described as 'a grand day's racing'.

At the 1956 Ulster Grand Prix Geoff (21) leads AF Martin (51 – Matchless). But again Geoff struck problems, this time a crash causing his retirement.

Ulster GP

After missing the Ulster GP the previous year following start money wrangles, Geoff returned to Dundrod for the 1956 event. Unfortunately, torrential rain showers punctuated the 500cc (and Sidecar) races.

Factory entries from BMW, Norton, Matchless, Gilera and Moto Guzzi made the 500cc race an exciting prospect. Gileras two riders were Geoff and Reg Armstrong.

Potentially a serious threat to the four-cylinder Gilera (and MV Agusta) machinery was the incredible V8 Moto Guzzi. However, continued teething troubles limited its success.

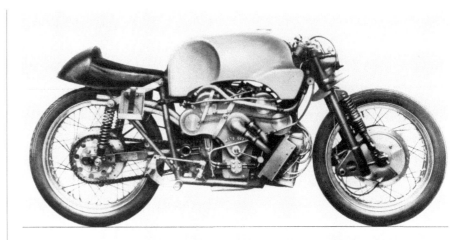

At the fall of the flag, John Hartle (Norton) rocketed away from the start, but Duke's engine hesitated and he was boxed in mid-field.

At the end of the first 7.23-mile lap Hartle still led, Jack Brett (Norton) second, Geoff third, Murphy (Matchless) fourth and Zeller (BMW) fifth. And with two laps completed, Duke's Gilera was the first machine to heel over round the long, sweeping right-hander before the pits. But Hartle was there, right in his slipstream. A lap later and the crowd were amazed, as it was Hartle who had gone back in front. At the end of the fourth circuit it was still the Norton rider. Geoff managed to regain the lead on the fifth lap. Meanwhile, Brett, who had been lying third, fell at Leathamstown. His right elbow had been severely cut – to an extent that eight stitches had to be put in afterwards – but the gritty Yorkshireman would not give in. He remounted and on the sixth lap passed Hartle and began to draw away, even though his gear lever was bent and he was changing gear by hand!

With Geoff 'riding at the top of his form' (*The Motor Cycle*), after 13 laps completed he led the second man Hartle (Brett having been forced to stop at his pit for repairs) by over 1½ minutes. By then, violent showers and high winds were making riding conditions difficult to say the least.

Then, fate struck both Gilera entries. First Geoff fell (badly bruising his shoulder) as he accelerated out of Leathamstown a shade too hard. Armstrong joined him in retirement a few minutes later with an inoperative clutch. Zeller and Lomas had already been forced to quit.

And so, for the first time in several seasons, British motorcycles took all top-six places in a Grand Prix counting towards Championship points, John Hartle tasting his first major success at this level. Geoff's only consolation was that he had been credited with a new lap record of 94.47mph.

Between the Ulster and forthcoming Italian round, Geoff had time to take in the Manx Grand Prix practising, the world champion having a personal

interest in the entry of F.A. Rutherford riding one of the Duke BSA Gold Star machines (destined to retire on the fourth lap of the Senior race). Geoff was also on the island to see his masseur Jack Griffiths, who needed to 'massage my shoulder back to normal again'.

First classic victory of the year
At Monza, Geoff scored his first classic victory of the year in the 500cc race after a hard race-long battle with the 350cc race victor Libero Liberati, Geoff's outing on one of the new, smaller fours having come to a halt after a broken clutch plate upset the gearchange of his machine.

With the streamlined
Gilera during his winning
ride in the 500cc Italian
Grand Prix, September
1956.

As an example of just how hard fought the Liberati/Duke battle had been is to realise that the two shared a new circuit lap record of 116.51mph. But Geoff had won the battle by being able to outfox the Italian star on his home patch.

Peace at last
As Geoff himself was later to recall after Monza, it was 'peace at last and only two more races to go – and these for the sheer fun of it'.

After a throughly miserable year, Geoff was able to score his first and only Grand Prix victory counting towards Championship points at the Italian round in September.

At Scarborough on 15 September 1956 Geoff convinced Bob McIntyre (left) to sign for Gilera instead of MV Agusta.

Scarborough on 15 September came first, winning the second heat by some 25 seconds from Alastair King (Norton), Geoff's fastest lap having been 65.33mph compared with Bob McIntyre's 64.36mph in the previous heat. The third heat was won by Bob Anderson.

In the final, McIntyre led Geoff for the first three laps, but then on lap four the Gilera man took the lead and the 'flying pair' (*The Motor Cycle*) were soon half a minute ahead of the rest. For many laps the two kept close company, but at the finish Duke was seven seconds ahead and his fastest lap was approximately 2mph slower than his own record speed.

At the finish, Geoff and Bob swapped machines to do a lap of honour – or so it seemed at the time. Actually, there was another purpose – Geoff had just persuaded Bob to join Gilera instead of MV Agusta! The whole story behind this is fully explained in my companion volume *Bob McIntyre: the Flying Scot* (Breedon Books).

Eight days later, following his victory at Scarborough, Geoff was competing in the Skaneloppett Races on 22 September, run over the narrow Kristianstad, Sweden circuit. Geoff had been joined by his Gilera teammate Reg Armstrong, and the two were without serious opposition in the 500cc race. The event was won by Geoff, with Armstrong 2.1 seconds behind, after the pair had lapped the entire field; the lap record fell no less than four times before finally being claimed by Geoff at 100.04mph. Other winners at this particularly well-organised meeting, which had attracted a number of works stars, were Romolo Ferri (Gilera) in the 125cc and August Hobl (DKW) in the 350cc.

The South African adventure

As Geoff was to admit, he 'believed in accepting every opportunity for world travel arising out of my motorcycling activities'. And so he readily accepted an offer to race in South Africa and Southern Rhodesia over the closed season of 1956–57.

Gilera prepared two five-hundred four-cylinder models, and these left Venice by sea for Cape Town on 5 December 1956 with mechanic Carlo Cazzaniga. Meanwhile,

Geoff, together with former racer Bob Foster, arranged to fly out from London to Johannesburg on 27 December.

After a shaky start, which included the machine, spares and mechanic going to the wrong destination and all Geoff's riding gear being left behind in Italy, eventually everything fell into place.

The actual racing began with the Port Elizabeth 200 on 1 January 1957. The remainder of the programme comprised meetings at Pietermaritzburg on 19 January, Johannesburg on 2 February, Salisbury (Southern Rhodesia) on 23 February and finally Cape Town on 2 March.

For the last month of the tour Geoff's wife Pat and their three-year-old son Peter joined him in Johannesburg, the party returning to England on Tuesday 5 March.

Both Geoff's machines wore the small top-half fairings for the trip down south and, as Geoff was later to admit:

I, personally, met some wonderful people out there – people who went to a great deal of trouble on my behalf, for which I was extremely

Following his earlier winter tour of Australia, Geoff visited South Africa and Rhodesia during the European closed season of 1956–57. He is seen here racing at Pietermaritzburg on the 19 January 1957, winning both the scratch and handicap events.

Geoff awaiting the start of a very wet handicap race at Belvedere (Salisbury, Rhodesia) on 23 February 1957.

In April 1957, following his return to Europe, Geoff's first outing was at Imola in Italy. He is seen here trying to catch Alano Montanari (Moto Guzzi) in the early stages of the 350cc race. Soon afterwards Duke crashed, while Montanari was runner-up to Libero Liberati.

grateful. By their kindness and hospitality, a trip which I had at first been tempted to terminate, almost before it began, finished on a very pleasant note indeed.

Of all the riders Geoff witnessed during his stay, it was Borro Castellani who he adjudged as 'outstanding, especially on the extremely-fast type of circuit'.

As for the results Geoff achieved during his South African and Southern Rhodesian races, these are fully catalogued in the appendices at the end of the book.

Back in Europe

Back in Europe, there had been several changes and events at Gilera. First, Piero Taruffi, 'a brilliant racing manager and engineer' (Geoff Duke), had made way for the younger and far less experienced Roberto Persi. Next, Reg Armstrong had retired from racing, his position effectively being replaced by Geoff Duke's own recommendation, Bob McIntyre. But probably the event which was to have the major effect on the company's racing plans was the unexpected death in October 1956 of Ferruccio Gilera. The 26-year-old, Giuseppe Gilera's only son, suffered a fatal heart attack while visiting the firm's Argentinian subsidiary in Buenos Aires. Ferruccio's untimely passing robbed the team of a most enthusiastic supporter (it was he who had inspired Ing. Passoni to design the new 125-twin and 350-four-cylinder models).

Libero Liberati

Libero Liberati during 1955, the year he became 500cc Senior Italian champion.

Even after winning the 1957 500cc World Championship title, to many people, at least outside Italy, Libero Liberati remained a mystery man. When he took the title at the final round at Monza he was almost 32 years old and had been racing for 12 years. In fact, he had enjoyed the backing of the Gilera factory since 1950 – and first rode a four the following year, so in reality his rise came slower than most.

Besides his racing contract with Gilera, he was also one of their dealers, with a showroom in Terni, near Rome. The son of a butcher, he left school at the age of 14 and began work as a mechanic. Even at this young age, he was keen on motorcycling and had already had his first ride – on a small capacity Mas – some two or three years earlier.

Then came the war, but when competition resumed after the conflict, Libero, then 20, made his debut on a Moto Guzzi flat single in a local hill climb. That model soon gave way to a Guzzi Condor, and, before 1946 was out, came the first of his victories.

Next, a Gilera Saturno Sanremo was obtained. At first, Liberati raced privately, but after a string of excellent results he eventually received help from the Arcore factory, followed by a works Saturno for the 1950 season.

At Monza in September 1951 came his debut on a four at the Grand Prix des Nations. During 1952 Gilera entered Libero in the Italian and selected World 500cc Championship rounds. He rode abroad in Holland, Spain and Switzerland. And it was in the latter country, at Berne, where he was to crash, sustaining a severe injury which left him with a 'bent arm' riding style for the remainder of his career.

One of the reasons why Libero Liberati was so little known outside his homeland was that he never raced in the Isle of Man (then the world's premier event) and only once in Ulster.

After being victorious in the 1955 and 1956 Italian 500cc Senior Championship titles, Libero scored his first Grand Prix victory on the new

350 four-cylinder machine in September 1956; he was also runner-up to teammate Geoff Duke in the 500cc race.

During his Championship year, Libero Liberati took victories at Hockenheim, Dundrod and Monza; he also won at Spa Francorchamps but was excluded from the results for entering on teammate Bob Brown's machine. A 350cc victory was notched up at Hockenheim on the smaller-engined four.

Some critics said that if Geoff Duke or Bob McIntyre had not suffered injuries, or that if so-and-so had not retired, Liberati would not have taken the title – but that is exactly what Libero did, he scored the most points.

After Gilera withdrew from racing at the end of 1957, Libero continued to compete in major events on his own Gilera Saturno single. It was a measure of his sportsmanship and enthusiasm for the marque that he persevered on what was, by then, an outdated bike.

Sadly, it was to be on his faithful Saturno that Libero Liberati was to meet his death on Monday 5 March 1962, while testing the Gilera on public roads near his home town of Terni in readiness for the coming season's racing.

The new 350 Gilera four made a winning debut to its career in the hands of Libero Liberati, at Monza on 9 September 1956.

Ferruccio's death was to be instrumental, in the author's opinion, in draining Giuseppe Gilera (then aged almost 70) of the determination and drive which had created what was, at the time, one of the truly great racing teams in existence. It was almost as if he had lost much of the will to live, so great did he feel his loss. As someone who has also lost a son at an early age, I can appreciate just what Giuseppe Gilera went through: it is truly heartbreaking.

1957 – A season of High Drama

And so to 1957, destined to be a year of high drama for both Gilera and Geoff Duke.

Things started to go wrong right from the start, at the European season's first major international event, the Shell Gold Cup, at Imola, Italy, on Easter Monday 22 April.

Even though official practice had gone well for the Gilera riders, including Geoff, McIntyre and Liberati, things did not pan out so well in the actual races (the company having entered riders in both 350 and 500cc events).

Geoff Duke had a miserable time. Getting a bad start on the smaller four, he came off early in the race due to oil spilled by another competitor. Then, in the 500cc event, after making another bad start (and probably feeling the effects of the earlier crash) to spill again after closing up on the leading pair of McIntyre and Umberto Masetti, but this time dislocating a shoulder. At first the medics said it would be 15 days, then 30 days, and finally, upon returning to the Isle of Man, bad news – he would be missing the TT.

McIntyre had been hampered by machine troubles at Imola (and other early season non-Championship meetings) but came good with not only an historic Junior/Senior TT double, but he also became the first man to lap the fearsome Isle of Man Mountain Circuit at 100mph.

Then, Bob crashed during the Dutch TT, effectively ruining his chances of World Championship glory. Although the Australian Bob Brown had backed up McIntyre at the TT, Gilera's main man (and ultimately the 1957 500cc World Championship winner) was the Italian Libero Liberati.

Things got even worse in the 500cc event at Imola. Here Geoff struggles to control his sliding machine in vain, suffering a badly-damaged shoulder which ruined his year, his last with Gilera.

Another reason for Gilera's problems, so Geoff revealed later, was that virtually no changes had been made to the 1956 machines. And, as Geoff recalled in his 1988 autobiography, 'the lack of his (Taruffi's) guiding hand found us at Imola in 1957 with no two frames alike, as far as the relative position of engine unit to wheel spindles was concerned'. And this stemmed not only because of Taruffi's departure, but Ferruccio Gilera's death. That all-important spark of genius, so long a feature of the Gilera camp, seemed to be missing. And now, years later, the reasons are much, much clearer than in 1957.

A lengthy lay-off

And so, for a second year, Geoff Duke was to remain a virtual spectator as the season unfolded, and was forced into a lengthy lay-off.

In fact, his first ride after the Imola debacle did not come until the Swedish Grand Prix (still a non-Championship event) at the Hedemora circuit in mid-July.

Geoff only rode in the 500cc race, and although he was first into the saddle and still led at the end of the first lap both Australian Keith Campbell (Geoff's brother-in-law) on a works Moto Guzzi and John Hartle (factory development Norton) forced past. By the 18th lap Duke was 34 seconds behind, and at that point Campbell pulled out the stops to tear ahead, a clear winner, with race and lap records (the latter at 106.54mph) in his pocket. Geoff's lack of riding for the past few months clearly showed.

Following his Imola nightmare Geoff was forced to sit out most of the year. He is seen here talking to Alastair King at Oulton Park that summer.

500cc Swedish GP – 30 laps – 135.3 miles

1st	K.R. Campbell (Moto Guzzi)
2nd	J. Hartle (Norton)
3rd	G.E. Duke (Gilera)
4th	G.A. Murphy (Matchless)
5th	V. Lundberg (Norton)
6th	J. Brett (Norton)

Ulster Grand Prix

The Gilera team was far from perfect when Geoff took part in his first classic road races of the season, over the 7.23-mile Dundrod circuit – home of the Ulster Grand Prix. McIntyre had ridden in practice and elected to start with the proviso that if his head troubled him (he had been suffering from headaches as an aftermath of his spill in the Dutch TT) he would retire. The Gilera team was completed by Libero Liberati. Keith Bryen and Keith Campbell (Moto Guzzis), and John Surtees (MV Agusta), seemed likely to provide the most serious opposition.

At the start of the 350cc race, Campbell 'rocketed into the lead' (*The Motor Cycle*) with Liberati and Surtees in hot pursuit. As for Geoff, he was way down in a midfield position, while McIntyre had been stranded at the start and was forced to change a plug before his machine would fire; things did not look too good.

First Geoff retired with suspension trouble, then McIntyre joined him after managing to close on the leaders. At the end of the 20-lap, 144.6-mile race, the two Guzzi riders Campbell and Bryen were first and second respectively, while Liberati brought the remaining Gilera home third.

A first, second and third for Gilera

In the 500cc race it was a Gilera first, second and third, with Libero Liberati taking victory, Bob McIntyre runner-up and Geoff third; MV's John Surtees set the fastest lap, a new record, at 95.69mph.

However, Surtees was destined to retire (with a faulty magneto) after looking clearly set for victory.

500cc Ulster GP – 20 laps – 144.6 miles

1st	L. Liberati (Gilera)
2nd	R. McIntyre (Gilera)
3rd	G.E. Duke (Gilera)
4th	G.B. Tanner (Norton)
5th	K. Bryen (Moto Guzzi)
6th	T.S. Shepherd (MV Agusta)

The start of the 500cc race at the Italian Grand Prix, Monza, 1 September 1957, Geoff is on row two, number 18.

Geoff crossing the line at Monza in 1957 to finish ahead of Alfredo Milani, the race was won by the newly-crowned 500cc world champion Libero Liberati. It was to be Gilera's final race prior to their withdrawal from the sport a short while later – and thus an end of an era.

Liberati wins the Championship

The final round of the 1957 World Championships was staged at Monza on Sunday 1 September. The meeting was dominated by rumours suggesting that one or more of the Italian marques was on the verge of withdrawal from Grand Prix racing.

Bob McIntyre won the 350cc race from Liberati and was then packed off to hospital by Giuseppe Gilera after being taken ill. In the 500cc race, Gilera took the first three places – Liberati (and the Championship title), Geoff and Alfredo Milani. Later, Geoff was to admit that he had to pull out all the stops to beat Milani that day, but in the end his vast experience paid off.

And when one takes into account the problems and lack of riding he had done that year, it was a fine result. What he did not realise at the time was that the 1957 500cc Italian Grand Prix was to be his last competitive ride on a four-cylinder Gilera.

500cc Italian GP – 35 laps – 125.05 miles
1st	L. Liberati (Gilera)
2nd	G.E. Duke (Gilera)
3rd	A. Milani (Gilera)
4th	J. Surtees (MV Agusta)
5th	U. Masetti (MV Agusta)
6th	T.S. Shepherd (MV Agusta)

The Gilera withdrawal

The truth concerning what might happen was not long in coming, and at the end of September 1957 came the official news that Moto Guzzi, FB Mondial *and* Gilera would not be racing in 1958. Various reasons were put forward, including, as the official communication for all three companies stated, that they had 'demonstrated the undeniable technical excellence of their products and that recently there had been no foreign opposition'. Added to this had been an outbreak in Italy of anti-racing public opinion, fuelled by the popular press and the restrictions of the authorities following the Mille Miglia car tragedy (where a car had ploughed into the crowd, causing several fatalities). But the *real* reason, which could not be disclosed at the time, was that motorcycling itself was in trouble. It was the beginning of a period in which customers would turn away from two-wheels to small cars, in ever-increasing numbers.

So came about the end of a truly golden era in the history of road racing, not witnessed on quite the same scale before or since. The decade of the 1950s was a time when motorcycle ownership was at a peak, and the racing matched this sales boom, with crowds flocking in their thousands to witness the top riders and machines of the day, all over Europe. During this time, the Gilera legend had been irrevocably welded together and, besides the mere masterpieces of metal, had spawned men such as Armstrong, the Milani brothers, Masetti, Colnago, Liberati, McIntyre and, of course, the maestro himself, Geoff Duke.

Left out in the cold

All of the above meant that Geoff was effectively left out in the cold. The first he officially heard from Gilera on the subject was when he received communications from the Italian company that there would not be any machines available for the traditional end-of-season British short-circuit meetings… and he had, in good faith, entered for Scarborough, Silverstone, Aintree and Oulton Park.

This meant he was forced to seek alternative machines. In the end, this turned out to be the Alan Holmes production Manx Norton, which had just won the Senior Manx Grand Prix. At Scarborough over Friday 14 and Saturday 15 September, Geoff struggled with what one commentator described as an 'off-tune Norton'. But, in truth, it was the first Norton he had ridden for some five years, so it was, perhaps, little wonder that he found the going tough, later commenting 'it's easier to switch from a single to a four, rather than the other way around'. He eventually rounded the weekend off with a seventh place in the 500cc final.

A week later, Geoff was at Silverstone on Saturday 21 September for the famous Hutchinson 100 meeting. But things were worse than Scarborough, *The Motor Cycle* describing what happened in their 26 September 1957 issue: 'Poor Geoff Duke: his Norton was noticeably down on power and, after slipping back through the field, he toured in to retire when placed no higher than 15th.'

There then followed rides, which, although not bringing rostrum positions, did give a bit of cheer at the season's end.

First, on Saturday 28 September, Geoff put in 'A meteoric ride' to secure eighth in the 500cc race at Aintree. Then, at Oulton Park on Saturday 5 October, came the last big British race meeting. And it was here that Geoff was to put in his best performance of the four meetings. The main event of the day was the 500cc Slazenger Trophy race. *The Motor Cycle* of 10 October 1957 takes up the story: 'Geoff Duke, starting badly, was 10th from last on lap one and began a long and heartbreaking struggle against hopeless odds, yet he pulled up to seventh position at the finish.'

And so the 1957 season came to an end. Certainly, it had been the most difficult in Geoff Duke's racing career, when his patience had been tested to the limit. However, his enthusiasm for motorcycle racing had remained undimmed. When many lesser mortals would have simply called it a day and hung up their leathers, Geoff was already making plans for continuing his racing without the benefit of a full factory Gilera contract into the 1958 season.

Chapter 6

Going it Alone

As Geoff was to admit in his autobiography, 'Gilera's withdrawal from racing in 1957, I suppose in retrospect, should have signalled the end of my racing career, but I still enjoyed racing.' And, as he went on to say, 'a considerable part of that enjoyment had been in assisting with the development of the machines I rode.' The *BP Book of Motor Cycle Racing* (1960) gave an excellent insight into his abilities in this direction, saying 'Geoff Duke is not only a brilliant rider. He is one of those rare beings that development engineers dream about – a man with an instinctive love and "feel" for machinery who can sense where modifications are needed and explain what should be done.'

This ability had prompted Norton's race supremo Joe Craig to comment that Geoff's analytical mind had simplified his job 'enormously', while Duke's advice to Gilera on how to solve its handling problems did virtually as much to bring the Italian marque their string of successes from 1953 to 1955 as his own mastery in the saddle.

Geoff would be the first to admit that he was not an engineer. However, he *knew* what was needed to achieve success on the race circuit. And, besides the guidance he was able to provide both Norton and later Gilera, he was also responsible for a number of interesting projects including a three-fifty Velocette, a brace of BSA Gold Stars and, most notably, a Lightweight three-fifty Norton. The latter (see separate boxed section within this chapter) shows several interesting design features, in which Geoff was able to use his vast riding experience to good effect. Also, the 1958 season saw a switch from fully enclosed 'dustbin' fairing to the new 'dolphin' type, after the FIM banned the former from international events at the end of 1957.

The machinery

Besides the Lightweight 350 Norton, what machinery could Geoff call upon for the 1958 season? Well, as we already know, three of the big four Italian factories had quit Grand Prix racing. And only MV Agusta had signalled their wish to continue. John Surtees was Agusta's number-one rider, with John Hartle about to join him. And by now British factory participation was limited to say the least.

As catalogued in the following chapter, a major part of Geoff's 1958 plans featured the German BMW company. But, for various reasons, Geoff's BMW experiences never matched the initial hype surrounding his signature for the Munich concern.

Joining up with Dearden

By January 1958 the BMW ride, plus 'at least one rather special Norton' (*Motor Cycle News*, 22 January issue), was public knowledge.

Next came news, in mid-March, that Geoff had purchased one of Derek Minter's Manx Norton models. Then, only a week later, *Motor Cycle News* in its 19 March edition carried a front page news item headlined 'Duke on Nortons'. *MCN* went on to say 'Geoff Duke will ride 350 and 500 Nortons at the Oulton Park Easter Monday meeting,' and 'both machines are the property of Reg Dearden, who is, in fact, entering Geoff for the meeting.'

An even bigger headline greeted *Motor Cycle News* readers in the 9 April 1958 edition: 'Duke is Back'. This was in response to his debut on the brace of Dearden Nortons at Oulton Park two days earlier, on Easter Monday 7 April.

Actually, although he led the 350cc race for several laps, it was the Scot Alastair King who not only won both races, but set the fastest laps in each.

A crowd, described as 'of near record proportions' (*MCN*), had crammed every vantage point round the 2.761-mile Cheshire circuit in slightly cool, but otherwise perfect, weather conditions to witness Geoff's return. There was certainly a top-class entry, with Bob McIntyre, Terry Shepherd, Frank Perris, Bob Anderson, Ray Fay, Alan Holmes, Bob Brown, plus Alastair King and Geoff himself. *Motor Cycle News* concluded by commenting that 'the way Geoff was dicing with these arch ear'olers of modern short-circuit racing proved to enthusiasts that road racer Duke is back in business with a bang!'

Then, in his *Paddock Gossip* column in *MCN* dated 16 April, Mick Woollett had this to say:

The smile on Geoff Duke's face at the end of the 350 final at Oulton Park on Easter Monday was well worth seeing. After months of wondering and waiting, Geoff had found form again and had obviously enjoyed his epic struggle with Alastair King, Ray Fay and

Norton Lightweight 350

Geoff Duke's interest in the design and development of the motorcycle led him to create a lightweight three-fifty machine, powered by a Manx Norton engine. This programme was financed by Geoff himself, and again displays his genuine enthusiasm for two wheels.

The frame itself was designed and built by Ken Sprayson of Reynolds, with input from Geoff, in Reynolds 531 aircraft-quality light-gauge tubing. As Geoff himself explained, 'the duplex-loop frame had a single front downtube, of 4in diameter, which was also the container for engine oil.' This latter feature alone saved some 5lb, compared with a conventional separate oil tank. This, combined with a longer rear swinging arm, helped achieve a 'more forward weight distribution'. Another advantage gained by the absence of an oil tank was 'plenty of breathing space around the carburettor intake'. Thus, as Geoff says, 'the air was cooler and it was easier to experiment with induction pipe length'.

Another area of change concerned the front suspension. In his 1988 autobiography Geoff revealed 'I was never completely happy with telescopic forks, which lacked rigidity and therefore suffered from stiction and the adverse effect under heavy braking of a fixed brake anchor.' In fact, Geoff 'favoured a trailing-link fork, which I had suggested to Joe Craig at Nortons.' But, as he recalled, 'However, as time and money were short, I eventually settled for the more conventional leading-link variety.' As with the frame, this was designed and produced by the Reynolds concern. As a point of interest, Woodhead-Monroe hydraulic suspension units were employed, front and rear.

Geoff, with his own special project, the lightweight Reynolds-framed 350 Manx Norton.

The very special Duke Reynolds-framed 350 Manx minus its bodywork. Although it showed considerable potential, Geoff eventually halted development, due to financial implications.

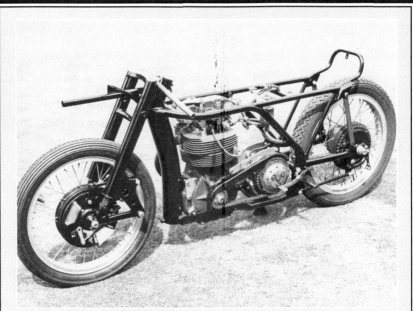

As for the brakes, the front was a twin-leading shoe Manx Norton component, while an AJS 7R unit was at the rear. As Geoff said, 'Direct anchorage of the plates to the rear fork arm or front fork link causes the rear wheel to hop and the front fork to lock under heavy braking, so a true parallelogram was used at the front, which isolated fork action entirely from brake torque.'

Although the Manx Norton was used as the basis of the motive power for the Duke 350 Special, it was not entirely standard. Geoff's 'old friend', Stan Hackett of Nortons, produced a set of drawings for a one-off unit, employing short-stroke dimensions of 80 x 69.5mm – with a one-piece forged crankshaft – a plain bearing big-end, aluminium (Jaguar) connecting-rod and an outside flywheel. Another notable feature was the cylinder barrel in aluminium alloy (manufactured specially by specialists Hepworths) featuring a bore chrome-plated directly on to the alloy. As for the cylinder head, this was a standard Norton component, suitably modified to accept American-made Withams dual coil valve springs. This latter change, as Geoff described, 'to facilitate the planned enclosure of the valve gear'. This would help prevent oil leakage from the cambox – a weakness with the standard Norton set-up. This set-up would also allow a freer fit for the tappets in their bushes. Geoff again: 'All the development work on the engine was carried out by that engineering wizard Bill Lacey.'

The 350cc Lightweight Duke Special was given its first real test (with a standard Manx engine) during practice for the 1958 German GP at the Nürburgring, where 'the spring poundage and hydraulic settings of the shock absorbers were found to be too high for a machine weighing only 262lb (some 50lb lighter than the production machine)'.

In an attempt to further reduce weight, Geoff acquired, from America, a twin disc and single disc brake assemblies – although these were never used.

As for the development engine, this, after 'showing great potential on

Bill Lacey's test-bench', was tested in the motorcycle around Oulton Park, but 'after a few laps, the big-end bearing showed signs of tightening up'.

But by now, with costs rapidly spiralling upwards and yet more development costs expected (5-speed gearbox, cylinder head valve gear enclosure – to say nothing of solving the insufficient oil pressure to the big-end), Geoff decided 'reluctantly' to 'cut my losses and call it a day' for the Lightweight programme.

A close-up showing the large diameter, oil-carrying front downtube, and cutaway to allow for an outside flywheel engine.

Bob Anderson. I think everyone at Oulton Park was hoping that Geoff would win, but after holding the lead for a short while he dropped back with a front brake which wouldn't brake.

A victory at Silverstone

And the Oulton Park meeting was quickly followed later the same month by Silverstone, where, in the 350cc Championship event, Geoff (riding a Dearden Norton) not only won but in the process passed the complete field from a poor start. One commentator described that the way he swept the 350 Norton through the Silverstone curves 'brought back memories of 1951'.

Geoff also set the fastest lap at 91.58mph.

350cc Silverstone – 17 laps – 50 miles
1st   G.E. Duke (Norton)
2nd   R. McIntyre (Norton)

3rd   K.E. Patrick (Norton)
4th   R. Fay (Norton)
5th   R. Anderson (Norton)
6th   D. Minter (Norton)

It was an impressive victory by any standards, with the *Motor Cycle News* race report headlined 'Duke shatters the opposition.'

Unfortunately, as related in Chapter Seven, Geoff had a poor start to his BMW career, retiring from the 500cc race when poorly placed.

Then came a period of BMW, rather than Norton, activity (covered in the next chapter).

The TT
The 1958 Isle of Man TT could not have been worse. First, Geoff suffered endless problems with his Junior (350cc) entry – largely because, instead of being allowed to race his Silverstone-winning machine, the Norton factory convinced Reg Dearden to use their experimental engines with disastrous results, both in practice and the race. In the latter, after a last-minute magneto swap, Geoff found the machine 'refused to exceed 6000rpm' and, although he 'continued in the hope of completing one lap, but at Sulby the valve gear decided to call it a day and I was forced to retire'.

And another retirement was posted in the Senior, when, after experiencing handling gremlins and brake fade on the BMW, Geoff was again forced to call it a day.

A Belgian interview
Towards the end of June, Geoff, together with Reg Dearden, visited the Brussels Fair as guests of the Federation Motorcliste de Belgique, where the opportunity was taken for that country's leading sports paper, *Les Sports*, to interview the ex-world champion.

Geoff was reported as saying that the special Lightweight 350 Norton, on which he was to be entered by Dearden, was 'very fast indeed', and that he was hopeful of beating John Surtees in the 350cc class of the Belgian Grand Prix. And in reply to the question 'Then you think you have a better chance in the 350cc race than in the 500cc?', Geoff was quoted as saying 'I think so. The Norton goes well and I have complete confidence in that machine.' But, of course, it was what he did not say which was most interesting – that, by now, he had become more than a little apprehensive about his chances of success with the BMW.

More retirements in Holland, but finishes in Belgium

Just after he had given the interview in Belgium, Geoff took part in the Dutch TT at Assen, only to retire in both the 350 and 500cc events. But things turned out better in the Belgian GP a few days later where Geoff finished both races, with a fourth on the BMW in the larger capacity event behind John Surtees and John Hartle (MVs), and Keith Campbell (Norton).

Earlier, on his Dearden Norton, Geoff had a fantastic four-way battle with fellow Norton riders Keith Campbell, Derek Minter and Dave Chadwick, with the result going down to the wire.

350cc Belgian GP – 11 laps – 96.32 miles

1st	J. Surtees (MV Agusta)	
2nd	J. Hartle (MV Agusta)	
3rd	K.R. Campbell (Norton)	
4th	D. Minter (Norton)	
5th	G.E. Duke (Norton)	
6th	D.V. Chadwick (Norton)	

Next came the German Grand Prix over the ultra-demanding Nürburgring circuit. But here there was a repeat of the Dutch round, with retirements in both races. This meeting also marked the end of Geoff's BMW outings, as the factory said it would not be contesting any more solo GPs that year.

So, for the remainder of the 1958 season, Geoff Duke was to be mounted exclusively on Norton machinery.

A double in Sweden

At the Hedemora circuit, the scene of the Swedish Grand Prix on Saturday 28 July 1958, in wonderfully sunny weather, Geoff twice snatched victory on the last lap in the 350 and 500cc events. In the former, Geoff was making his first actual race appearance on the Reynolds-framed machine (but powered by a standard Manx engine), whereas he rode a conventional Featherbed-framed works experimental model in the 500cc. This double victory was also noteworthy as it was Geoff's first Grand Prix double on Nortons since 1951!

350cc Swedish GP – 25 laps – 113.02 miles

1st	G.E. Duke (Norton)	
2nd	R. Anderson (Norton)	
3rd	S.M.B. Hailwood (Norton)	

Swedish Grand Prix, Hedemora, 26 July 1958. 500cc: Terry Shepherd (11), Bob Anderson (15) and Geoff with the Doug Hele works experimental Norton. Geoff won both the 350 and 500cc races. This was notable as it was his first GP double on Nortons since 1951.

4th	A. Trow (Norton)
5th	G. Monty (Norton)
6th	M.P. O'Rourke (Norton)

500cc Swedish GP – 30 laps – 135.38 miles

1st	G.E. Duke (Norton)
2nd	R.H. Dale (BMW)
3rd	T.S. Shepherd (Norton)
4th	G. Hocking (Norton)
5th	E. Hiller (BMW)
6th	R.N. Brown (Norton)

The five-hundred model Geoff used to win the Swedish GP used a Doug Hele-developed 93mm bore engine, and, at the time, he reported it was the smoothest Norton he had ever ridden and that it had excellent power characteristics with practically no 'meggaphonitis' – power coming in at below 3000rpm, and it could be driven out of slow corners without giving the clutch a beating. Unfortunately, in the race the machine was over-jetted and thus ran far too rich. This seriously impaired the performance, for the big-bore Nortons were very critical on jet sizes.

Ulster Grand Prix

Compared with the warm, sunny weather experienced in Scandinavia, conditions at the Ulster round at Dundrod a couple of weeks later in early August were absolutely atrocious, with unrelenting rain and thick mist all round the 7.5-mile Irish road course. Anyone who took part in this meeting can only be described as a real hero. There were 51 starters for the 20-lap, 148.32-mile 350cc event, and Geoff's ultimate fourth place behind the two MVs of Surtees and Hartle, plus third-place man Terry Shepherd (Norton), can only be seen as a good result.

Save for the presence of Ernst Hiller and Dickie Dale on BMWs and the absence of Dave Chadwick (who had had to retire from the 350cc race with cramp), the field for the 500cc race (again of 51 riders) was similar to the earlier race. Again, the race distance was 20 laps. So, like the other riders taking part in both races, Geoff would be taking in almost 300 miles of racing in a single day. Not unusual in those days, but not pleasant with the prevailing conditions to contend with. And fifth place was Geoff's when the flag finally came down.

500cc Ulster GP – 20 laps – 148.32 miles

1st	J. Surtees (MV Agusta)
2nd	R. McIntyre (Norton)
3rd	J. Hartle (MV Agusta)
4th	D. Minter (Norton)
5th	G.E. Duke (Norton)
6th	R.H. Dale (BMW)

Terry Shepherd finished third in the 350cc 1958 Ulster GP at Dundrod, behind the MVs of John Surtees and John Hartle and in front of Geoff, who finished fourth.

Third place in Italy

A third place in the 350cc Italian GP at Monza in mid-September, behind the works four-cylinder MVs of Surtees and Hartle, was a truly excellent result, and a hard one too. A titanic scrap between Geoff and Bob Anderson (both riding Nortons) was only settled at the final bend (the famous Parabolica). This is how the *MCN* race report saw it:

> *Anderson comes in with Duke just a few inches behind him, but the 'maestro', with a wonderful manoeuvre, manages to come out in front of the valiant rival and beats him on the line by a margin of just one-fifth of a second.*

350cc Italian GP – 27 laps – 96.41 miles
1st	J. Surtees (MV Agusta)
2nd	J. Hartle (MV Agusta)
3rd	G.E. Duke (Norton)
4th	R. Anderson (Norton)
5th	D.V. Chadwick (Norton)
6th	R.H. Brown (AJS)

Moto Morini test session

While in Italy, Geoff also tested a works two-fifty Moto Morini dohc at Monza. As he told Mick Woollett at the time, he was impressed with its power and handling, while its top speed was within a couple of miles-per-hour of Geoff's 350 Norton. He also told Mick that he hoped to go to Italy 'within a month or so' and visit the Morini factory in Bologna and 'perhaps' try a model if they have one ready to 'fit' him, as the Monza test machine was a 'little cramped'.

Scarborough

Over the years, the Oliver's Mount road circuit, Scarborough, had often proved a happy hunting ground for Geoff, so it was no surprise that he had entered for the traditional September Gold Cup meeting at the North Yorkshire seaside venue. But it was not to prove a successful return, being troubled by clutch slip in the 350cc final on the Friday, while on Saturday in the 500cc final Geoff could only manage 10th.

At the beginning of 1959, Geoff's father-in-law, the Revd R.H. Reid, was injured quite seriously in a road accident on his Velocette LE motorcycle. After being transported to Geoff's hotel, the Arragon, at Santon, Isle of Man (which Geoff had purchased in the spring of

1958), Revd Reid was transferred to Noble's Hospital in
Douglas.

As was often the case, Geoff
Duke's fame meant he was in
demand to perform at various
functions throughout the closed
season. For example, in February
1959 he crossed to Ulster, when he
officially opened a new garage and
showrooms owned by Malcolm
Templeman. Also in attendance was
Geoff's old Norton teammate and
friend, Artie Bell.

Although nothing ever came of
the possible Moto Morini tie-up, Geoff did join forces with another old
friend and teammate, Reg Armstrong. The result, as detailed in the next
chapter, was the construction of a special Reynolds framed two-fifty,
housing an ex-works NSU Renmax dohc twin-cylinder power-plant.
However, this technically-interesting project was not destined to be a
success. So it was again back to mainly campaigning 350 and 500cc Nortons
for 1959 – plus some outings later in the year on a factory Benelli two-fifty
(see Chapter Seven).

Although he journeyed to the Austrian GP (a non-Championship
event) held near Salzburg on 1 May, and to the North West 200 shortly
afterward with the NSU special, his first Norton outing – and then on a
borrowed bike – did not come until the Les Graham Trophy meeting at
Oulton Park later that same month. But here Geoff was forced to ride a
standard Manx borrowed from Reg Dearden at the last minute, after
mechanic Charlie Edwards found that the plain bearing big-end of
Duke's Lightweight 350 Norton was about to expire the night before the
race.

Oulton Park, 4 August
1958. Bob Anderson (15)
leads Geoff (130), both on
348cc Nortons – Duke
riding the Reynolds-
framed Special.

The Isle of Man TT

Geoff was entered in two races at the 1959 Isle of Man TT, the Lightweight
(NSU) and the Junior (Norton). But after the engine seized during his first
practice lap (on the Clypse circuit) on the NSU, he was left with one ride
only – on his Reynolds-framed Norton Special.

1959 was a significant year in TT history as it saw the start of the
Japanese invasion of European racing, with a team of Honda twins in the

For the last two seasons
of his career, Geoff
returned to Norton
machinery, albeit privateer
rather than works entries.

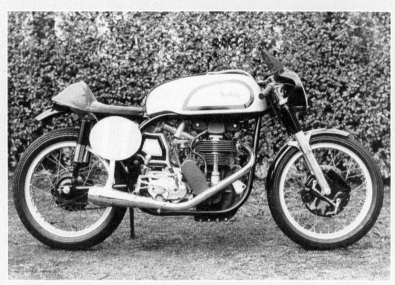

Featherbed Manx Norton

Ulsterman Rex Candless was responsible for the design of the Featherbed frame, and, powered by a works dohc Norton single-cylinder engine, this made its debut in the spring of 1950. Initially ridden only by the works riders, such as Geoff Duke and Artie Bell, the first over-the-counter 'customer' examples arrived the following year. In both cases this signalled the end of the old plunger-framed 'Garden Gate' models (which in works guise had debuted during the 1936 TT and in production form had been sold from 1946).

The Featherbed (thus named thanks to rider Harold Daniell saying it felt like a 'feather bed' during a test session) created a sensation when it made its winning entrance at the Blandford Camp circuit in April 1950. Geoff Duke was in the saddle that day, as he was when, wearing his innovative one-piece skin-tight leathers, he won the Senior TT a couple of months later. Although Geoff did not win the 1950 World Championship (due to a succession of tyre problems), the same rider/machine combination took the 350/500cc World Championships double in 1951, retaining the 350cc crown for Norton in 1952.

For 1951 the production Manx models were given the Featherbed chassis for the first time, together with several other improvements pioneered on the 1950 works models. It is also worth pointing out that the production machines were constructed in a different area of the Bracebridge Street, Birmingham, factory and were the responsibility of Edgar Franks (later design chief at the Ambassador works) rather than Joe Craig.

The pukka works specials were raced until the end of 1954. Then, with Joe Craig in charge, works development versions of the standard production version were entered in selected meetings by the trio of Surtees, Hartle and Brett. The over-the-counter customer Manx 40M (350cc) and 30M (500cc) continued with yearly updates until production

A 1958 Manx from the Norton factory brochure of that year.

finally came to an end in 1962. During the 1950s, 'customer' meant someone who was approved by the company. This approval meant the rider had to use his new machine in an international event, such as the TT, Ulster Grand Prix or a Continental European Grand Prix.

The first (1951) production Manx models displaced 499cc (79.62 x 100mm) and 348cc (71 x 88mm). Then, for the 1954 season there was a major engine redesign, with shorter-stroke dimensions: 86 x 85.62mm for the larger unit and 76 x 76.85mm on the three-fifty.

There were also detail changes in most years: Amal GP carburettors (1952); rotating-magnet magneto (1956); redesigned vertical drive shaft (1959); Amal GP2 carb (1961); dual 7in front brakes (1962).

During much of the 1950s, Norton engines were widely used in Formula 3 (500cc) racing cars. But Norton would not supply separate engine and transmission, instead customers had to purchase a complete bike and dispose of the cycle components themselves. This meant that redundant Norton Featherbed frame assemblies were used to house a variety of other engines, notably 500 and 650cc Triumph twins. And thus the now-famous Triton special was born.

The 1959 five-hundred Manx engine, with rotating-magnet magneto and Amal GP carburettor.

There is no doubt that top entrants, such as Joe Potts, were able to enjoy a liaison with the Norton works, which was useful to that entrant's riders – in Potts's case Bob McIntyre and Alastair King. During the late 1950s, development engineer Doug Hele carried out an extensive programme of improvements to the Manx, which benefitted the marque and those who rode the twin-cam Manx racers.

Geoff accelerating out of the Governors Bridge Dip during the 1959 Junior TT on his Lightweight 350 Norton Special. He went on to finish an excellent fourth in his last ever Isle of Man race.

Geoff with this go-kart, built locally in the Isle of Man at Peel.

Ultra Lightweight (125cc) event – and they went home with the Manufacturer's Team Prize to give a glimpse of what was to come.

As for Geoff's Junior race, he finished fourth, behind the two MVs of Surtees and Hartle, with the Scot Alastair King third. As for our hero, his years of campaigning for a grading system according to previous TT performances was introduced, in this his last Isle of Man race. Incidentally, Geoff's starting number was four, and there is no doubt he benefitted from Bob McIntyre's retirement after 'a fantastic ride' at the end of the fourth lap, when a fairing mounting bracket fractured on the Scottish rider's Norton. But Geoff enjoyed a 'wonderful scrap' with Bob Anderson, which the former won while he rode the Reynolds-framed Lightweight Norton bike.

Junior TT – 7 laps – 264.11 miles

1st	J. Surtees (MV Agusta)
2nd	J. Hartle (MV Agusta)
3rd	A. King (Norton)
4th	G.E. Duke (Norton)
5th	R. Anderson (Norton)

Reg Dearden

This famous Manchester-based tuner and dealer had a quite remarkable Isle of Man record, for, by the end of 1961, his bikes had won no less than 186 TT and Manx GP awards!

But, although today Dearden is best remembered for his Norton expertise, it was Velocette and Vincent with which he first became established – initially preparing one of the Stevenage v-twins and a very fast Velocette KTT Mark VIII. This latter machine featured dohc, as on the works bikes. Ridden by Les Graham, the Velo proved incredibly quick for a private entry. One of the secrets of its success was the special Dearden-designed cylinder head with an inlet port 1$\frac{9}{32}$in diameter, a far larger size than the Velocette factory's own development team had ever dared to try on its own engines.

As for the Vincent, this 998cc v-twin was built for an attempt on the world speed record during the early 1960s.

But it was the Norton single with which Dearden gained the majority of his successes. One of the first came when George Catlin won the 1954 Senior Manx Grand Prix using a virtually untested motor that had been built behind the Castle Mona Hotel, Douglas, just prior to the start of practice. In fact, Dearden believed that many of his best results had come as 'the result of mistakes and often they had never been bench tested before'. Typical of this was at Motor Cycling's 1958 Silverstone Saturday, when Dearden had our hero, Geoff Duke, mounted on one of his 350 Manx models (see elsewhere in this chapter for details). During the final practice session on the day prior to the race, Geoff had bent one of the special inlet valves Dearden had fitted. It was a unique design and no spares were available, so Reg grabbed a hammer and sat in his van tapping at the valve all night – until it was straight! And although he got the engine running, it sounded very flat when Geoff took it to the line. Then, to cap it all, the multi-time world champion had a terrible start and was almost last away. As recorded elsewhere, flat-sounding or not, the Manx engine went like a rocket once off the mark, with the result that Geoff overtook rider after rider to score a sensational victory – one of the most popular ever witnessed at the Northamptonshire speed venue.

As for helping up-and-coming youngsters, this was another area in which Reg Dearden was a past-master. Probably the greatest example was another future world champion Gary Hocking. In fact, if it had not been for Reg Dearden it is unlikely that the world would ever have seen the combination of Hocking and the four-cylinder MV Agusta. The young Rhodesian had wandered into Dearden's shop one day and, wistfully viewing a line-up of Manx Nortons, asked Reg if he would sponsor him. There was the usual discussion and then Hocking pulled out a return ticket to Rhodesia. 'If you don't sponsor me, Mr Dearden,' he said, 'this is all I've got left and I'm going to use it.' Reg recalled later 'He looked so keen that I couldn't let him go, so I called him back and told him to take a Norton with him.' That began an association which lasted until Hocking was signed up by Count Agusta. Besides Duke and Hocking, other riders who benefitted from Dearden-tuned Nortons included Dave Chadwick, John Hartle, Ralph Rensen, Fred Fisher, Keith Terretta and Terry Shepherd.

6th   D.V. Chadwick (Norton)

7th   R.N. Brown (Norton)

8th   D. Minter (Norton)

Following the TT came a succession of Continental European meetings, beginning with one at the Karlskoga circuit in central Sweden, where Geoff came home fifth in the 350cc event. The up-and-coming Gary Hocking won both the 350 and 500cc races on Dearden Nortons.

Then came the German Grand Prix at Hockenheim, where, as recorded in the following chapter, Geoff made his debut on the works two-fifty Benelli single (finishing sixth), with fourth (350) and ninth (500) on Nortons. He also finished third (again on the Benelli) in the Swedish GP, but did not ride his Nortons.

The Ulster Grand Prix

The Ulster Grand Prix, held over the 7.42-mile Dundrod road circuit, proved to be one of the highlights of Geoff's final year, with two rostrum finishes in the 350 and 500cc races. And for once the meeting was held in fine, sunny weather. The 125 and 250cc races had seen victories for Mike Hailwood (his first in an event counting towards World Championship points) on a 125cc Ducati, while Gary Hocking won the 250cc clash on a works MZ twin.

In the 350cc race Geoff finished third behind the winner John Surtees (MV Agusta) and Norton-mounted Bob Brown, while in the 500cc event it was another win for Surtees, with Bob McIntyre (Norton) runner-up and Geoff third once again.

350cc Ulster GP – 20 laps – 148.32 miles

1st   J. Surtees (MV Agusta)

2nd   R.N. Brown (Norton)

3rd   G.E. Duke (Norton)

4th   R.H. Dale (Norton)

5th   T. Phillis (Norton)

6th   J. Hempleman (Norton)

7th   J. Redman (Norton)

8th   E.G. Driver (Norton)

500cc Ulster GP – 20 laps – 148.32 miles

1st   J. Surtees (MV Agusta)

2nd   R. McIntyre (Norton)

3rd	G.E. Duke (Norton)
4th	T.S. Shepherd (Norton)
5th	R.N. Brown (Norton)
6th	A. King (Norton)
7th	R.H. Dale (BMW)
8th	J. Hempleman (Norton)

Geoff riding a hastily borrowed Manx Norton in the Les Graham Trophy race at Oulton Park on the 16 May 1958. The bike belonged to Reg Dearden, Geoff's mechanic Charlie Edwards had discovered the big-end of Geoff's Norton special was ready to disintegrate.

Monza

Monza, the scene of the Italian Grand Prix throughout Geoff's career, saw the former champion make a final visit to the rostrum in an event counting toward World Championship points, when he finished third behind the four-cylinder MV Agustas of John Surtees, the race winner, and Remo Venturi. Meanwhile, he had ridden the works Benelli into 10th in the 250cc race, but been a retirement in the 350cc event.

500cc Italian GP – 35 laps – 125.05 miles

1st	J. Surtees (MV Agusta)
2nd	R. Venturi (MV Agusta)
3rd	G.E. Duke (Norton)
4th	R.N. Brown (Norton)
5th	E.G. Driver (Norton)
6th	J. Hempleman (Norton)

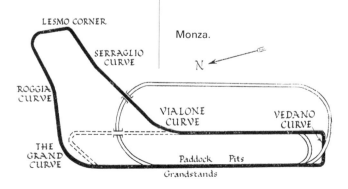

Monza.

Technique

As the title of this book quite clearly states, Geoff Duke was 'the Stylish Champion'. And, in the author's mind, Geoff's smooth style and professional approach to racing played a major role – together with great natural riding ability – in him becoming one of the truly great motorcycle racers of all time.

Another major factor was that he was probably the best all-rounder motorcycle sport has ever seen. As, without doubt, he could have also risen to the very top in trials and motocross. This, together with his ability to drive cars at high speed, marks Geoff Duke out above many other top motorcyclists.

His dirt-bike experience gave Geoff a great sense of throttle control, something which the Americans were to benefit from in their tarmac racing experiences in a later generation, having come up through the ranks of the AMA National Championships, where riders had to undertake various disciplines of the Stateside motorcycle sport including action on both tarmac and dirt.

But there were many other facets which played an important part in Geoff's success, including knowing when to put in an extra effort, tucking himself away on the machine, his ability to understand how to maximise his performance (examples being the innovation of tight-fitting, one-piece leathers and improving the machines he rode) and lightning reactions when faced with a dangerous situation.

Typical of his attention to detail were the hours spent helping to perfect streamlining of the Peel fairings (made in the Isle of Man by Cyril Cannell). Whereas other riders would soon loose interest, Geoff Duke was both patient and meticulous.

He also had the sense to realise when a machine had a problem or was not competitive – the latter being the reason why he ultimately made the switch from Norton to Gilera.

During the Geoff Duke era, the Isle of Man TT was the world's premier racing event. This meant (unlike other events) racing against the clock. And it was from 1951 onwards that Geoff 'consciously started making a big effort on the opening lap of each TT I contested with a capable machine, with the intention of demoralising the opposition'.

As for circuits, Geoff considered 'the TT course, although not quite as difficult to learn as Germany's Nürburgring, is unique. There are so many blind, or near-blind bends'.

There is no doubt that Geoff also realised the importance of 'putting in as much practice as possible'. This meant that right from the start of his Isle of Man career he spent many hours simply learning the course before he ever attempted to race around the 37.73-mile long Mountain lap. Using the same common-sense approach, Geoff also studied other riders and machines throughout his career. He might have been the best of his generation, but he was always keen to learn.

Another aspect of Geoff's success was his genuine enthusiasm for motorcycles. This explains why, when he could have safely retired at the end of 1957 following Gilera's withdrawal, he chose to continue with far less competitive machines.

Another facet of the Duke technique – aided by his smoothness – was that he was appreciative of the machinery. As an example of how easy he was on the motorcycle are the following words from the Regina chain engineer Ercole Villa: 'Geoff Duke was the best. The chain on his Gilera was always perfect and would have lasted for five TT races. But, at Monza, where it is much easier for the machines, Alfredo Milani (another Gilera works rider of the same era) would use 10 chains to Duke's one.'

Only one aspect of Geoff's racing did not seem to be perfect – this concerning his ability to get the motorcycle off the line first time, like John Surtees for example. In Geoff's case, his starts seem to not have received the same level of perfection. Even so, he had the ability to still pull out all the stops and win. The sign of a true master.

7th   E. Hiller (BMW)

8th   J. Hansgünther (BMW)

A dramatic final meeting

And so, a week after Monza came Geoff's final motorcycle race meeting, the non-Championship Swiss Grand Prix at Locarno. And what a dramatic event it turned out to be… three victories in three rides! The setting was a gloriously sunny day on Sunday 13 September 1959. As *The Motor Cycle* reported in its 17 September issue, it truly was 'Duke's Day'.

Considering that the opposition included the likes of Gary Hocking and Dickie Dale (to say nothing of his Italian Benelli teammate Silvio Grassetti), it was a wonderful performance – and achieved on a riders' circuit rather than one which simply gave the advantage to the fastest motorcycle.

1959 Junior TT, the first three finishers; left to right Alastair King (9) John Surtees (5) and John Hartle (1).

Geoff retired from racing after scoring three wins in three rides at the Swiss Grand Prix at Locarno on 13 September 1959. He rode 350 and 500 Norton, plus a works 250 Benelli. The smaller Norton is shown here.

Besides the Benelli, Geoff also rode his Lightweight 350 Norton and a standard Manx model in the 500cc race. Also, to ride in three different classes in a single day was unusual. As Geoff was later to recall:

I had only done it twice before, and it was strange that it should occur at my last event. Charlie Edwards accompanied me to look after the Nortons, and, always the perfectionist, his work was faultless.

And so the curtain came down on a glittering career. Even so, in the author's opinion, Geoff Duke's achievements would probably have been even greater had he not been a victim of FIM politics, which, together with his Imola crash at the beginning of 1957 and Gilera's subsequent retirement from the sport at the end of the same year, conspired to limit his successes from the end of 1955.

One of the top-line riders which Geoff defeated that day was none other than future world champion Gary Hocking.

Chapter 7

BMW, NSU and Benelli

Besides his Nortons (covered in the last chapter), during the final two seasons of his long career Geoff Duke also raced three other makes of machinery: BMW, NSU and Benelli.

BMW sign Duke

First rumours that the famous German BMW factory was about to sign Geoff came right at the end of 1957 – and at first were largely disbelieved, even by the press themselves. For example, *Motor Cycle News* Italian correspondent Carlo Perelli sent the newspaper a story saying that Geoff would be riding for the BMW company in 1958, but it was to be some weeks later, in the journal's 15 January 1958 issue, that *MCN* covered the news. This came a week after rivals *The Motor Cycle* had already told the British motorcycling public about not only his decision to carry on racing, but that he had signed for the Munich-based firm.

Walter Zeller

All this came as a surprise to most pundits, who had fully expected BMW to quit its official participation in solo racing events following their long-time number-one rider Walter Zeller's retirement at the end of 1957. Yes, BMW were masters of the sidecar class (going on to win no less than 19 World Championship titles in 21 years between 1954 and 1974 inclusive), but even Zeller had not been able to repeat the performance in the 500cc solo class. Added to this, by the beginning of 1958 BMW, like the other remaining German motorcycle brands, was struggling commercially.

So why, one asks, was BMW (and Duke, for that matter) to join forces? The answer to this question is quite simple: as of October 1957, both Gilera

First rumours that Geoff might sign for the famous BMW factory began to circulate towards the end of 1957, but it was not until early January 1958 that this became official and he had agreed to race for the German team.

and Moto Guzzi had announced that they would not be competing in 1958. So, apart from the by now ageing British singles, this left MV Agusta and BMW as effectively the only contenders for the 500cc World Championship crown. And one must also remember that Walter Zeller had finished runner-up to John Surtees (MV) in the 1956 title rankings.

These, therefore, are the reasons which brought BMW and Geoff together.

Debut day

Geoff's BMW debut came on Saturday 17 April 1958 at an international permit Silverstone meeting. Held in fine conditions, it brought huge crowds to see the former world champion making a bid to prove he was still a force to be reckoned with after almost two years away from regular weekly competitive riding.

His first ride that day was not on the BMW, but instead aboard a three-fifty Norton (see Chapter Six), with a superb victory against serious opposition. However, the race which everyone had really come to see was the big one: the blue riband 500cc clash. Geoff's BMW had, it was revealed, only been collected in Munich a few days before. Clad in the new-for-1958 dolphin fairing, it was reputed to be the ex-Zeller bike.

A poor start

During practice for the Silverstone meeting, Geoff had decided to replace the original shock absorbers for both the front and rear suspension systems and instead used British Girling dampers. It was then very much a wait-and-see approach by both Geoff and his fans to see how his BMW went.

Forty-three starters pushed their mounts into life as the flag dropped. The pack snarled and weaved away from the start line in a close-knit bunch, with Geoff and the German horizontally opposed dohc twin among the initial leaders. However, this early promise was not to be maintained, and at the completion of the first lap Geoff came past the packed grandstand opposite the pits in eighth position with, as *Motor Cycling* reported, 'the BMW's acceleration making no visible impression on the majority of the singles'. Next lap and Geoff was down to 11th place. Three laps later, he halted a silent BMW just past the start line. It was not a promising start. Geoff's own view of the race as expressed in 1988:

> *Silverstone was also my first outing on the BMW which, after the euphoria of my win on Dearden's Norton, served to dampen my ardour. After struggling through practice, trying to come to terms with its peculiarities in the handling department, I was totally uncompetitive in the race.*

BMW Renn Sport

The works BMW twin, which Geoff Duke rode in 1958, was closely related to the Renn Sport model of 1954 – all subsequent factory and privateer machines being a development of this basic design.

Originally, the Renn Sport flat-twin dohc (itself following the traditional BMW layout which had begun back in 1923 with the R32) engine was a long-stroke unit, with bore and stroke dimensions of 66 x 72mm (displacing 492cc). In this guise, maximum power was produced at 8,000rpm. Later, however, with the need for more power, the measurements were altered to 68 x 68mm (493.9cc), resulting in the engine revolutions going up to 9,500rpm.

The centre of any engine is its crankshaft, and, in the case of the BMW racing unit, this featured 180-degree throws and was of built-up construction. The mainshafts were hollow and integral with their flywheels, which embodied balance weights.

Like the mainshafts, the hollow crankpins were of 35mm diameter, one of each being pressed into the crank web and locked into position by a solid, forced-in expander plug.

After the big-end bearings and connecting rods (of an unusual flat-section) had been assembled on the pins, the cheeks were pressed on and further expander plugs driven in.

There were three crankshaft bearings. The one at the rear was of the self-aligning type, embodying a special type of roller, while the one at the front was a conventional ball-race. Another conventional ball-race bearing was housed in the front engine cover as an outboard support for the timing pinion.

View of the Renn Sport engine assembly with its horizontally-opposed cylinders and massive Italian Dell'Orto carburettors.

The crankcase was a one-piece electron casting and featured a pair of 35mm main bearings, which were fitted into separate housings. These housings were manufactured from different materials – cast iron at the front, steel at the rear.

Integral with the forward main bearing housing was the rear wall of the oil pump – the aluminium-alloy pump body carrying the gears being fitted into a recess in the housing to which it was bolted.

The pump itself was of the duplex-gear type, one part feeding the main bearings and big-end, while the other supplied the cam gear. Wet-sump lubrication was employed, a 2.8 litre sump (again in electron) was bolted to the base of the crankcase.

The gear case at the front of the engine contained three pairs of spur gears. A steel gear on the crankshaft drove an aluminium half-speed gear immediately above it – the gears being lubricated by a jet from the front main bearing housing. Also on the crankshaft was a steel gear, which meshed with the alloy oil pump driving gear. BMW found it necessary to embody a cushdrive in the steel gear to prevent the teeth of the alloy gear from breaking under the load produced by full throttle acceleration or deceleration of the crankshaft.

A steel gear on the half-speed shaft meshed with the alloy magneto gear, which was equipped with slotted holes for timing adjustment. In front of the half-speed gear, and driven from it by a pair of pegs, was a ported sleeve which ran in the electron front cover and served as an engine breather.

At the rear of the half-speed shaft, which was carried in a pair of ball bearings in a duralumin housing, was a bevel gear. This meshed with two more bevel gears embodying short, hollow shafts, which transmitted the drive, via solid shafts, to the camshafts.

The BMW engineering team had employed a most unconventional arrangement for the double-overhead-camshaft system. In each head, the two camshafts lay close together within a split housing, and each operated its respective valve through a short, straight rocker. The design was a compromise between the usual sohc and the conventional 'double knocker' layouts because, although the reciprocating weight with the rockers was higher than with directly-operated valves, there was less power loss since two spur gears replaced the normal five. No doubt, this helped the Renn Sport engine achieve its higher engine revolution figures.

Camshafts and rockers ran on needle rollers, while the rocker spindles were carried in the cam housings and had eccentric ends for valve clearance adjustment.

Each cylinder head contained a part-spherical combustion chamber, which provided quite a wide valve included angle of 82 degrees. Inlet and exhaust valve seats were of different materials: manganese steel for the inlet, bronze for the exhaust. Both valve guides were also of bronze.

Valve diameters were 40mm inlet, 36mm exhaust, the latter being sodium-cooled: duplex coil valve springs and a stepped form of split collet were employed to keep the cylinder head width to a minimum.

The piston design was interesting: almost fully-skirted, these were forged and featured an oil scrapper ring below the bosses of the gudgeon pins. Three compression rings were also fitted in the conventional position, the lowest of these having a tapered face and drainage holes to assist oil control.

The piston crown was of almost pent-roof shape and fitted closely into the head space at each side to promote squish. To accommodate the contour of the valve head, the valve cutaways under the inlet and exhaust valves were convex and concave respectively.

The cylinder barrels normally featured shrunk-in cast-iron liners, but BMW also tried chromium-plated bores, the finish being applied directly to the aluminium, with complete success.

A taper at the rear of the crankshaft accommodated a flywheel car-type clutch, while the gearbox was of conventional, all-indirect design – normally with five ratios, although four were used for some circuits. Final drive was by shaft.

The cycle parts

The complete engine and transmission was supported at three points in the cradle-type frame. A new, specially-designed dolphin fairing was evolved for Geoff Duke to use. Previously the works models were either naked or with the fully streamlined 'dustbin' fairing, the latter having been banned by the FIM from the end of 1957. Other details included Earles-type pivoted front forks, swinging arm rear suspension and massive drum brakes (a 2LS device at the front).

With their only works rivals for the 1958 season being the four-cylinder MVs, BMW considered that its twin could be competitive. However, as Geoff Duke was to prove, the German design was little, if any, better than the best of the privateer British Norton singles. Even so, BMW did add a touch of flavour to racing, which had seen the withdrawal of both Moto Guzzi and Gilera from the Senior (500cc) class a few months before.

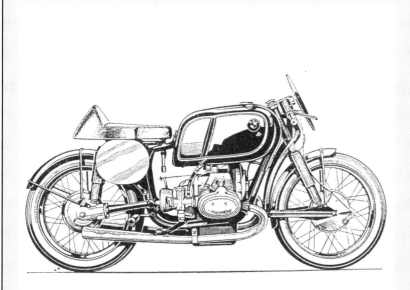

A drawing of the BMW works Renn Sport of the type raced by Geoff Duke during 1958. Features included swinging fork front and rear suspension, shaft final drive and duplex streel-tube frame.

A much better result came just over a week later at the German Hockenheim circuit, where Geoff won the 500cc race by a narrow margin, from Ernst Hiller (seen here at Thruxton the same year) on another BMW twin.

Salzburg and Hockenheim

Next came visits to Salzburg, for the non-Championship Austrian Grand Prix, followed by Hockenheim in Germany.

In Austria Geoff was eighth, but a few days later in Germany he seemed to have resolved the problems, when, in one of the closest and most hotly contested races of his career, he scored an impressive victory over the ultra-fast Hockenheim circuit, the Englishman leading Ernst Hiller on a production (but equally quick) Renn Sport BMW production racer over the finish line by little more than four lengths.

500cc Hockenheim – 20 laps – 95.94 miles

1st	G.E. Duke (BMW)
2nd	E. Hiller (BMW)
3rd	H. Hinton Jnr. (Norton)
4th	A. Huber (BMW)
5th	G. Klinger (BMW)
6th	K.R. Campbell (Norton)

A schoolboy dream

The first race counting towards the 1958 500cc World Championship was the Isle of Man TT. Commenting upon his choice of the BMW, Geoff offered some personal views in an article published in the *Motor Cycling* of 22 May that year:

This wonderful action shot of Geoff
and the BMW was taken by Wolfgang
Gruber at the Austrian Grand Prix on
1 May 1958. The former world
champion finished eighth on the day.

After all the hype surrounding Geoff's Senior TT entry on the BMW, the actual performance was very much an anti-climax. Although the official reason for his retirement in the race was braking problems, as he was to admit later, Geoff never really adapted his riding style to the German bike.

When I was a child my family frequently took me to the Isle of Man, but I was 16 before I saw my first TT race there. This was in 1939, when Georg Meier, on a German BMW, won the Senior at 89.38mph and achieved the fastest lap of 90.75mph. I am accepting this as a happy omen – because, unfortunately missing the TT for two seasons, I am, in June this year, returning to what I regard as the world's greatest event on a BMW. If 19 years ago, as I stood amazed and thrilled by Meier's performance, someone had suggested that one day I also would be riding a works entered BMW and in the fabulous TT too… well, I would have just told them that they were quite mad!'

Added expectations

Perhaps it was the added expectations heightened by memories of Meier's 1939 victory, but Geoff, except for that solitary victory in Germany, never really adapted to the BMW. In his autobiography *In Pursuit of Perfection*, published in 1988, he had this to say of his 1958 TT ride on the German bike:

Switching to the BMW for the Senior race [he rode a Norton in the Junior], *we settled down to serious work with the race machine after a preliminary canter with the practice BMW. The race bike was even smoother than the original and was certainly quicker. The extra speed, however, heightened my navigation problems – it was surprising what devastating effect another 5mph could have. On two occasions I all but lost the plot on the way down to Brandish corner from Creg-ny-Baa, and at one place, near the top of Creg Willey's Hill, a wobble developed on almost every lap I did! The limited modifications which could be carried out in the Island made little difference. And yet there was no getting away from the fact that, in previous years, Walter Zeller had put up a superlative performance on virtually the same machine, although the full streamlining he used in 1957 may perhaps have created a downforce which helped to keep the front wheel on the ground. The main problem, however, obviously lay in my inability to adapt myself to the unusual handling characteristics of a machine which had an in-line crankshaft and shaft drive. My admiration for Walter, always high, grew day by day.*

The race

If Geoff hoped for better things in the race, he was to be disappointed, as he described later, 'At the fall of the flag, I set off with every intention of relaxing and giving the machine its head, but by the time Ballacraine was reached I had started to wrestle with it. This was fatal. My shoulders soon began to ache as I rode with muscles tensed.' And after what *The Motor Cycle* described as 'two slowish laps', the former world champion retired with braking problems.

Following his TT experiences, Geoff compiled what he described as a 'long letter' to BMW, 'suggesting many modifications which would, I felt, enable me to do reasonable justice to a basically fine machine'. But, because of the company's continuing financial problems and outstanding engineering work with production vehicles, many of these suggested changes were not possible. Geoff's next outing at the Assen Dutch TT saw a repeat of the brake gremlins, and so another retirement was eventually posted.

However, he had the riding position altered to suit himself (Walter Zeller was much taller than Geoff) and found that the general handling was considerably improved. The footrests had been moved forward about three inches, while a wider fuel tank, that allowed the rider to grip it with his knees, and wider handlebars had been fitted.

For the Belgian round the double-sided front brake had been converted to twin leading shoe operation (and was also now heavier), so at least the braking deficiencies had been cured. And at Spa Geoff enjoyed a duel between himself, Dickie Dale (on a production RS BMW) and Bob Anderson (Norton) – which Geoff won, to come home fourth, which, except for Hockenheim, was to be Geoff's best BMW performance.

500cc Belgian GP – 15 laps – 131.34 miles

1st	J. Surtees (MV Agusta)
2nd	K.R. Campbell (Norton)
3rd	J. Hartle (MV Agusta)
4th	G.E. Duke (BMW)
5th	R.H. Dale (BMW)
6th	R. Anderson (Norton)

Sadly, the following week the Australian Keith Campbell (married to

Geraldine, the younger sister of Geoff's wife Pat) was killed while competing in the 500cc race at Cadours, in France. As the couple had only married late the previous year this was particularly sad for all the family.

The German Grand Prix

The German Grand Prix, held at the Nürburgring on Sunday 20 July 1958, was not to prove a very successful event for Geoff, as first he was forced to retire from the 350cc race after his rear wheel was smothered in oil – due to the oil tank breather on his Norton coming loose. Then, in the 500cc race, after handing over his works BMW engine to sidecar-star Walter Scheider and having a standard Renn Sport engine fitted into his frame, the carburation proved too rich, and Geoff retired early on. He later commented 'not that I was too sorry, for later in the race the rain came down in torrents'.

Just before the German GP, news had been received that BMW would not be supporting any more solo races that year, so Geoff asked for and received permission to use Norton bikes in the subsequent races that year. The story behind this and the races themselves are covered in the previous chapter.

The NSU saga

Geoff had first come into contact with NSU when the German factory team had competed in the Isle of Man TT, during June 1953. At that time the Englishman was contracted to the Italian Gilera firm but his teammate, Irishman Reg Armstrong, was also an NSU rider (from the Dutch TT that year).

During the TT period Geoff was able to test one of the German dohc twins, which, at the time, were generally seen as the most advanced machinery in its class.

But it was not for another six years, in the spring of 1959, that the combination of Geoff Duke/NSU was to be seen in a race programme, when Geoff and his old Gilera teammate Reg Armstrong (now retired) joined forces.

Reg had managed to obtain the Rennmax as a result of his business connections with the German factory – he being at the time NSU's Southern Ireland distributor, assembling the company's two and four-wheelers in Dublin.

Originally, so the story goes, both Geoff and Reg had expected one of the 1954 models, but what they got was actually a less powerful 1953 bike, which also had the disadvantage of only a four instead of six-speed gearbox.

Geoff first came into contact with NSU when the German works team competed in the 1953 TT. And he was able to ride (but not race) one of the firms Rennmax twins, which at the time was seen as the most advanced bike in its class.

NSU Rennmax

Designed by Dipl. Ing. Walter Froede, the R22 Rennmax double-overhead camshaft two-fifty parallel twin was a purpose-built Grand Prix machine, which debuted in 1952.

Designed by Dipl. Ing. Walter Froede, the R22 Rennmax dohc two-fifty twin was a purpose-built Grand Prix machine. Debuting in the spring of 1952, the Rennmax shared the square 54 x 54mm bore and stroke dimensions of both the 125 Rennfox single and the R54 500 four. Initially, the power output was 25bhp at 9000rpm, improving to 29bhp at 9800rpm by the season's end.

The engine was of full unit construction, with primary drive by enclosed chain, to a four-speed close ratio gearbox. The crankshaft was a pressed-up assembly supported by a trio of roller bearings. Early failure of light alloy big-end cages at high-engine revolutions was overcome by the use of an improved alloy and by anodising the friction surfaces. There was an Alfin cylinder with an aluminium alloy head. The twin overhead camshafts were driven on the offside (right) of the engine by separate 'Y' bevel shafts, in the same manner as the earlier, supercharged 350/500 twins. A feature of the early Rennmax was the use of torsion bar valve springs, but after initial glitches these were exchanged for conventional hairpin components, which remained thereafter on all Rennmax engines.

Twin single float chamber 24mm (later 25mm) Amal RN carburettors were fitted, inclined at 30 degrees downdraught. Ignition was by a pair of 6-volt, 7-amp hour batteries, wired in parallel, with twin ignition coils. A distributor, housing the points and condenser, was mounted in the timing chest and driven by a skew gear from the lower bevel for the inlet camshaft drive coupling.

For the 1953 season the Rennmax was considerably modified, certainly with regard the cycle parts – there being a brand new pressed steel chassis, leading link front forks and wrap-around miniature fairing. As for the engine, the compression ratio had been increased to 9.8:1, bigger 25.4mm RN9 carburettors and a hotter camshaft profile –

The Rennmax engine shared its 54 x 54mm bore and stroke dimensions with both the 125 single (Rennfox) and the 500 four, giving a capacity of 247.34cc.

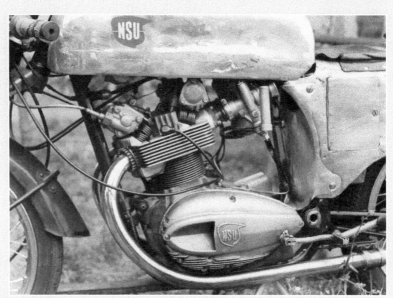

these changes resulting in the power being increased to 32bhp at 10,000rpm.

Even though Werner Haas had won the 1953 250cc World Championship title, the Rennmax was extensively redesigned for the 1954 season. In spite of appearing to be larger, the new machine was actually 8.5lb lighter than the 1953 version, weighing in at 258lb (dry). The most noticeable difference between the latest bike and its predecessor was that the former's separate shafts and bevel overhead cam drives, which were on the right of the engine, had been replaced by a single shaft on the other side at the rear of the cylinder. In turn, this drove the inlet camshaft and was driven from the immediate gear of the primary train. Spur gears transmitted the drive from the inlet camshaft to the exhaust camshaft. In addition the rev counter drive was taken from the exhaust cam.

A revised bore and stroke was another major change, these now being oversquare at 55.9 x 50.8mm. The engine was also narrower due to the elimination of the bevel drives from the right-hand side of the crankcase. The new camshaft drive allowed a shallower casting. Battery/coil ignition was retained. There was now also a six-speed gearbox, while the power figure was now given at 39bhp at 11,500rpm. As for maximum speed, this, said NSU, approached 200kmh (125mph).

After emerging victorious from the 1954 season, with both the 125 and 250cc titles, NSU announced their intention of not contesting the 1955 series of road-racing World Championship meetings with a works team. But, in part compensation for the void left by this decision, the German company announced that distribution of the 247cc single-cylinder Sportmax production racing motorcycle was to begin in early 1955. And, as history records, with one of these Herman Peter Müller gave NSU their third consecutive 250cc world crown that year.

As for the Rennmax (and its 125cc single-cylinder brother, the Rennfox), these acted as an inspiration to Soichiro Honda – and look what happened there!

Exploded view of the Rennmax power unit, showing bevel gear and shafts employed to drive the camshafts, unit construction, twin carbs and hairpin valve springs.

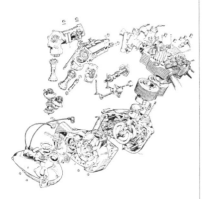

An exciting prospect

In Geoff's own words 'an exciting prospect loomed for 1959 when Reg Armstrong announced that he had obtained the loan of a 250 NSU Rennmax, asking me if I would be interested in riding it – sure thing! But this turned out to be a bit of a damp squib.' He continued 'this was a bitter disappointment to us both, but, nevertheless, the services of Ken Sprayson of Reynolds were called upon to design a lighter, more up-to-date frame and forks.'

Besides the new Reynolds frame, swinging arm and front fork assembly (the latter of the type already in use on Geoff's 350 Norton), the NSU featured a Manx Norton front brake and a Lyta aluminium fuel tank.

The debut for the Reynolds-framed Rennmax twin came at the Austrian Grand Prix at Salzburg, which, although then a non-Championship event, was still a relatively important fixture on the racing calendar, where many teams were able to test their machines in GP-like conditions. And in the 250cc race, there were factory entries from MZ, Benelli and Jawa among others. In what Geoff was later to describe as 'foul conditions', water in the ignition on the first lap of the race brought the debut to an early end.

Another Wolfgang Gruber shot of Geoff, this time about to make his debut on the Reynolds-framed NSU Rennmax twin at Salzburg on the 1 May 1959.

The TT

And, although entered for the North West 200 later that month, it was not until the TT that the machine was ready again, with race number five for the bike. But, as Geoff described himself, 'entry in the Lightweight TT on the Clypse circuit terminated when the engine seized at Creg-ny-Baa on my first practice lap'.

When stripped, it was discovered that the gudgeon pin of the offside (right) cylinder had broken. Fragments of metal had then found their way into the oil pump, and, starved of lubrication, the gears shattered. With spares of this nature unavailable, at least on the island, Geoff had no alternative but to advise his sponsor that he would be a non-starter for the race.

Unfortunely Geoff's NSU debut was marred by wet weather and a mechanical breakdown which forced his retirement. This potentially exciting project was a joint venture between Geoff (rider) and former teammate Reg Armstrong (entrant).

After the TT, Geoff was to accept an offer of a works ride on a Benelli dohc single and so the NSU went back to Reg Armstrong. It was subsequently sold to Glen Henderson from Ayr in Scotland. After this, in 1963 it passed on again, this time to North Shields rider Eddie Johnson. Finally, in early 1969, it was sold to Gloucestershire rider/dealer John Kidson, who was to retain the machine for the next quarter of a century – using it for parades and the like in the classic era – from the late 1970s.

Switching to Benelli

And so Geoff made a switch from German NSU to Italian Benelli in the 250cc class for the remainder of 1959. The technical details and its development history are covered separately in a boxed section within this chapter, but suffice to say, as with the NSU Rennmax, the twin cam Benelli single was in reality an obsolete design. In fact, it could trace its origins much further back than the German design – to pre-war days!

Packing away the results

Beginning with the German Grand Prix in mid-June 1959, Geoff gained some useful results with the Benelli.

At the 4.77-mile high-speed Hockenheim circuit he began his use of the Italian single by finishing sixth.

German GP – 20 laps – 95.4 miles
1st   C. Ubbiali (MV Agusta)

Benelli 250 Double Overhead-Cam Single

Pre-war Benelli had often won at Grand Prix level, with a range of overhead camshaft single-cylinder machines. Then riders Ciai, Francisci Martelli, and most of all Dario Ambrosini, had donned their leathers to give Benelli its first post-war success in the late 1940s.

Then, in 1948, Ambrosini had rejoined Benelli – following a short spell at rivals Moto Guzzi – and immediately brought international acclaim. Victories in the Swiss and Italian GPs, and the Lightweight TT in the Isle of Man, culminated in this talented rider winning the 250cc World Championship in 1950.

In 1951, after winning the Swiss Grand Prix at a soaking Bremgarten circuit in Berne, and finishing runner-up – only seconds behind winner Tommy Wood (Moto Guzzi) – in the TT, Ambrosini was killed when his machine skidded on molten tar while practising for the French round at Albi. This tragedy hit the Benelli family hard and resulted in their virtual withdrawal from racing.

Not until 1959 did they fully feel inclined to pick up the threads again. That year Benelli came back with a strong effort, consisting of a considerably revised double-knocker two-fifty single and a trio of top riders – Geoff Duke, plus Dickie Dale and the young Italian star, Silvio Grassetti.

The pre-war and early post-war Benellis had long-stroke 65 x 75mm engines, giving a displacement of 248.8cc and a power output of 25bhp at 8,000rpm when Irishman Ted Mellors won the 1939 Lightweight Isle of Man TT; power was increased to 27bhp at 8,700rpm by 1948. Then, in 1951 the bore and stroke dimensions were changed to square 68 x 68mm measurements, long favoured by rivals Guzzi, and the power boosted to 29bhp at 9,400rpm.

For its comeback in 1959, Benelli's then chief engineer Ing. Aulo Savelli carried out a number of technical changes to the dohc single cylinder engine, including new short-stroke 70 x 64.8mm dimensions, giving a displacement of 248.1cc.

For its comeback in 1959, chief engineer Ing. Aulo Savelli carried out a number of changes, including a short-stroke 248.1cc (70 x 64.8mm) engine with a totally new appearance to provide neater, more modern lines. These modifications combined to give more power and yet higher engine revolutions (33bhp at 11,500rpm), while a six-speed gearbox was added. The running gear was also updated with new telescopic front forks, a duplex tubular chassis, swinging-arm twin-shock rear suspension, full-width alloy brake hubs and an aluminium dolphin fairing. Tests were also carried out on a desmodromic version, too.

But, in truth, it was still an outdated design, and one of the very few successes for the revised single came in Geoff Duke's hands in the non-Championship Swiss Grand Prix at Locarno, where, on a tight and twisting circuit, the old master scored one of the last victories of a glittering career.

It was soon realised that the single, even in revamped form, could scarcely be expected to hold its own against the latest crop of multi-cylinder models, which, by 1960, included MV Agusta and Ducati twins, to say nothing of the new four-cylinder Japanese Honda. So, in response, Benelli set to and built its own four-cylinder machine, but this bike, which made its race debut in the hands of Grassetti in 1962, is outside the scope of this book.

Geoff's teammate Silvio Grassetti with one of the revamped Benelli singles.

2nd	E. Mendogni (Moto Morini)
3rd	H. Fugner (MZ)
4th	L. Liberati (Moto Morini)
5th	S.M.B. Hailwood (FB Mondial)
6th	G.E. Duke (Benelli)

Next came the Swedish Grand Prix (now having Championship status) at Kristianstad instead of the popular Hedemora circuit, the latter having not been allowed to take place due to the local police chief refusing to sanction the event.

And it was at Kristianstad that Geoff had one of his very best rides since

After the NSU came the offer of a works Benelli 250 dohc single. Geoff is seen here on the machine at the German GP at Hockenheim on the 16 June 1959; he finished sixth.

Like Geoff Duke, Dickie Dale rode a BMW twin in 1958 (and again in 1959) But unlike Geoff's model, Dickie's was a production Renn Sport. He is seen here (11), competing in Germany, during 1959.

Dickie Dale

A works rider during the glory days of the 1950s for MV Agusta, Gilera, Moto Guzzi, BMW, Benelli and Norton, Dickie Dale's career period was very similar to Geoff Duke's. And the two men rode against each other in countless races both in Great Britain and in Continental Europe.

Born at Wyberton near Boston, Lincolnshire, on 25 April 1927, Dickie was drafted as a flight mechanic into the Royal Air Force during 1945 and served three years. He worked on a wide variety of aircraft from Tiger Moths to Meteors. While stationed at RAF Cranwell, Dickie bought his first motorcycle, a 1939 AJS Silver Streak, for transport between the base and home. But like many before and since, he soon found bikes more than simply a means of getting from A to B and started competing in grass-track events organised by the local Boston Motorcycle Club.

His first road race took place at Cadwell Park in 1946, on a Norton single, and his performances that year caught four-times Manx Grand Prix winner. Then came more sponsorship from Munks's long-time friend and racing colleague Sam Coupland, whose house was in the middle of the seven-mile Frithville straight, and this section of the road was utilised for unofficial testing with the local policemen turning a blind eye!

Dickie won the 1948 Lightweight Manx Grand Prix (on a Munks-entered Moto Guzzi) at record speed. He also rode a Munks-tuned five-hundred Norton and a Coupland-owned KTT Velocette that year.

Dickie Dale's TT debut came in 1949, when he rode a Moto Guzzi in the Lightweight and a Velocette in the Junior. And even though he retired from both, he caught the eye of Norton team manager Joe Craig. This resulted in an offer of a team ride for 1950. Dickie's best results that year were a pair of fourth places – on the three-fifty at Monza and on the five-hundred in Ulster.

The following year he spent most of his time in a sanatorium in Dorchester, after contracting tuberculosis.

Many riders would probably have quit the sport, but not Dickie Dale, who, by 1953, was back in the saddle, first with Gilera, followed by an MV contract for 1954. Then, in 1955 he joined Moto Guzzi, with whom he stayed until the Mandello del Lario concern quit racing at the end of 1957. Probably his most well-known Guzzi performance was bringing home a very sick V8 to fourth position in that years eight-lap Senior TT.

In 1958 Dickie rode a BMW Renn Sport (together with Geoff Duke) and in 1959 (again with Geoff) a Benelli 250 dohc single. For 1960 he went back to being a privateer with a pair of production Manx Nortons, having ridden the same bikes for Bob Foster of Parkstone, on the occasions when the BMW and Benellis were not available.

Then, in 1961, while racing at the Nürburgring in Germany on 30 April, in horribly wet conditions, he crashed fatally (caused by, it is believed, oil on the track). After a cremation ceremony in Bournemouth, his ashes were put under Sam Coupland's lawn.

Again, like Geoff, Dickie Dale had some rides on the revised Benelli 250 single during the 1959 season.

Geoff's Italian teammate
with the Benelli was the
young Silvio Grassetti.

his glory days with Norton and Gilera, by finishing a magnificent third behind the winner Gary Hocking, riding a works MZ twin for the first time, and reigning world champion Carlo Ubbiali (MV Agusta).

Geoff brought his Benelli home in front of several works machines and a host of top riders.

250cc Swedish GP – 20 laps – 81.19 miles

1st   G. Hocking (MZ)
2nd   C. Ubbiali (MV Agusta)
3rd   G.E. Duke (Benelli)
4th   E. Degner (MZ)
5th   S.M.B. Hailwood (FB Mondial)
6th   R.H. Dale (Benelli)

Mixing it in Italy

The final Grand Prix counting towards World Championship points was held over the 3.57-mile Monza circuit on the outskirts of Milan. And what a race it turned out to be, with the Italian factories bringing a variety of foreign stars to add to the local aces – plus, of course, interest from foreign factories such as MZ. Just look at the results list to see what I mean!

At the end Geoff came home 10th, but, at a speed venue such as Monza, this was not perhaps a surprise. He was also the first Benelli finisher.

Italian GP – 22 laps – 78.6 miles

1st	C. Ubbiali (MV Agusta)
2nd	E. Degner (MZ)
3rd	E. Mendogni (Moto Morini)
4th	D.W. Minter (Moto Morini)
5th	L. Taveri (MZ)
6th	T.H. Robb (MZ)
7th	G. Milani (Paton)
8th	A.F. Wheeler (Moto Guzzi)
9th	S.M.B. Hailwood (MZ)
10th	G.E. Duke (Benelli)

A final victory

Then came Geoff's final race on the Benelli at Locarno, Switzerland, on Sunday 13 September 1959. And what a day this turned out to be. Not only did he win both the 350 and 500cc races on Norton machines (covered in the previous chapter), but he made it a treble with victory on the Benelli.

Actually, he almost did not ride the Italian bike, simply because he considered that attempting three long races in a single day (he was then 36 years of age) would be too much. But the Benelli people pleaded with Geoff to the point where he relented. And in retrospect he made the right decision, as what other rider in history has retired with three wins in three rides?

Although not a Championship event, the Swiss Grand Prix at Locarno was still a prestigious meeting with several top-star riders entered. So, all-in-all, it was a day which Geoff Duke was to remember with considerable pride and satisfaction.

An offer from Honda

An interesting and little-known postscript is that, the following year, Geoff received an 'open cheque' offer to race for the Japanese Honda company. But, as he was later to recall, 'I somewhat reluctantly declined – "comebacks" rarely work.'

But this does prove that the Geoff Duke name and reputation were still held in the highest regard, Honda, after all, by then having become the world's number-one motorcycle manufacturer.

Geoff bowed out of a glittering racing career with a trio of victories at the non-Championship Swiss Grand Prix at Locarno. He is seen here after winning the 250cc event on the Benelli single.

Chapter 8

Scuderia Duke

As Geoff was to reveal in his autobiography, the agreement between FB Mondial, Moto Guzzi and Gilera to quit Grand Prix racing at the end of the 1957 season came as 'a complete surprise to me, for Gilera had suggested that I might retire from riding at the end of that season with a view to taking over from Roberto Persi as the racing manager for 1958'.

He also revealed that 'we had also discussed a major redesign of the four-cylinder 500cc engine, as it was then felt that Remor's ten-year-old design had reached the limit of development'. This, Geoff explained, would have included revised bore and stroke dimensions, four valves per cylinder – and possibly even fuel injection. The former world champion was 'also keen for a monocoque chassis with trailing-link front forks', and that disc brakes were a 'must'.

However, with Gilera's announcement, this ambitious plan was shelved.

But, as Geoff also explained, 'It was during a visit to the factory at Arcore in 1959, and later with Reg Armstrong, that I tried to persuade

The Gilera 1957-type four which the factory sent to England for Geoff Duke to parade at the Bob McIntyre Memorial meeting in October 1962, a few weeks after the former Gilera star's fatal accident at the Cheshire circuit. In the background is the works BMW, which was ridden by Georg Meier at the same event.

Commendatore Giuseppe Gilera to provide machines for Bob McIntyre to race.' But, despite his admiration for the Scott, Senor Gilera refused. But Geoff persisted, and, although he did eventually agree, the plan was 'scuttled' when Bob signed with Honda – and Gilera would not consider any other rider at that time.

And strangely, Bob McIntyre did play a part in bringing Gilera back to racing in 1963. Following his tragic death, resulting from a crash at Oulton Park in August 1962, as Geoff says, 'a tribute to this fine and most determined rider was held at the circuit [in October that year], where I was asked to demonstrate the 1957 four-cylinder Gilera.' And the Italian factory responded by providing 'a most beautifully-prepared fully-streamlined 500 – identical to McIntyre's 1957 TT mount – and they sent it along with "my" race mechanic, Giovanni Fumagalli, for the Bob McIntyre Memorial occasion.'

The Gilera race shop gathering dust in the autumn of 1962. After five long years away from the circuits the disorganised remains of what were once the best team in the world is evident.

As someone who was there that day, among the record 60,000 plus crowd at Oulton Park, I can well remember the impact Geoff and the Gilera (and that of the German Georg Meier – the 1939 Senior TT winner – with a work BMW) made. As for Geoff:

I thoroughly enjoyed my outing, which was further enhanced the next day when Avons booked the track for a tyre-testing session. With the machine fitted with the then-revolutionary 'cling' tyre compounds, I could hardly believe the grip I was getting, and, after a few laps, I recorded my fastest-ever lap time around Oulton Park.

Geoff (left), Derek Minter (centre) and journalist Charlie Rous, together at Monza during testing, which preceded Gilera's comeback under the Scuderia Duke banner in 1963.

This experience fired Geoff with enthusiasm to the point where he arranged a visit to Arcore to see Giuseppe Gilera himself on the subject of a return. The outcome was that if Geoff could find backers for the project and the right riders (Derek Minter and John Hartle were Geoff's choices), and that subsequent tests at Monza proved the machines were still competitive, Gilera would sanction the venture.

And so, as Geoff was to recall, 'It was a historic moment when the old machines, with new [dolphin] fairings to comply with 1963 regulations, the latest Girling rear-suspension struts and Avon racing tyres, were wheeled out for that high-speed testing session at Monza.'

As for the riders, he described Derek Minter as 'an

Derek Minter, pictured after winning the 1962 250 (Lightweight) TT on a semi-works Honda four, beating all the official team members at the same time.

Derek Minter

Of the three riders who rode for Geoff Duke's Scuderia Gilera during 1963, it was 'King of Brands' Derek Minter who most observers, including the author, expected to offer the biggest challenge to reigning 500cc world champion Mike Hailwood.

And, at Silverstone in April of that year I was there to see Derek give the Italian marque its first victory, after six years away from the sport. But, unfortunately, as explained elsewhere in this chapter, Geoff Duke's attempt to attract sponsorship for the fledgling team was less successful than hoped for, resulting in the riders Derek plus John Hartle (and later Phil Read) being allowed to compete on their own machinery when not riding for Scuderia Gilera. And this resulted in Derek riding his Petty-tuned Norton at Brands Hatch the following month, with fateful, far-reaching consequences.

Then the undisputed star at his local circuit, Derek was also at the height of his form – the only man who was considered to be likely to match 'Mike the Bike'. But before the World Championship class between Minter (Gilera) and Hailwood (MV Agusta) even began came that race at Brands in May 1963. A youngster named Dave Downer was riding Paul Dunstall's six-fifty Domiracer twin, the combination being evenly matched against Derek's five-hundred Norton single. For almost the entire race distance a pattern unfolded where the lead swapped many times – Downer overtaking on acceleration, Minter on the corners. And, as journalist Charlie Rous was later to describe, 'it was the fiercest two-bike battle I ever saw and it ended in a last lap collision in which Downer died'. Derek Minter himself was seriously injured, and although he was recovered enough to ride later that year his chances and those of the Duke Scuderia team were ended on that fateful day.

Right up to his eventual retirement at the end of 1967 he was still racing on the British short circuit, but after the 1963 Brands Hatch crash somehow the ultimate sharpness was not quite there as it had been before.

Derek had begun his motorcycling career back in 1954 at the age of 22 on a BSA Gold Star. And it was on the same machine that he made his racing debut the following year, in what he was subsequently to admit as 'a complete novice'.

Even so, he soon became a regular at his local Brands Hatch circuit, and in 1956 his then employers, Wincheap Garage, bought him a 350cc Norton, and the following year one of the larger Norton singles.

The real breakthrough came when Steve Lancefield took over the preparation of Minter's Manx engines. The Lancefield–Minter alliance brought a period of real achievement: victory over world champion John Surtees (MV) at the final Brands Hatch meeting of 1958, while in 1960 Derek became the first man to lap the TT Mountain Circuit at 100mph on a single-cylinder machine. This period also brought the first works rides, including Bianchi, MZ and Morini.

After 1961, Derek began his association with tuner Ray Petty, and it was a much closer personal relationship than had been the case with Lancefield. On his Petty-tuned Manx models, the 'Mint' ruled much of the short-circuit scene, collecting victories all over the British Isles.

In 1962 he rode for the then British Honda importers Hondis to win the Lightweight (250cc) TT on a two-fifty four – against factory team orders – which ensured he did not ride for the Japanese giant again.

Then, at the beginning of 1963 he signed for the Geoff Duke Scuderia Gilera team, the details of this being recorded elsewhere in this chapter.

Derek at Silverstone on his three-fifty Lancefield-tuned Manx Norton. There is no doubt that at the time, when the Scuderia Duke Gilera team came into being, he was the only rider capable of challenging world champion Mike Hailwood for the 500cc title. Unfortunately, these hopes did not materialise due to a crash on one of his own machines, prior to the start of the GP season.

Gilera mechanics readying the fours for testing at Monza in early 1963.

exceptionally talented rider regarded more as a short circuit ace, yet overlooked as a TT winner [the 1962 250cc on a Honda] and the first rider to lap the TT at 100mph on a single-cylinder machine.' And also 'the very experienced John Hartle, for whom I had the greatest respect'.

In the Monza test session both riders were soon circulating at 115mph, and Minter eventually put in a lap of 118mph, just outside the John Surtees MV record. And, as these tests took place at the tail end of winter, they were good enough to convince the Gilera camp.

Lack of sponsors means future problems

But, unfortunately, as Geoff was later to reveal, most of the 'anticipated sponsors I approached for financial help did not share my enthusiasm and confidence'. This meant that Geoff soon 'realised I would have to bear the brunt of the cost myself. I was therefore unable to pay for anything beyond the cost of keeping the machines in race trim.'

It also meant that 'development work was out of the question'. Worse still to the ultimate fortunes of the team, but not fully appreciated at the time, was that this lack of money (Gilera were, effectively, only loaning machines and mechanics) meant that the riders' contracts allowed both Minter and Hartle 'to ride other machines when the Gileras were not available'.

Silverstone

In early March 1963 came the news that every enthusiast had waited for – the famous Gilera fours were to come out of retirement to do battle once again after a five-year absence. The private Scuderia Duke team of Minter and Hartle made their public debut at Silverstone, on Saturday 6 April.

I was there that day and can still vividly recall the expectant buzz all around the Northamptonshire circuit, which everyone in the vast crowd experienced in the build up to the 500cc race. But, although Minter put in a race-winning performance, it was the sight of Norton-mounted Phil Read splitting the Italian multis on what was after all a speed circuit (although Hartle finally got the better of the Norton privateer), which put the question on everyone's lips – would Gilera really do as well as the pundits had been forecasting when they came up against the World Championship pairing of Mike Hailwood and MV Agusta?

I for one rated Derek Minter highly, having seen him give Mike Hailwood serious opposition when both had been Norton-mounted. But I was less than convinced of Hartle's chances.

A serious setback

But then, after Minter scoring victories at Brands Hatch on Good Friday and Imola shortly thereafter (where he beat Mike Hailwood and the MV), came a fateful day on Sunday 12 May 1963 at Brands Hatch, which was to see Minter, mounted on his Ray Petty-tuned privately-owned 499cc Norton,

The Gilera four in its 1963 guise, with dolphin fairing, but little else changed from 1957.

Mike Hailwood in his early Ecurie Sportive days, at the beginning of his career, during the late 1950s; just as Geoff Duke's racing activities were coming to a close.

Mike Hailwood

Many consider S.M.B. (Stanley Michael Bailey) Hailwood to have been the greatest motorcycle racer of all time. He was born in Oxford on 2 April 1940, the son of a self-made millionaire motorcycle dealer. His father Stan had competed pre-war on two, three and four wheels, before going on to build up the largest grouping of dealerships seen up to that time in Great Britain.

Mike began his racing career aboard an MV Agusta 125 single overhead camshaft production racer, loaned to him by family friend Bill Webster (also a close friend of Count Domenico Agusta). This debut occurred on Easter Monday 22 April 1957 at Oulton Park in Cheshire, only a few miles from Webster's base.

Unlike Geoff Duke's early racing days, there is absolutely no doubt that Stan Hailwood went about buying success for his son, with the best bikes, the best tuners and a huge media hype. However, in fairness, Mike did not really need this vast support, as he had natural talent in abundance. An example of Stan Hailwood's 'methods' is displayed by a story concerning the NSU Sportmax Mike rode during the early part of his career. In 1955 John Surtees had raced the then new German bike thanks to his employers Vincent (who were the British NSU distributors). John was given a bike plus a spare engine. Then, towards the end of 1957, John received a telephone call from Stan asking 'Can we borrow the NSU for Mike to use in South Africa this winter?' John agreed and the machine went to the Hailwood equipé. Later, another call from Stan: 'Can we use the engine too?' Again John Surtees agreed. Now Stan had both bike and engine – and John was never to see either again. Because Stan conveniently became an NSU dealer – the 'deal' with new London-based importers meaning that King's of Oxford would only become agents if Stan could keep the racer and the engine – even though it had been given to John Surtees.

In many ways Mike was embarrassed by his father's wheeler dealings, and as soon as he could he became self sufficient – his race results giving him freedom from his father's overpowering attention. In fact, Mike nicknamed his father 'Stan the Wallet'. But this was not before Stan had bought bikes such as a 125 Paton, a 125 Grand Prix Ducati, various Desmo Ducati twins and singles for the 125, 250 and 350cc classes, a couple of ex-works FB Mondial 250 singles, a squadron of Manx Nortons and an AJS 7R. In 1958 Mike was able to score a trio of British ACU Star titles (125, 250 and 350cc).

Mike's first Grand Prix victory came aboard a factory 125 Ducati Desmo single during the 1959 Ulster – the man he beat that day was none other than his future teammate at MV Agusta Gary Hocking (riding an MZ). That year he also won all four ACU Stars – adding the 500cc to the classes he had retained for a second year. He repeated this feat the following year, one which no man before or since has equalled.

For 1961 Mike rode 125 and 250cc works Hondas, plus a 350cc AJS 7R and a 500cc Manx Norton. He gained his first world title, the 250cc, on the four-cylinder Honda, taking the 125 and 250cc Isle of Man TTs and the Senior race on his Norton. On the latter machine (tuned by Bill Lacey) Mike averaged over 100mph for the six-lap, 226-mile race.

At the end of 1961 he signed for MV Agusta – going on to win the 500cc world title four years in a row (1962–65). In 1964 Mike set a new one-hour world speed record (at Daytona), thus breaking the existing record set by Bob McIntyre on a 350cc Gilera four at Monza in November 1957.

In 1966 Mike rejoined Honda, winning both the 250 and 350cc classes on the new six-cylinder models, equalling his feat the following year before switching his attention to four wheels. But even he could not tame the wayward 500cc four-cylinder Honda, with MV (ridden by Giacomo Agostini) retaining the title.

For more than a decade Mike largely stayed away from bikes (except for a couple of outings on BSA and Yamaha machines) before making a historic comeback TT victory on a Ducati v-twin in 1978. The following year, 1979, he rode a Suzuki to a final TT victory. Then he retired once more, becoming a partner in the Hailwood & Gould business (with fellow world champion Rod Gould). By a twist of fate the premises they used had formerly been the home of the Birmingham branch of King's of Oxford (part of father Stan's dealership chain).

Mike died tragically (with his younger daughter Michelle) while driving home in his Rover car after collecting a fish and chip supper on 14 March 1982.

Mike, racing his three-fifty Norton at Aintree, autumn 1958.

Another view of the 1963 Scuderia Duke Gilera. Unfortunately, an accident at Brands Hatch (while racing his own Norton) sidelined Minter for the majority of the season.

have a race-long battle with Dave Downer – the latter aboard Paul Dunstall's 647cc Norton Domiracer twin. But, as the *Motor Cycle News* report explains:

Tragedy struck the most terrific race I have every seen …On the last lap of what was possibly the fastest and closest, and certainly the most tremendous race ever at the track, Dave Downer crashed fatally in a pile up with Derek Minter, who sustained head and back injuries.

So Minter was out of action, even before the World Championship series had begun, thus at a stroke denying Scuderia Duke of the one man who could have seriously challenged Hailwood. Geoff Duke responded by signing the up-and-coming Phil Read as Minter's replacement.

More problems
The next problem arose at the first Grand Prix, the West German round at Hockenheim. Here, the smaller Gilera four was totally outclassed for speed, not just by the full works-backed Honda fours and Bianchi twins, but also by the pre-production Honda CR77 twin. Even though Hartle subsequently brought a 350 Gilera home runner-up in the Junior TT, the writing was clearly on the wall and the smaller four was withdrawn so the team could concentrate on the 500cc class.

A victory in Holland
However, except for the previously mentioned victory at Imola, the larger Gilera simply could not match the lone MV of Mike Hailwood. And Scuderia Duke's sole GP victory – in the Dutch TT at Assen – only came courtesy of Hailwood's MV blowing up on the second lap of the race. Read finished runner-up in Holland – and in the next round in Belgium.

Minter returned to the squad in time for the Ulster Grand Prix in August, but even this failed to bring any real improvement in the team's fortunes, with Hailwood still victorious. For the record, Hartle came in second and Minter third. Then Minter finished runner-up (to Hailwood) at the Sachsenring in East Germany. But after that there were no more top-six finishes in the final three rounds of the Championship (Finland, Italy and Argentina).

Looking back, Hartle's best performance came in the Isle of Man where, besides being runner-up in the Junior, he was also runner-up in the Senior race.

Uncertainty again

There then followed a period of uncertainty as to whether or not Gilera would race in 1964. It carried out yet more testing at Monza – this time with several Italian riders, including Gilberto Milani, Franco Marcini and Renzo Rossi. John Hartle was also on hand, riding one of the fours equipped with a British-made Reynolds leading-link fork assembly. Finally, the following year, the little-known Argentinian Benedicto Calderella shot to fame by holding Hailwood in the first GP of the year at Daytona, before being slowed by gearbox problems. Thereafter, first Calderella, and subsequently several riders (including Derek Minter), had occasional Gilera rides, the last coming at the end of 1966 with the Canadian Frank Perris and Italian Remo Venturi as pilots. But all these later efforts were not to involve Geoff Duke.

Phil Read (499cc Norton) harries the Scuderia Duke rider, John Hartle, Hutchinson 100, Silverstone, April 1963. Already the warning signs were there to say that Gilera's return could be in trouble.

John Hartle was born in 1933 at Chapel-en-le-Frith in the English Peak district. His racing career spanned the early 1950s until the late 1960s. But although highly experienced, Geoff Duke later revealed that although 'John was good', he 'could not ride ultra-hard to win'.

John Hartle

Mike Hailwood's father Stan is on record as saying that John Hartle's 105mph lap from a standing start, on the Scuderia Duke Gilera four in the 1963 Senior TT, was one of John's finest performances.

Hailing from Chapel-en-le-Frith in the English Peak District, John Hartle was born in 1933. And in a career which spanned the early 1950s until the late 1960s he rode a variety of machinery, including not only four-cylinder MV Agustas and Gileras, but BSA, AJS, Norton and Aermacchi singles, plus Bob Geeson's REG twin, and even being a TT winner for Triumph aboard a Thruxton Bonneville.

For a couple of years after leaving school, John took a job in a local garage where, as he once described, 'I was required to delve into the internals of cars and lorries'. But his interest, however, lay more with two wheels than four, and with a certain degree of what he described as 'hero worship', the young Hartle visited various trials and scrambles in which local star Eric Bowers was competing.

The lure of motorcycle sport proved too strong to resist and so, in 1950, then aged 17, John joined Bowers's Chapel-en-le-Frith dealership. By this time Bowers had retired from active competition, but was sponsoring a couple of road racers, including Eric Houseley; John was recruited as a 'weekend race mechanic'. When Houseley subsequently won the 1952 Junior Clubman's TT on a BSA Gold Star, the young Hartle was there to look after the spanners and pitboard.

The following year, John made his own race debut at Brough airfield circuit in East Yorkshire on a BSA single – alongside the likes of Houseley,

Peter Davey and Ken Kavanagh (the latter on a works Norton). In September 1953 John found himself competing in the Manx Grand Prix, on an AJS 7R in the Junior and a Manx Norton in the Senior. But after refuelling the 7R in around 10th position, he braked too hard at Quarter Bridge and fell off. Undaunted, he then remounted to come home 21st. In the Senior event he did better, finishing a respectable 15th on the Norton and, as a result of these two finishes, collected that year's Newcomer Award.

But even better was to come the following year, when not only did Eric Bowers provide new machinery (still an AJS and Norton), but, after finishing third on the 7R in the 1954 Junior Manx GP, John led the Senior race in truly awful weather conditions until suffering the huge disappointment of running out of fuel on the last lap. Later that same month he also had the distinction of finishing third behind Geoff Duke (Gilera) and Bob Keeler in the Hutchinson 100 meeting at Silverstone.

These outstanding performances led to John being invited to join the Norton team alongside Jack Brett and John Surtees for 1955.

A close friendship between John Surtees and John Hartle transpired and this played a part in Hartle later joining Surtees in the MV Agusta team for the 1958 season. Prior to that, he continued to ride for Norton in 1955 and 1956, while in 1957 he had the use of a fully streamlined Norton bike.

His MV contract continued into 1959 and he rode for the Italian factory in the 1960 TT, but was subsequently sacked, which John Surtees told the author he thought 'unjust'. There is no doubt that Lady Luck seemed to desert Hartle during his MV days – he suffered more than his fair share of crashes, breakdowns and even a fire.

After MV John went back to racing as a privateer on his own Norton machinery. He was recalled as a works rider for the Geoff Duke Scuderia Gilera squad in 1963. And it was during this year that he became the main challenger to Mike Hailwood in the World Championship series. But the combination of Mike and the MV simply proved too strong, this resulting in the Scuderia team being disbanded at the end of 1963.

Then it was back to Norton, but by the midle960s he had switched to Italian Aermacchis, riding for the British importer Syd Lawton.

Then came a period riding factory-supported Triumph production bikes. In 1967 he set up a racing spares service business, but was to be fatally injured while racing at Scarborough the following year, aged 34.

John Hartle with the works 350 MV Agusta on which he finished runner-up to race winner John Surtees on a sister machine during the 1959 Junior TT

Geoff Duke with one of the 350 Gilera fours, at the Isle of Man TT in June 1963, and chief mechanic Giovanni Fumagalli.

There is no doubt that the Scuderia Duke team was a valiant but ultimately unsuccessful effort. Unfortunately, too much was left to Duke himself and no man, however enthusiastic, can hope to have the clout of the factory itself.

In his autobiography, Geoff commented:

Of course, it is easy to be wise after the event. Derek [Minter], with the prospect of a great Grand Prix season ahead of him and the possibility of the 500cc world title, should perhaps have been more restrained and settled. But he hated to be beaten, especially at Brands, and in the heat of battle it is sometimes difficult to think logically.

Geoff went on to say:

To say that I was shattered when I heard the news would be an understatement. I had pinned my faith on Minter who, at the peak of his racing career, was the only rider capable of beating Mike Hailwood. I had a gut feeling there and then that my plan for a victorious return by Gilera had been dealt a mortal blow.

As for John Hartle, although Geoff 'was reasonably sure' that he could 'battle with Hailwood on a road circuit, especially the TT,' but 'I always had a lingering doubt in my mind about John's ability to sustain the pressure of

John Hartle during the 1963 Isle of Man TT, he finished runner-up behind Jim Redman, Honda (Junior) and Mike Hailwood, MV (Senior). Gilera's only GP win that year came at Assen when Hartle won the 500cc race, with Phil Read on another Scuderla machine second.

Hartle (with crew-cut) and Minter at Oulton Park in August 1963, following the latters return to the saddle earlier that month.

cut-and-thrust racing in the massed-start Grand Prix. Whether this was due to lack of stamina or some obscure psychological factor is debateable. The fact remains that John was good, but not superb, and could not ride ultra-hard to win.'

So, with Minter injured, Geoff then turned to the 'still young and comparatively inexperienced Phil Read' who he considered 'even then a rider of exceptional ability'. But, Geoff was 'totally unprepared for the effect that subsequent success would have on his ego! Read was an individualist, not a team man. Worst of all, though, he seemed incapable of accepting advice from any quarter, no matter how well intentioned or informed.'

Scuderia Duke was a brave try, but not ultimately successful, due to the reasons outlined above. But this failure was certainly not due to any lack of enthusiasm or commitment on Geoff Duke's part.

Mallory Park Race of the Year, September 1963. The Scuderia Duke Gileras of Derek Minter (4) and Phil Read (6). The race was won by world champion Mike Hailwood (MV), followed by Minter; Read was fourth.

Chapter 9

Industry Politics

Besides the actual racing, Geoff Duke always took a great interest in his surroundings (he greatly enjoyed travelling to different places and meeting new people). In addition, he took notice of the various motorcycles – and their development. This, in turn, proved of great value to both the factories he rode for and his on-track performances.

Geoff was also someone who both the fans and his sponsors admired, the latter also valuing his clean-cut image and technical interest. After all, some riders can ride a motorcycle, but are not what we would refer to in modern day terms as media friendly.

So it will probably come as no surprise to readers that Geoff was a sought-after figure. This, in turn, meant that a combination of his own enthusiasm and his reputation saw him involved in several projects – which I have put under the general heading of 'Industry Politics', because, in several cases, this was precisely what transpired.

The BSA MC1 Project

Geoff's first real taste of the complexity and problems associated with an industry project came via the BSA company, and its MC1 250cc Grand Prix design.

And, as he was to discover, the MC1 saga was to highlight the lack of determination and commitment, certainly at senior management level, which was so prevalent within the British motorcycle industry during the 1950s. Sadly, like John Surtees (see *John Surtees: Motorcycle Maestro*, Breedon Books), Geoff was to experience at first hand a lack of official interest or backing.

He had first learnt of the BSA two-fifty racing project in early 1953 – before he signed for the Italian Gilera marque. And, as he recalled in his autobiography, *In Pursuit of Perfection*, 'the prospect of a British 250 appearing on the Grand Prix scene filled me with hope and enthusiasm.' He continued: 'so, anxious to do all I could to assist this forward-looking policy,

No less a rider than Geoff Duke himself rated BSA's two-fifty MC1 single, the most promising design 'never to see the light of day'. BSAs management, rather than the engineers, killed off the project in the mid-1950s.

I went to see Bert Hopwood (BSA's design chief), telling him of my interest and offering my support.' Hopwood gave Geoff 'a brief rundown of the engine's development,' and 'this was the first of many such visits as I tried to keep him up to date with Grand Prix activity, particularly with the progress of NSU and other competitors in the 250cc class.' But, although Geoff considered Hopwood 'a good listener', he also had the 'feeling that my words were bouncing off a wall.'

But, despite Geoff's serious interest (and one must take into account that during the early–mid 1950s he was the world's biggest road-racing star), in his own words 'slow progress was made'. And it was not until late 1954 that he eventually was able to ride the machine, this being at Oulton Park in Cheshire, where the world champion covered some 30 laps 'in far from ideal conditions'. But, even so, Geoff found the engine 'exceptionally smooth', with it 'revving to 10,000rpm'.

The MC1 was the joint work of Doug Hele and Hopwood, the former Geoff described as 'Hopwood's brilliant and phlegmatic deputy', and after the Oulton Park test session was 'quietly pleased'. As for Geoff himself, he 'was convinced that with a little more development, five gears [when tested it had only four ratios] and better brakes, this 250 BSA had excellent potential in Grand Prix road racing, and it could have formed the basis of a production sports machine that would have sold like the proverbial hot cakes.'

Actually, the initial concept was even older than Geoff himself had thought. Bert Hopwood had joined BSA, from Norton, in March 1949 and

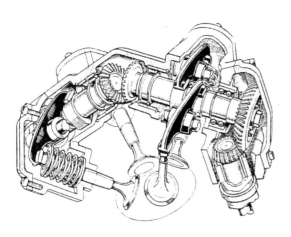

Drawing of the MC1's valve layout, with its radically dispersed 4-valves, rockers and bevel gears.

was provided with an office deep within the vast Small Heath Birmingham works. Very soon he was to be appointed chief designer, but not before he had drawn out the design of an entirely new 250cc engine unit.

Beginning with a clean sheet of paper, Hopwood's drawings included a four-valve single cylinder, the valves being radically disposed. He also opted for twin overhead camshafts. The layout chosen saw two longitudinal cams in the form of an inverted V, coupled together. A third shaft in the apex of the V supported the chain drive sprocket. A sketch of the engine at this time showed it was to be mounted in a duplex steel tubular frame, with a front fork of the type devised by the Birmingham engineer Ernie Earles. The engine, with an almost horizontal cylinder, gave the impression from the nearside of being a unit construction design, but in fact a separate gearbox was fitted at the rear offside (right). This gearbox (made by BSA themselves) was to prove one of the few weak points of the original design (and still in place when Geoff carried out the tests referred to earlier). Also, this points to the fact that Hopwood intended the design for road use rather than racing.

Then, for some years the four-valve single project was quietly put to one side. And it was not until Doug Hele joined BSA (after spells with Norton and Douglas) that another look was taken at what is now known as the MC1. Fellow author Jeff Clew described Hele's involvement thus: 'Hopwood put him [Hele] in charge of a separate design team to concern itself with forward projects, shielded from day-to-day problems.'

Whether Hele uncovered the 250cc project on his own, or whether Hopwood passed the drawings over, is not known as both men have since died. But what is certain is that Hopwood did give Hele authority to update and improve upon the original.

Essentially, Hele decided to broadly stick to Hopwood's specifications. However, he did redesign the layout of the camshafts so they lay transversely across the cylinder head, and were driven by a vertical shaft and bevel gears with an Oldhams coupling (similar to a Manx Norton).

When interviewed before his death, Hele gave two main reasons for this change: to prevent the camboxes from obstructing the flow of cooling air over the cylinder head and to provide room for a pair of carburettors.

The cylinder head is a critical area in the design of any four-stroke engine. And Hele received help here from the respected BSA specialist in the field, Donald Bastow. Bastow was employed in the Small Heath R&D department, having at one time worked for W.O. Bentley of the legendary automobile company. Not only this, but Bastow had seen service with a wide range of British motor companies and was widely respected. Flow tests of the MC1 engine showed that parallel inlet tracts provided the best results and Bastow provided Hele with an optimum layout. Bore and stroke dimensions were finalised at 70 x 64.5mm giving 248.5cc, and the engine also featured an outside flywheel.

Another feature of the Hele redesign came in the shape of cantilevered rear suspension, which now featured a single Girling-sourced shock absorber.

The front fork carried on the unusual nature of the machine. This pivoted around the fixed steering head rather than the conventional practice of the other way round. But its lower structure was still modelled on the Earles leading-link type.

It was not until the middle of 1953 that the cycle parts were ready to receive the redesigned power unit. The frame was actually the work of BSA's brilliant trials rider and engineer Bill Nicholson.

By this time bench testing of the engine had begun – this and the fine tuning being entrusted to Roland Pike. Problems centred around broken valve springs, sheered Oldhams coupling and lubrication glitches. The sealed, oil-filled primary chain case was equipped with finning – to get rid of excess heat – generated by the primary chain itself.

The BSA development team also encountered difficulties with the ignition, with even a racing magneto seeming hard pushed to keep pace with the high engine revolutions.

Serious track testing took place during the summer of 1954 – mainly at the MIRA (Motor Industry Research Association) near Nuneaton, Warwickshire, the riders involved being Charlie Salt and Roland Pike himself, followed by the Geoff Duke tests (in September and December 1954).

And then comes the controversy.

Geoff's version of events is that, early in 1955, he, together with BSA's competition manager Bert Perrigo, had another meeting with Hopwood, where it was agreed that the machine should be entered for Silverstone in April, using the Rudge name which BSA owned. After visiting Bert Perrigo, it was also agreed that Geoff should submit a TT entry, describing the bike as a GDS (Geoff Duke Special) purely to avoid premature disclosure of BSA's involvement. Streamlining was produced, and the machine made ready for its first race. However, the day before everyone was ready to depart to Silverstone, Doug Hele telephoned Geoff Duke, totally unexpectedly, and told him that the BSA board of directors had decided that the MC1 should not be raced!

Geoff pictured in early March 1964, after taking up a consultancy role at the Royal Enfield works in Redditch, south west of Birmingham.

John Hartle testing the original Villiers-Starmaker powered GP5 prototype at Oulton Park in March 1964.

Why?

Why? Well, it transpired later that Bert Hopwood had been called to the managing director James Leeke's office and had been asked for a guarantee that the machine would win. This, of course, was a totally unreasonable demand. Instead of standing his ground, Hopwood had taken the easy route, quietly succumbing to a defeatist attitude.

Hopwood's capitulation not only resulted in the MC1 being shoved in a corner and forgotten, but a great chance of British pride being reinstated in the Lightweight racing class had been lost.

Who today, one may ask, would have told Valentino Rossi to go away – but that is exactly what happened to Geoff Duke and BSA half a century ago …it also led to key men such as Nicholson, Pike and Amott quitting the BSA empire.

The Japanese visit

Shortly after his retirement from racing, Geoff took up an offer from Fumito Sakai, president of the Japanese Motorcycle Federation and publisher of the *Motorcyclist* magazine. Geoff was also asked to ship a Manx Norton to Japan so he could give riding demonstrations. This was done, and on 13 April 1960 Geoff left London bound for Tokyo on a BOAC (British Overseas Airways Corporation – forerunner of British Airways) de Havilland Comet 4B.

Upon his arrival in Japan, Geoff was received in a truly royal fashion – and throughout his three-week stay in the country. During this time Geoff not only visited Suzuki, Honda and Yamaha (Kawasaki were not manufacturing complete motorcycles at this time, only engine units) and the NGK spark plug factory, but also a motocross meeting, plus what passed for a road race in Japan at that time – where Geoff demonstrated the Norton to several thousand enthusiasts. But, as he admitted later:

in my three short weeks there it was hard to do more than just scratch the surface.' And 'on the plane home, I had some time to think and made certain notes which I thought might serve to stir some of our manufacturers out of their complacency. But alas, this was not to be. Edward

Turner of Triumph/BSA later visited Japan on a fact-finding tour, but appeared to be unmoved. Perhaps the 'facts' were too shattering!

AMC

Shortly after Geoff's return from Japan, he received 'an unexpected telephone call, followed by a letter, inquiring if I might be interested in accepting a high-level appointment with a major British motorcycle manufacturer'. Although, as Geoff was to admit, 'I did not know the caller personally, he was well known and I knew of him'. He was, in fact, Lt Col. 'Goldie' Gardiner (a very successful world-record car driver with the MG company). But, in Geoff's case, Gardiner had contacted the former world champion from his position as chairman of the shareholders committee at AMC (Associated Motor Cycles), who manufactured AJS, Matchless, Norton, Francis-Barnett and James.

These shareholders had become increasingly worried regarding AMC's performance and profitability. This, in fact, was well founded as, although the group made a profit of £219,000 in 1960, this turned into a loss of £350,000 the following year and accelerated thereafter until finally, in August 1966, a receiver was appointed, before being sold to Denis Poore – the chairman of Manganese Bronze – later still the remains of AMC became Norton Villiers.

As for the shareholders committee's attempt to save AMC, this, unfortunately, never got off the ground. But again it shows in what high regard Geoff Duke was held.

With the arrival of German two-stroke engineer and tuning wizard Hermann Meier, in late spring 1964, a new engine was designed and built to replace the original Villiers unit. Unfortunately, Meier was saddled with an Alpha bottom-end, so he was restricted in what he could achieve.

Geoff with one of the development GP5 racers at Brands Hatch, later in 1964.

After Geoff Duke recruited Percy Tait into the Enfield team, results, if not reliability, improved. A hightlight was Tait's magnificent third, behind the works Yamaha twins of Phil Read and Mike Duff at the international Silverstone meeting 17 August 1965.

Royal Enfield

Yet another British company to be involved with Geoff Duke was the Redditch-based Royal Enfield marque. As Geoff was to comment in his 1988 autobiography, 'After the demise of Scuderia Duke [see Chapter Eight] my spirits were raised by an invitation in 1964 from Leo Davenport, winner of the Lightweight TT on a New Imperial in 1932, and then managing director of Royal Enfield, to assist in the design of a 250cc road-racing machine powered by a single-cylinder two-stroke engine.' And although primarily intended as an over-the-counter production racer, Leo had promised Geoff that there would be a 'limited programme of racing with factory support'.

Ken Sprayson of Reynolds (who had worked with Geoff on his Lightweight 350 Norton) was responsible for the frame design, while, at Geoff's instigation, a clever one-piece fibreglass fuel-tank-cum-seat (containing around six imperial gallons) not only helped reduce the height of the tank, but distributed the fuel load over approximately two-thirds of the machine's length.

Geoff was also instrumental in bringing in Hermann Meier, the famous two-stroke specialist, to look after engine development. A little-known fact is that Geoff was also in touch with his old friend Leo Kuzmicki, the gifted Polish engineer, from his days at Norton.

During his time at Royal Enfield, Geoff also suggested 'a design for a very simple and inexpensive car'. The engine for this was to be an Austrian Styr Daimler Puch air-cooled, horizontally-opposed ohv twin. In the Royal Enfield, the engine would have been front-mounted, driving the front wheels via simple automatic transmission of the belt and expanding-pulley type employed on the DKW hobby scooter. But, because of financial implications, this interesting project was to be stillborn.

As for the racer, by now called the GP5, this was raced both by the works – notably by first John Hartle and later Percy Tait, and small quantities were sold to customers. The first prototype employed a bought-in Villiers Starmaker engine, but most machines were equipped with the Meier-designed air-cooled single-cylinder unit. But reliability was to prove a major problem, although while it kept going the Enfield proved the quickest of the then current breed of British-built 250cc racers including DMW, Greeves and Cotton.

As Geoff was to comment later, 'Conscious of the engine's limitations,

Meier proposed the design of an in-line, liquid-cooled, twin-cylinder two-stroke engine, with disc valves, for which he produced a general layout and specification. Funding of the project, though, was not forthcoming.'

Interestingly, just such a layout was used by the Japanese Kawasaki marque to win several World Championship-titles in the 250 and 350cc classes during the late 1970s and early 1980s...

By the end of 1965 Leo Davenport pulled the plug on the GP5 – Hermann Meier having left a few months earlier and Geoff Duke following him.

Other interests

In late 1964 Geoff had become involved in the task of planning routes (in excess of 1,000 miles) for the ISDT, to be held in the Isle of Man the following year. As he had already been the clerk of the course 'for several Manx Two Days Trials', Geoff did have 'some knowledge of trials organisation, plus a good knowledge of the island's terrain'.

The subsequent success of the trial was down, no doubt, to Geoff's abilities in this area, both of actual trials experience and his organisational skills.

Thereafter, Geoff returned to his various business ventures, which by the late 1970s included the Manx Line shipping company (not successful) and later still Duke Video (very successful and still very much alive and being run by Geoff's son, Peter). And so Geoff's involvement continued in subsequent decades, showing his talents far exceeded simply riding skills.

Unlike many others, Geoff Duke was able to make the transition from champion sportsman to successful businessman.

AJS was part of the giant AMC (Associated Motor Cycles) group of companies, which Geoff came close to a major involvement; shortly after he quit competing himself, during 1960.

Geoff's widespread fame, both during his racing career and in the years thereafter, meant that he was in constant demand. He is seen here (astride the famous vintage Norton 'Old Miracle') at the opening of the National Motor Museum, with Lord Beaulieu (centre) and Lord Brabazon.

Chapter 10

A Place in History

There is little doubt in the author's mind that Geoff Duke could, equally, have reached the very top in not only road racing, but trials and scrambling (motocross). In fact, he can well lay claim to being the most successful all-rounder motorcycle sport has ever seen.

Geoff began his competitions career as a trials expert in the BSA works team after being demobbed from the Royal Signals. Later he joined Nortons, mainly to achieve his ambition to go road racing, and from his first tarmac event, the Junior Manx Grand Prix in 1948, it was patently obvious that he had a natural talent destined to sweep him to the very top of his chosen profession. However, it should be remembered that he not only rode works Norton racing models, but he represented the famous old Birmingham marque in both trials and scrambles too.

Amazingly, certainly if one compares him to the likes of John Surtees or Mike Hailwood, Geoff became a works rider almost immediately, whereas the other two stars rode countless races before they were offered works machinery.

But few of Geoff Duke's many successes came easily, however. His greatest triumphs were achieved against considerable odds. For example, when, as a new recruit to the Norton team, he alone succeeded in regularly vanquishing the much faster four-cylinder Italian machines.

In the six years from 1950 when he made his dramatic debut as a works rider under the management of the legendary Joe Craig, on the then new Featherbed Norton, Geoff Duke won six World Championships, five TTs and many international Grands Prix. And all with the characteristically easy grace and supreme style that impressed everyone who was fortunate enough to see him ride.

Geoff affectionately pats an ex-works Norton single of the type he rode in the early 1950s, following a demonstration run at the 1965 Silverstone Hutchinson 100 meeting.

The 1977 Earls Court Show, London; Geoff talks to world champion Barry Sheene about the latter's Heron Suzuki machine.

Advertisement from the 1979 Isle of Man TT race programme, promoting one of Geoff's business ventures.

A natural

Geoff Duke was a natural. Unlike some top names, he was not manufactured or honed, but simply a *born* rider, and was not just a brilliantly gifted rider but also someone with the ability to judge to perfection exactly when he needed to put in that little bit extra to overcome whatever opposition there was ranged against him. Not only this, but he was one of those rare beings who development engineers love – a man with an instinctive love and ability to sense exactly what changes and modifications are needed and be able to explain precisely what should be done.

Joe Craig soon realised this and stated that Geoff's analytical mind simplified his job greatly, while Duke's advice to Gilera soon solved the Italian company's handling problems – which actually did almost as much to bring them their string of successes from 1953 until 1957 as Geoff's mastery in the saddle.

But, as the *BP Book of Motor Cycle Racing* (Stanley Paul, 1960) stated:

Classic Lap action, at the Nook, during the 1981 Isle of Man TT week when Geoff paraded a Gilera four.

Geoff astride the Norton International, on which he won his first TT (the Senior Clubman's in 1949), following its restoration in 1986.

Lady Luck has not always smiled on him and since 1955 he has suffered misfortunes which might well have discouraged or embittered lesser men. Always, however, his natural determination and good humour have risen above them to maintain unsullied his reputation for being not only a truly great rider, but an equally great sportsman.

Looking, with the benefit of hindsight, at his involvement in the private riders' strike at the 1955 Dutch TT – and his subsequent six-month ban from 1 January 1956 – this proved a major setback. As were the crashes he sustained at the Imola circuit in spring 1957, which sidelined him for most of that year. Then came the shock withdrawal of Gilera at the end of the same year. And if Gilera had continued, Geoff would have become the firm's team manager.

Again, in retrospect, his signing for BMW at the beginning of 1958 was doomed to failure, as he had picked the exact period when the famous German corporation was going through the toughest financial period in its history and was virtually bankrupt.

Even Geoff was later to admit that he should have quit when Gilera retired. However, his genuine enthusiasm and love of motorcycles made him carry on.

But even then he was able to bow out in September 1959 with three wins

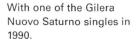

With one of the Gilera Nuovo Saturno singles in 1990.

Opening the National Motorcycle Museum, Birmingham, in October 1984.

in three rides at the Swiss Grand Prix at Locarno. And, one has to ask, what other rider has pulled off such a coup at their last meeting?

As for his car career, even though on results alone this does not seem significant, people who really mattered, the team owners, managers and technicians, all regarded him highly.

And, finally, in business and as an ambassador to motorcycling itself Geoff Duke has proved that he could achieve success beyond his riding career. Very few others can match Geoff in this respect.

Quite simply, there is only one Geoff Duke.

Centenial TT at Assen, May 1998. Rivals years ago, Umberto Masetti (in the helmet), who won world titles for Gilera in 1950 and 1952, and Geoff; at the time Geoff was 75, Umberto 72. Umberto Masetti died in 2006.

Geoff pictured in his Isle of Man home having reached 80 years of age, spring 2003.

Appendices
Geoff Duke Motorcycle Road Racing Results

RL + Record Lap; FL = Fastest Lap.

1948

Position	Class	Machine	Circuit	Date
Retired (split oil tank, seized engine)	Junior Manx GP	Norton (350cc)	Isle of Man	7 September
4	350cc	Norton	Ansty	23 October

1949

Position	Class	Machine	Circuit	Date
2	350cc Heat	Norton	Haddenham	3 April
1	350cc Final	Norton	Haddenham	3 April
1	350cc Heat	Norton	Blandford	18 April
2	350cc Final	Norton	Blandford	18 April
1	Up to 1000cc Non Experts	Norton	Blandford	18 April
3	350cc	Norton	North West 200	14 May
1	Senior Clubman's TT	Norton (500cc)	Isle of Man	15 June
1	350cc Heat	Norton	Ansty	25 June
1	350cc Final	Norton	Ansty	25 June
Retired (crash)	350cc	Norton	Skerries 100	2 July
2	Junior Manx GP	Norton (350cc)	Isle of Man	13 September
1	Senior Manx GP	Norton (500cc)	Isle of Man	13 September RL
1	350cc	Norton	Scarborough	23 September
1	500cc	Norton	Scarborough	24 September RL

1950

Position	Class	Machine	Circuit	Date
2	350cc	Norton	Blandford	1 April
1	500cc	Norton	Blandford	1 April
1	350cc	Norton	Thruxton	10 April
1	500cc	Norton	Thruxton	10 April
1	350cc	Norton	Silverstone	22 April
1	1000cc	Norton	Silverstone	22 April
3	350cc	Norton	Blandford	29 April
1	500cc	Norton	Blandford	29 April FL
1	350cc	Norton	North West 200	13 May RL
2	Junior TT	Norton (350cc)	Isle of Man	7 June
1	Senior TT	Norton (500cc)	Isle of Man	11 June RL
3	350cc Belgian GP	Norton	Spa Francorchamps	2 July
Retired (tyre problems)	500cc Belgian GP	Norton	Spa Francorchamps	2 July FL
2	350cc Dutch TT	Norton	Assen	8 July
Retired (crash)	500cc Dutch TT	Norton	Assen	8 July
3	350cc Swiss GP	Norton	Geneva	23 July
4	500cc Swiss GP	Norton	Geneva	23 July
1	500cc Heat	Norton	Blandford	8 August
1	500cc Final	Norton	Blandford	8 August FL
1	500cc Ulster GP	Norton	Clady	19 August FL
2	350cc Heat	Norton	Thruxton	27 August
1	350cc Final	Norton	Thruxton	27 August FL

Position	Class	Machine	Circuit	Date
1	500cc Heat	Norton (350cc)	Thruxton	27 August
Retired (not allowed to race, undersized engine)	500cc Final	Norton (350cc)	Thruxton	27 August
1	350cc Italian GP	Norton	Monza	17 September
1	500cc Italian GP	Norton	Monza	17 September
1	350cc	Norton	Scarborough	22 September FL
1	500cc	Norton	Scarborough	23 September FL
Retired (did not race due to heavy standing water)		Norton	Silverstone	30 September

1951

Position	Class	Machine	Circuit	Date
2	350cc	Norton	Brough	24 March
2	Festival of Britain Ch'ship	Norton (500cc)	Brough	24 March
3	350cc Heat	Norton	Thruxton	26 March
2	350cc Final	Norton	Thruxton	26 March
2	500cc Heat	Norton	Thruxton	26 March
1	500cc Final	Norton	Thruxton	26 March
1	350cc Marseilles GP	Norton	Marseilles	7 April
1	500cc Marseilles GP	Norton	Marseilles	7 April
1	350cc	Norton	Goodwood	14 April
1	500cc	Norton	Goodwood	14 April
3	350cc	Norton	Mettet	29 April FL
1	500cc	Norton	Mettet	29 April FL
Retired (plug trouble)	350cc	Norton	North West 200	10 May FL
1	500cc	Norton	North West 200	12 May RL
1	350cc Heat	Norton	Blandford	14 May
1	350cc Final	Norton	Blandford	14 May
Retired (magneto failure)	350cc Swiss GP	Norton	Berne	26 May
Retired (magneto failure)	500cc Swiss GP	Norton	Berne	27 May
1	Junior TT	Norton (350cc)	Isle of Man	5 June RL
1	Senior TT	Norton (500cc)	Isle of Man	8 June RL
1	350cc Belgian GP	Norton	Spa Francorchamps	1 July FL
1	500cc Belgian GP	Norton	Spa Francorchamps	1 July FL
Retired (crash)	350cc Dutch TT	Norton	Assen	7 July
1	500cc Dutch TT	Norton	Assen	7 July RL
5	500cc French GP	Norton	Albi	15 July
2	350cc	Norton	Thruxton	6 August
1	Festival of Britain Invitation	Norton (500cc)	Thruxton	6 August FL
1	1000cc	Norton (500cc)	Thruxton	6 August FL
1	350cc Ulster GP	Norton	Clady	16 August RL
1	500cc Ulster GP	Norton	Clady	18 August
1	350cc German GP	Norton	Solitude	26 August RL
1	500cc German GP	Norton	Solitude	26 August
1	350cc Italian GP	Norton	Monza	9 September FL
4	500cc Italian GP	Norton	Monza	9 September
1	350cc	Norton	Silverstone	6 October FL
1	500cc	Norton	Silverstone	6 October FL

350cc and 500cc World Champion

1952

Position	Class	Machine	Circuit	Date
1	350cc	Norton	Silverstone	19 April
1	500cc	Norton	Silverstone	19 April
1	500cc	Norton	San Remo	20 April
1	500cc	Norton	Codogno	27 April
1	350cc Swiss GP	Norton	Berne	17 May

Position	Class	Machine	Circuit	Date
Retired (exhaust valve)	500cc Swiss GP	Norton	Berne	18 May
1	Junior TT	Norton (350cc)	Isle of Man	9 June FL
Retired (misfiring and clutch)	Senior TT	Norton (500cc)	Isle of Man	13 June
1	350cc Dutch TT	Norton	Assen	28 June
2	500cc Dutch TT	Norton	Assen	28 June
1	350cc Belgian GP	Norton	Spa Francorchamps	6 July
2	500cc Belgian GP	Norton	Spa Francorchamps	6 July
Retired (crash)	350cc	Norton	Schotten	13 July

350cc World Champion

1953

Position	Class	Machine	Circuit	Date
7	350cc	Norton (Manx)	Silverstone	18 April
Retired (crash)	Senior TT	Gilera (500cc)	Isle of Man	12 June
1	500cc Dutch TT	Gilera	Assen	27 June
Retired (throttle cable nipple)	500cc Belgian GP	Gilera	Spa Francorchamps	5 July RL
Retired (teams withdrew)	500cc German GP	Gilera	Schotten	18 July
1	500cc French GP	Gilera	Rouen	2 August
2	500cc Ulster GP	Gilera	Dundrod	15 August
1	500cc Swiss GP	Gilera	Berne	23 August
1	500cc Italian GP	Gilera	Monza	5 September
1	500cc Heat	Gilera	Scarborough	19 September FL
1	500cc Final	Gilera	Scarborough	19 September FL
Retired (crash in practice)	500cc	Gilera	Silverstone	25 September

500cc World Champion

1954

Position	Class	Machine	Circuit	Date
1	500cc	Gilera	Silverstone	10 April
Retired (machine trouble)	500cc	Gilera	North West 200	15 May RL
Retired (engine)	500cc	Gilera	Rheims	29 May
2	Senior TT	Gilera (500cc)	Isle of Man	18 June
1	500cc Belgian GP	Gilera	Spa Francorchamps	4 July FL
1	500cc Dutch TT	Gilera	Assen	10 July RL
1	500cc German GP	Gilera	Solitude	25 July RL
Retired	500cc	Gilera	Senegallia	1 August RL
1	500cc non-Championship	Gilera	Silverstone	7 August FL
1	500cc Championship	Gilera	Silverstone	7 August
1	500cc Swiss GP	Gilera	Berne	22 August FL
1	500cc Italian GP	Gilera	Monza	12 September RL
1	500cc	Gilera	Scarborough	18 September RL
1	500cc	Gilera	Casale Monferrato	19 September RL
1	1000cc	Gilera (500cc)	Aintree	25 September FL

500cc World Champion

1955

Position	Class	Machine	Circuit	Date
Retired (crash)	500cc	Gilera	Imola	11 April
1	500cc	Gilera	Silverstone	23 April RL
Retired (misfire)	500cc Spanish GP	Gilera	Barcelona	1 May
1	500cc	Gilera	Hockenheim	8 May
1	500cc French GP	Gilera	Rheims	15 May FL
1	500cc	Gilera	North West 200	21 May RL
1	Senior TT	Gilera (500cc)	Isle of Man	10 June RL
1	500cc German GP	Gilera	Nürburgring	26 June RL
Retired (timing gears)	500cc Belgian GP	Gilera	Spa Francorchamps	3 July RL

Position	Class	Machine	Circuit	Date
1	500cc Dutch TT	Gilera	Assen	16 July FL
1	500cc Swedish GP (non-Championship)	Gilera	Hedemora	24 July RL
3	500cc Italian GP	Gilera	Monza	4 September FL
1	500cc Heat	Gilera	Scarborough	16 September FL
1	500cc Final	Gilera	Scarborough	17 September RL
1	500cc	Gilera	Aintree	25 September RL
2	Solo Handicap	Gilera	Aintree	25 September FL
1	500cc (5 laps)	Gilera	Silverstone	1 October FL
2	500cc (20 laps)	Gilera	Silverstone	1 October RL
3	1000cc	Gilera (500cc)	Brands Hatch	20 October

500cc World Champion

1956

Position	Class	Machine	Circuit	Date
Retired (non-starter)	350cc	Velocette	North West 200	12 May
1	500cc	Gilera	Aintree	19 May
1	Aintree 90	Gilera (500cc)	Aintree	19 May
1	500cc Heat	Gilera	Oulton Park	21 May
1	500cc Final	Gilera	Oulton Park	21 May
Retired (broken piston)	500cc Belgian GP	Gilera	Spa Francorchamps	8 July RL
1	500cc Swedish GP (non-Championship)	Gilera	Hedemora	15 July RL
Retired (magneto)	500cc German GP	Gilera	Solitude	22 July
1	1000cc Heat	Gilera	Oulton Park	4 August
1	1000cc Final	Gilera	Oulton Park	4 August
Retired (crash)	500cc Ulster GP	Gilera	Dundrod	11 August
1	500cc Italian GP	Gilera	Monza	9 September
1	500cc	Gilera	Scarborough	15 September
1	500cc	Gilera	Kristianstad	22 September

1957

Position	Class	Machine	Circuit	Date
2	Port Elizabeth 200 Handicap	Gilera	Uitenhage	1 January
1	500cc Scratch	Gilera	Pietermaritzburg	19 January
1	Handicap	Gilera	Pietermaritzburg	19 January
1	500cc Scratch	Gilera	Grand Central (Johann'burg)	2 February
4	5-lap Handicap	Gilera	Grand Central (Johann'burg)	2 February
Unplaced	12-lap Handicap	Gilera	Grand Central (Johann'burg)	2 February
1	500cc Scratch	Gilera	Belvedere (Salisbury)	23 February
Unplaced	Handicap	Gilera	Belvedere (Salisbury)	23 February
1	500cc Scratch	Gilera	Cape Town	2 March
1	Handicap	Gilera	Cape Town	2 March
Retired (crash)	350cc Shell Gold Cup	Gilera	Imola	22 April
Retired (crash)	500cc Shell Gold Cup	Gilera	Imola	22 April
Retired (clutch)	350cc Swedish GP (non-Championship)	Gilera	Hedemora	14 July
2	500cc Swedish GP (non-Championship)	Gilera	Hedemora	14 July
Retired (suspension)	350cc Ulster GP	Gilera	Dundrod	11 August
3	500cc Ulster GP	Gilera	Dundrod	11 August
Retired (engine)	350cc Italian GP	Gilera	Monza	1 September
2	500cc Italian GP	Gilera	Monza	1 September
7	500cc	Norton	Scarborough	15 September
Retired (power loss)	500cc	Norton	Silverstone	21 September
8	500cc	Norton	Aintree	28 September
7	500cc	Norton	Oulton Park	5 October

1958

Position	Class	Machine	Circuit	Date
3	350cc	Norton	Oulton Park	7 April
3	500cc	Norton	Oulton Park	7 April
1	350cc	Norton	Silverstone	19 April FL
Retired (suspension/gearing)	500cc	BMW	Silverstone	19 April
8	500cc Austrian GP (non-Championship)	BMW	Salzburg	1 May
1	500cc	BMW	Hockenheim	11 May
Retired (valve trouble)	Junior TT	Norton	Isle of Man	2 June
Retired (front brake problems)	Senior TT	BMW	Isle of Man	6 June
Retired (poor engine performance)	350cc Dutch TT	Norton	Assen	28 June
Retired (brake fade)	500cc Dutch TT	BMW	Assen	28 June
5	350cc Belgian GP	Norton	Spa Francorchamps	6 July
4	500cc Belgian GP	BMW	Spa Francorchamps	6 July
Retired (oil breather pipe)	350cc German GP	Norton	Nürburgring	20 July
Retired (carburation)	500cc German GP	BMW	Nürburgring	20 July
1	350cc Swedish GP	Norton	Hedemora	26 July FL
1	500cc Swedish GP	Norton	Hedemora	26 July FL
4	350cc	Norton	Oulton Park	4 August
3	500cc	Norton	Oulton Park	4 August
2	Les Graham Invitation	Norton (500cc)	Oulton Park	4 August
4	350cc Ulster GP	Norton	Dundrod	9 August
5	500cc Ulster GP	Norton	Dundrod	9 August
3	350cc Italian GP	Norton	Monza	14 September
7	500cc Italian GP	Norton	Monza	14 September
Retired (clutch)	350cc	Norton	Scarborough	19 September
10	500cc	Norton	Scarborough	20 September

1959

Position	Class	Machine	Circuit	Date
Retired (engine)	250cc Austrian GP (non-Championship)	NSU	Salzburg	1 May
Retired (non-starter)	250cc	NSU	North West 200	9 May
Retired (broken oil pipe)	350cc	Norton	North West 200	9 May
8	Les Graham Invitation	Norton	Oulton Park	16 May
Retired (engine seized in practice)	Lightweight TT	NSU (250cc)	Isle of Man	2 June
4	Junior TT	Norton (350cc)	Isle of Man	7 June
5	350cc	Norton	Karlskoga	9 June
6	250cc German GP	Benelli	Hockenheim	16 June
4	350cc German GP	Norton	Hockenheim	16 June
9	500cc German GP	Norton	Hockenheim	16 June
3	500cc Belgian GP	Norton	Spa Francorchamps	6 July
3	250cc Swedish GP	Benelli	Kristianstad	20 July
3	350cc Ulster GP	Norton	Dundrod	9 August
3	500cc Ulster GP	Norton	Dundrod	9 August
6	350cc	Norton	Silverstone	22 August
Retired (sump plug)	500cc	Norton	Silverstone	22 August
10	250cc Italian GP	Benelli	Monza	6 September
Retired	350cc Italian GP	Norton	Monza	6 September
3	500cc Italian GP	Norton	Monza	6 September
1	250cc Swiss GP (non-Championship)	Benelli	Locarno	13 September
1	350cc Swiss GP (non-Championship)	Norton	Locarno	13 September
1	500cc Swiss GP (non-championship)	Norton	Locarno	13 September

Index

Aberdare Park 155
Aberdare, Lord 97
ACU 36, 38, 62, 90, 143, 228–9
Adelaide Bandiana 146
Agostini, Giacomo 229
Agusta, Count Domenico 155, 164, 228
Agusta, Mario 155
Ahearn, J.J. 153
Ainsdale 8
Aintree 139, 143–4, 158, 162–3, 177–8, 229, 250–1
AJS 13–14, 16–17, 22–3, 28–30, 33–5, 40, 45, 51, 58–64, 68–9, 71, 73, 76, 78, 80–1, 85, 88–94, 97, 102, 114–16, 120–1, 125, 131–2, 134–41, 143–4, 148, 158–60, 164–5, 182, 188, 218, 228–9, 232–3, 241, 243
AJW 74
Alan Trophy Trial 23
Allison, R. 133
Alves, Phil 22
Amal 50, 191, 211
Ambrosini, Dario 215
AMC 14, 17–18, 21, 29, 160, 241, 243
Amm, Ray 87, 104–6, 116, 119, 121–3, 129, 131–7, 139, 141, 143
Anderson, Bob 163, 165, 168, 180, 183–6, 188–9, 192, 209
Anderson, Fergus K. 78, 120, 135–7, 141
Andrew, E. 40, 45
Ansty 28, 40, 248
Antice, Vic 40
Antoni, Gianni Degli 164
Archer, I.K. 37
Archer, Les 36, 56, 105
Arcore 111, 118, 125, 130, 158, 171, 222, 223
Ardennes 63, 134
Argentina 230
Armstrong, Reg 34–5, 61, 63–4, 78, 85, 89, 91, 93, 97, 102–4, 113–16, 121, 124–8, 131, 133, 136–7, 139, 141, 143–4, 147–54, 157, 163–5, 168, 170, 189, 210, 213–14, 222
Arragon 189
Artesiani 64, 69
Ashgrove 22

Assen 66, 116, 120, 134–5, 154, 185, 209, 230, 234, 247–52
Aston Martin 95, 98–101, 108, 109
Auchterarder 159
Austin 109, 112–13, 162
Australia 145–6, 149, 169
Austria 59, 87, 206
Austrian Grand Prix 189, 206, 207, 213, 252
Auto Cycle Union 36
Avon Tyre Company 7, 127
Ballacraine 25, 209
Ballaugh 25
Ballymena 87
Baltisberger, H. 126
Bandirola 64, 69, 101, 127, 135–7, 141, 147–8, 152–3
Bandirola, Carlo 64, 69, 127, 135–6, 137, 141, 147, 152–3
Barcelona 77, 87, 107, 130, 147, 250
Barker, Frank 53
Barnett, S.T. 40, 45, 68, 129
Barrington, M. 81
Bastow, Donald 238–9
Bates, Vic 7
Beart, Francis 41, 44, 67, 82
Beaulieu 162, 243
Belfast 17, 34, 54, 55, 87
Belgian Grand Prix 63, 65, 84–6, 110, 134, 153, 156, 184, 209, 248–52
Bell, Artie 17, 18, 32, 34, 48–9, 53–7, 60–6, 76, 79, 87, 189, 190
Belle Vue 13
Bellshill 160
Belvedere 170, 251
Bemrose Trial 22, 29
Bennett, Alec 21
Bennett, Dave 73, 101
Beveridge Park 159
Biggin Hill Airfield 155
Bills, Ken 34, 44
Birmingham 15, 17, 18, 20–2, 24, 28–9, 34, 41, 51, 55–6, 62, 80, 96, 109, 123, 137, 190, 229, 238, 240, 244, 247
Blackwell, A.J. 29, 33
Blanchard, Jim 7
Blandford 33, 56–8, 67, 77, 190, 248–9
Bluith Wells 28

BMW 7, 47, 92, 117, 120–1, 125–7, 141, 152–3, 165, 166, 180, 184–7, 195, 197, 200–11, 213, 215, 217–19, 221–3, 246, 252
BOAC 240
Bob McIntyre Memorial 222–3
Bologna 188
Bombay 74
Boston Motorcycle Club 218
Bournemouth 219
Bowers, Eric 232–3
Brabazon, Lord 99, 162, 243
Bracebridge Street 18–19, 21, 24, 54, 103, 190
Bradden Bridge 25
Brands Hatch 158, 161, 224–5, 227, 230, 241, 251
Brandywell 25
Bremgarten 77, 98, 99, 101, 125, 138, 215
Brett, Jack 45, 80, 85, 88, 89, 91–93, 121, 124, 125, 129, 133, 136–7, 139, 141, 143, 149, 151, 155, 157, 165–6, 174
Brewster, Percy 20
Brierlow Bar 52
Briggs, Eric 36
Britannia Vase Trophy 163
British Empire Trophy 95
British Experts' Trial 28, 51, 71
British Motor Cycle Racing Club (BMCRC) 44, 94, 131, 147
BRM 34, 156
Brooklands 20–1, 48, 82–3
Brough Airfield 73, 232
Brown, Bob 172, 173, 180, 194
Brown, David 99
Brown, George 40, 44, 102
Brown, R.H. 188
Brown, R.N. 154, 186, 194, 195
Brussels 78, 184
Bryen, Keith 174–5
BSA 11, 14–18, 22–3, 33, 36–7, 51, 71–2, 146, 149, 159, 161, 167, 179, 225, 229, 232, 236–41, 244
Cadwell Park 218
Calderella, Benedicto 118, 231
Campbell, Keith 134, 164, 174, 185, 206, 209

Candless, Rex 190
Cannell, Cyril 196
Cape Town 168, 169, 251
Carr, C.B. 60
Carter, P.H. 40, 144, 163
Casale Monferrato 250
Castrol R 8
Catlin, George 193
Catterick Camp 12, 13
Cazzaniga, Carlo 168
Chadwick, D.V. 185, 188, 194
Chadwick, Dave 185, 187, 193
Champion of champions 120
Chapel-en-le-Frith 232
Cheney, Eric 36
Cheshire Centre Championship 15
Chesterfield 37
Chiswick 100
Chrysler 75
Church Stretton 52
Circuito di Napoli 118
Clandeboye Estate 19
Clark, 'Nobby' 12
Clark, Bill 28
Clark, Harold 36
Clew, Jeff 238
Clifton 70
Clubman's TT 17, 18, 24, 35–8, 40, 41, 159, 232, 248
Clypse circuit 189, 213
Codogno 98, 249
Coleman, Rod 89, 93, 102, 125, 134–6, 139–40, 143–4
Coleraine 149
Collot, J. 148
Colmore Cup 19, 72
Colnago, Giuseppe 116, 120–1, 124–5, 153, 177
Colombo 146
Columbo, Sandro 118
Cooper Brothers 159
Cordey, Georges 77
Cotswell Cups Trial 72
Cotswold Cup Trial 22, 52
Cotswold Cups Trial 52
Coupland 109, 113, 219
Coupland, Sam 109, 113, 219
Coventry 28, 50
Cox, M. 23
Craig, Joe 17–19, 21, 28, 34, 48–9, 54, 56–7, 63, 67, 85, 87–8, 95, 97, 123, 179, 181, 190, 219, 244–5
Craner, Fred G. 70
Crebbin, T.P. 40

Creg-ny-Baa 26, 208, 213
Cronk-ny-Mona 26, 35
Crossley, Don 36
Crystal Palace 155
Czechoslovakia 59
Dale, Dickie 27, 45, 67–70,
    76, 77, 80, 88, 113, 125,
    127–9, 133, 135–6, 141,
    141, 143, 186–7, 194–5,
    197, 209, 215, 218–20
Daniell, Harold 20–1, 33–5,
    55–8, 62–3, 66, 70, 86–7,
    190
Daniels, J.D. 36
Darbishire, Dr Steve 94
Darbishire, Steve 94, 103
Dauwe, F. 148
Davenport, Leo 242–3
Davey, Peter 233
Daytona 160, 229, 231
Dear, L.A. 73
Dearden, Reg 180, 183–5, 189,
    193–5, 202
Degner, E. 220, 221
Dibben, Stan 47
DKW 168, 242
DMW 242
Dobelli, Lorenzo 46
Donington Park 13, 70, 82–3
Doran, Bill 45, 61, 73, 76,
    80–1, 90–1, 93–4, 121
Dorchester 219
DOT 11, 12
Downer, Dave 224, 230
Draper, G.J. 71
Driver, E.G. 194, 195
Dublin 41, 115, 210
Ducati 164, 194, 216, 228,
    229
Duff, Mike 242
Duke, Mrs 94, 130
Dundrod 124, 165, 172, 174,
    187, 194, 250–2
Dunlop 50, 66
Dunstall, Paul 224, 230
Duplex 72, 112, 118, 204–5,
    216, 238
Dutch TT 66, 86, 115–16,
    120–1, 134–5, 153–4, 163,
    173–4, 185, 209–10, 230,
    246, 248–52
Earles, Ernie 238
East Germany 230
Edinburgh 59
Edwards, Charlie 48, 189, 195,
    198
Elmdon Airfield 96
Emerton, Jack 20
Empire Trophy Race 99
Enfield 51, 240, 242
Ennett, D. 151

Evans, E.R. 80
Farrant, Derek 125, 131, 139,
    143
Fay, R. 184
FB Mondial 148, 177, 216,
    220, 222, 228
Featherstone, Mick 73, 76, 80
Federazione Motociclistica
    Italiana 127
Ferodo 50, 151
Ferrari 156
Ferri, Romolo 168
Ferriday, James R. 55
Ferruccio 111, 170, 173–4
Festival of Britain Invitation
    event 90
FIM 86, 90, 92, 115, 118, 121,
    161, 163, 179, 198, 205
Finland 230
Firth, F.L. 35
Fisher, Fred 193
Forconi, T. 141, 148
Foster, A.R. 64, 80
Foster, Bob 28, 56, 59, 61, 63,
    66, 75, 168, 219
Fox, F.M. 143, 163
Fraineuse, La 23
Francis-Barnett 82, 241
Frank Jones Cup 28
Franks, Edgar 19, 190
Freestone, B. 129
French Grand Prix 86, 88, 89,
    121, 124, 130, 131, 134,
    148, 150, 162, 249, 250
Frend, Ted 28, 58, 61, 64
Frith, Freddie 21, 34, 87, 94,
    112
Fugner, H. 216
Fumagalli, Giovanni 113, 127,
    146, 167, 223, 234
Gardiner, Lt Col. 'Goldie' 241
Gawler Airstrip 146
Geeson, Bob 232
Geminiani, S. 85
Geneva 66, 248
Genoa 146
Geoff Duke Ltd 95, 113
George Reynolds Trophy 138
German Grand Prix 91–2, 117,
    135, 137, 151–3, 165, 182,
    185, 194, 210, 214, 217,
    249–52
Gilera 31, 46, 64, 68–9, 73,
    78, 84–6, 89, 91, 93, 97–9,
    104, 109–39, 141–9,
    151–68, 170–9, 196–8, 200,
    205, 210, 218–20, 222–7,
    229–34, 236, 245–7, 250–1
Gilera, Ferruccio 170, 173–4
Gilera, Giuseppe 109–12, 117,

142, 158, 170, 173, 176,
    223
Girling 137, 151, 202, 223
Glasgow 37, 159, 160
Glasgow Mercury Club 37
Glazebrook, A.J. 60
Glencrutchery Road 2–6, 62
Godber-Ford, G.E.H. 52
Goffin, Auguste 45
Goodwood 73, 75, 249
Gould, Rod 229
Governor's Bridge 26, 41, 63
Graham, Robert Leslie 17–18,
    29, 30, 33, 61–4, 67–9,
    76–8, 81, 88, 104, 120, 123,
    165, 189, 193, 195, 252
Graham, Mrs Edna 165
Grand Prix des Nations 68, 93,
    126, 171
Grand Prix of Europe 87
Grant, E.M. 154
Grassetti, Silvio 197, 215, 216,
    220
Great Brickhill 29
Griffiths, Jack 167
Gruber, Wolfgang 7, 207, 213
Guthrie, Jimmy 21, 86–7, 117
Hackett, Stan 182
Hailwood, Mike 156, 160,
    185, 194, 216, 220–1, 224,
    225, 227, 228, 230,
    232–235, 244
Hall, B.W. 23
Hall, Ginger 25
Hansgünther, J. 197
Hartle, John 138, 143, 155,
    157–8, 164, 166, 174, 180,
    185, 187–8, 192–3, 197,
    223, 224, 226, 231–234,
    240, 242
Heath, Phil 36
Hedemora 115, 156, 164, 174,
    185–6, 216, 252
Hele, Doug 186, 191, 237–9
Helkama, Jukka 7
Hempleman, J. 194–5
Hesketh 75
Hillberry 26, 30, 116
Hiller, Ernst 186–7, 197, 206
Hinton, Harry 40, 69, 79, 146,
    206
Hockenheim 147, 172, 194,
    206, 209, 214, 217, 230,
    250, 252
Hocking, Gary 186, 193, 194,
    197, 199, 220, 229
Hodgkin, J.P.E. 45
Holcombe Moor 51
Holland 104, 121, 134, 164,
    171, 185, 230
Holmes, Alan 177, 180

Honda 31, 110, 115, 156, 160,
    189, 212, 216, 221, 223–6,
    229–30, 234, 240
Hooghalen 135
Hopwood, Bert 237, 240
Horn, C. 73
Horsman, Victor 24
Houseley, Eric 37, 159, 232
Humber 8, 75, 82
Humphries, A.J. 29
Hunt, Tim 21, 86, 87
Hurst Cup Trial 19, 72
Imola 123, 146, 170, 173,
    174, 198, 227, 230, 246,
    250, 251
Inter-Centre Team
    Championship Trial 94
International Gold Cup 128, 141
International Shell Gold Cup
    123
Isle of Man 9, 17, 20, 24–5,
    27, 31, 36–8, 43, 46, 53, 78,
    82, 90, 94, 96, 99, 102–3,
    111, 113, 120, 129, 136,
    138, 150, 152, 156, 159,
    161, 164, 171, 173, 184,
    189, 192–3, 196, 206, 208,
    210, 215, 229–30, 234, 243,
    245–50, 252
Isle of Man TT 20, 25, 31,
    103, 113, 120, 156, 184,
    189, 196, 206, 210, 215,
    234, 245–6
Italian Grand Prix 69, 92, 93,
    106, 126, 128, 139–2, 154,
    157, 176, 188, 195, 220,
    249–52
Italy 46, 75, 86, 93, 112, 123,
    137, 139, 146, 163, 169–71,
    173, 177, 188, 220, 230
Jackson, B.A. 37
Jaguar 182
James, K.R.V. 37
Janson, N. 23
Japan 240, 241
Jefferies, Allan 36, 37
Johannesburg 169
John Douglas Trial 16–17, 28,
    70
Johnson, Eddie 214
Johnson, Harry 14
Junior Manx Grand Prix 24,
    27, 82, 160, 233, 244, 248
Junior TT 37, 60, 79–81, 102,
    123, 146, 173, 192, 197,
    230, 233, 248–50, 252
Karachi 146
Karlskoga 100, 194, 252
Kavanagh, Ken 90–3, 97, 121,
    124–5, 129, 134–5, 137,
    141, 151 147, 153, 233

Kawasaki 240, 243
Kay, Dave 7
Keeler, Bob 136, 233
Kentish, J.F. 35, 60
Kerromoar 25
Keys, Basil 36
Kickham Trial 19, 72
Kidson Scramble 28
Killin 59
King, Alastair 160, 168, 174, 180, 191–2, 197
Kirkcaldy 159
Kirkmichael 24–5, 78
Kläger, J. 92
Klinger, G. 206
Krasnowodst 74
Kristianstad 168, 216, 251, 252
Kuzmicki 73–77, 79, 85, 93, 242
Kuzmicki, Leo 73–76, 85, 93, 242
Lacey, Bill 182, 183, 229
Laing, G. 133
Lancashire Grand National Scramble 28, 51
Lancefield, Steve 20, 34, 83, 225
Langton, Eric 28
Lawton, Syd 36, 102, 233
Leathamstown 166
Leeke, James 240
Les Graham Invitation 252
Les Graham Trophy 165, 189, 195
Liberati, Libero 118, 128, 147, 167, 170–176, 216
Lightweight TT 30, 189, 213, 215, 224–5, 242, 252
Liverpool 24, 28, 34, 74, 94, 119, 139
Liverpool Motor Club's Reliance Trial 28
Locarno 197, 198, 216, 221, 247, 252
Lockett, J. 63, 64, 68, 73, 80, 85Lockett, J.H. 68
Lockett, Johnny 34, 56, 58, 63–4, 66–8, 70, 73, 76–7, 80, 82–3, 85, 88, 89, 91–2
Lomas, Bill 7, 41, 64, 66, 69, 80, 102, 141, 151, 164
London 14–15, 17–18, 21, 29, 51, 54, 70, 95–7, 99–100, 155, 169, 240, 245
London's Earls Court Motorcycle Show 51
Longford 146
Lorenzetti, Enrico 75, 85–6, 120

Louis, Harry 56, 82, 107
Low, M.E. 149
Lyons, Ernie 22
McCandless, Crommie 41, 43, 44, 81, 88
McCandless, Rex 17, 32, 54–56
McEwan, T. 81
Macgregor, Robert 159
McGuffie, I. 37
McIntyre, Bob 36–7, 111, 115, 118, 132, 134, 136–8, 141, 143–4, 147, 151, 156, 158, 159, 163, 165, 168, 170, 172, 175–6, 180, 183, 187, 191–4, 222–3, 229
Manchester 13
Manns, S.B. 51
Manx Grand Prix 11, 24, 27–8, 34, 41, 43–5, 82–4, 160, 166, 177, 193, 218, 219, 233, 244, 248
Marcini, Franco 231
Markham, Charles 13, 18, 29
Marseilles Grand Prix 73
Martelli, Francisci 215
Martin, Luis 134, 153
Masetti, Umberto 64, 68–9, 85, 89, 91, 93, 104, 118, 120, 141, 147, 153–5, 165, 173, 176, 247
Matthews, R.T. 60, 165
Meier, Georg 92, 208, 222, 223
Meier, Hermann 241–3
Mellors, Ted 215
Mendogni, E. 216, 221
Merrick, Tom 10
Mettet circuit 75
MG 241
Middlesbrough 13, 23
Milan 110, 113, 130, 161, 220
Milani, Alfredo 86, 93, 101, 113, 116, 125, 127, 134, 153, 176, 197
Milani, Gilberto 120, 221, 231
Mille Miglia 177
Miller, Sammy 158, 163
Minter, Derek 180, 184–5, 187, 194, 221, 223–5, 227, 230, 231, 234–5
Monneret, G. 45
Monneret, Pierre 45, 128, 134, 138–9, 143, 148, 153, 165
Montague, Lord 162
Montanari, Alano 170
Montjuich Park 114, 147
Montlhéry 46–50, 53, 56
Monty, G. 73, 186
Monza 68–9, 92–3, 106, 111–13, 118, 126–9, 134,

139–41, 154–5, 157–8, 160, 163, 167, 171–2, 175–6, 188, 195, 197, 219–20, 223, 226, 229, 231, 249, 252
Monza Autodrome 93, 113
Monza Park 68
Mooliabeenie circuit 146
Morini 188–9, 216, 221, 225
Moscow 74
Moss, Stirling 100
Moto Guzzi 73, 75, 78, 85–6, 93–4, 121, 126–7, 134–8, 140–1, 147–8, 151, 153, 157, 164–6, 170–1, 174–5, 177, 202, 205, 215, 218–19, 221–2
Motor Industry Research Association (MIRA) 56, 239
Moule, Albert 35, 80
Mountain Course 25, 36, 118, 150
Mudford, K.H. 125
Müller, Herman Peter 128, 212
Munich 180, 202
Munks, Austin 109, 112, 113
Murphy, G.A. 134, 174
MV 30–1, 64, 69, 78, 81, 93, 101, 104, 110–11, 116–18, 120, 123, 126–8, 133–7, 141, 143, 147–8, 152–7, 163–6, 168, 174–6, 180, 185, 187–8, 192–5, 202, 209, 214, 216, 218–21, 224–30, 232–5
MZ 194, 213, 216, 220–1, 225, 229
National Motorcycle Museum 247
New York 20
News Chronicle Trophy 70
Nicholson, Bill 15, 16, 22, 28, 71–2, 239
North Shields 214
Northern Experts' Trial 15, 28, 29, 52
Northern Ireland 19, 54, 60, 77, 83, 87
Norton 9, 11, 17–25, 27–9, 31–8, 40–1, 43, 45–53, 55–93, 95–9, 101–9, 111, 114–18, 120–5, 127, 129, 131–9, 141, 143–5, 147–9, 151, 153–5, 157–66, 168, 174–5, 177–96, 198, 202, 205–6, 208–10, 213, 218–21, 224–5, 227, 229–33, 237–8, 240–4, 246, 248–52
NSU 114, 158, 163, 189, 200, 203, 205, 209–15, 217, 219, 221, 228, 237, 252

Nuneaton 56, 239
Nürburgring 24, 100, 151–153, 182, 185, 196, 210, 219, 250, 252
Nygren, O. 165
O'Donovan, Daniel 20
O'Rourke, M.P. 163, 186
Oliver's Mount 44, 70, 129, 141, 158, 188
Oliver, Eric 46, 48–9, 64, 84, 86, 95, 118
Oliver's Mount 44, 70, 129, 141, 158, 188
Olympia 15
Oulton Park 160, 162–3, 165, 174, 177–8, 180, 183, 189, 195, 223, 228, 235, 237, 240, 251–2
Oxford 228–9
Pagani, Nello 64, 78, 85, 89, 93, 97–8, 127, 135, 137, 141
Paris 48, 94
Parkinson, D. 129
Parkinson, Denis 36, 129
Parry, Len 81, 97
Passoni, Francesco 130
Passoni, Franco 118
Patrick, K.E. 184
Perrigo, Bert 14–16, 239
Perris, Frank 180, 231
Persi, Roberto 170, 222
Perth 146, 159
Petch, W. 92
Petty, Ray 225
Phillis, T. 194
Piaggio 7, 111
Pietermaritzburg 169, 251
Pike, David 7
Pike, Roland 239
Pilling, R.K. 51
Pirelli 66
Poore, Denis 21, 241
Pope, Noel 56
Portrush 149
Portstewart 34, 76, 149
Potts, Joe 147, 160, 191
Prescot 11
Purslow, Brian 37
Quincey, Maurice 135, 149
RAF Cranwell 218
Raleigh 9, 10
Ratcliffe, L.A. 52, 59, 71
Ray Bailey Cup 51
Ray, C.M. 51, 71
Raymond, William 122
Read, Phil 224, 227, 230–1, 234–5, 242
Redditch 240
Redman, Jim 194, 234
Reeve, Peter 7
Reid, Mr Guy 94

Reid, N. 94
Reid, Revd R.H. 188
Rennfox 211–12
Rennmax 210–214
Rensen, Ralph 193
Rheims 134, 148, 250
Rhodesia 122, 168–70, 193
Rist, Fred 16
Robb, T.H. 221
Roche, M.P. 149
Rogers, Stu 7
Romaine, Peter 67
Rossi, Renzo 231
Rous, Charlie 223, 225
Rover 229
Royal Air Force 30, 54, 218
Royal Corps of Signals 12
Royal Enfield 51, 240, 242
Royal Signals 13, 15, 244
Rudge 13, 239
Ruffo, B. 94
Ruffo, Bruno 86
Sachsenring 230
St Helens 8, 10, 11, 15, 53, 76,
    95, 107
Sakai, Fumito 240
Salisbury 122, 169, 170, 251
Salzburg 189, 206, 213, 252
San Remo 97, 249
Sandford, Cecil 31, 58, 68–9,
    73, 77, 128
Savelli, Aulo 215–16
Scarborough 40, 44–5, 69, 70,
    128, 129, 141, 158, 168,
    177–8, 188, 233, 248–52
Scheider, Walter 210
Schotten 104–5, 109, 121,
    145, 250
Scotland 59, 159, 214
Scottish Six Days Trial 33, 59
Scuderia 118, 222–5, 227,
    229–35, 242
Seagrave Trophy 105, 107
Senior Manx Grand Prix 44–5,
    177, 193
Senior TT 9, 21, 30, 44, 53,
    61–3, 80–1, 84, 92, 104,
    116, 118–19, 132–3, 138,
    150–1, 156, 165, 173, 190,
    208, 219, 223, 232, 246,
    248–50, 252
Serafini, Dorino 117
Sharatt, Frank 48

Sheene, Barry 245
Shell Gold Cup 123, 147, 173,
    251
Shelsley Walsh Hill 83
Shepherd, Terry 165, 175–6,
    180, 186–7, 193
Shipston-on-Stour 19, 72
Sidecar TT 47
Silverstone 57, 59, 70, 94,
    97–9, 108–9, 114, 130–1,
    137, 147, 158, 161, 177–8,
    183, 193, 202, 224–5, 227,
    231, 233, 239, 242, 244,
    248–52
Simpson, Jimmy 21
Simpson, Leo 134
Singapore 146
Smith, Gilbert 18, 21, 24, 27,
    54, 84, 96, 108–9
Smith, Jeff 72
Solo GPs 185
South Africa 88, 168–9, 228
South Eastern Centre trials 82
Southampton 57
Southport 107, 137, 161
Soviet Union 75
Spa Francorchamps 110, 134,
    153, 163–4, 172, 248–52
Spain 147, 171
Spanish Grand Prix 107, 114,
    147, 250
Sportsman of the Year 7, 96,
    99
Sprayson, Ken 181, 213, 242
Starr, L. 40
Stenning, Canon E.H. 94
Stocker, W.J. 51
Stonebridge, B.G. 51
Storr, John 164
Streatham Club 82
Streatham Trophy Trial 71
Sulby Bridge 25, 41
Sunbeam 22, 82
Surtees, John 31, 87, 90, 99,
    129, 138, 141, 143–4, 147,
    152, 155–8, 164–5, 174–6,
    180, 184, 185, 187–8, 192,
    194–5, 197, 202, 209, 225,
    226, 228, 233, 236, 244
Sutherland, A.R. 149
Suzuki 31, 229, 240, 245
Sweden 100, 157, 164, 168,
    185, 194

Swedish Grand Prix 115,
    156–7, 164, 174, 185–6,
    216, 220, 251–2
Swiss Grand Prix 66, 77–8, 95,
    98–9, 125, 138–9, 197–8,
    215–16, 221, 247–50, 252
Tait, Percy 242
Tanner, G.B. 175
Taruffi, Piero 109, 113, 117,
    121, 133, 137, 170
Tasmania 145
Tasmanian TT 146
Tattershall, Chris 30
Taveri, Luigi 137, 141, 221
Templeman, Malcolm 189
Terretta, Keith 193
Thomson, Dick 164
Thruxton 56, 68, 73, 89–90,
    206, 232, 248–9
Tokyo 240
Topham, Mrs Muriel 139
Trial, Half-Crown 82
Triumph 10, 11, 15, 21–3, 37,
    40, 45, 51, 54, 191, 232–3,
    241
Troon 159
Trow, Alan 161, 164
TT Mountain Circuit 24, 225
Tuck, Fred 100
Tyrrell, Ken 156
Ubbiali, Carlo 214, 220–1
Uitenhage 251
Ulster 30, 34, 54, 67–8, 76,
    83, 87, 90–1, 117, 124, 131,
    134, 148, 157, 165–6, 171,
    174–5, 187, 189, 191, 194,
    219, 229–30, 248–52
Ulster Grand Prix 30, 67, 68,
    83, 87, 91, 117, 124, 134,
    157, 165, 174–5, 187, 191,
    194, 230, 248–52
Upshaw, Don 7
Valdinosi, O. 97
Valenti Brothers 159
Vandervell, C.A. 95
Vandervell, Tony 74
Vanhouse, Norman 28
Veer, H. Drikus 135, 154
Velocette 8, 28, 34, 35, 41,
    45–6, 56, 59–61, 63, 66,
    68–9, 73, 75–7, 80, 82, 115,
    161–2, 165, 179, 188, 193,
    219, 251

Venturi, Remo 195, 231
Villiers 21, 241–2
Vincent 36, 40, 44, 90, 155,
    193, 228
Viney, Hugh 12–14, 16–18,
    22–3, 28, 33, 52, 71
Walker, Graham 12, 108
Walker, R.F. 45
Warner, Graham 100
Watling Street 75
Welsh, Rita 7
West, Jock 18, 68
Wheeler, Arthur 36, 60, 221
Whitfield, Don 11
Whitworth, David 28, 59
Wickstead, Ivor 37
Williams, Frank 156
Willoughby, Vic 115
Wilson, George 57
Wincheap Garage 225
Wisbech 7
Wise, Mrs Pat 47
Wood, Jackie 149, 161–2
Wood, Tommy 56, 215
Woods, Stanley 21, 61, 86–7,
    103
Woollett, Mick 7, 27, 75, 180,
    188
Woolwich 21
World Championship 7, 21,
    26, 30, 46, 54, 63, 66, 68,
    74–5, 77, 83, 90, 92, 104,
    112, 114, 118, 125–6, 132,
    155–6, 158, 161, 164, 171,
    173, 190, 194–5, 200, 202,
    206, 212, 215, 220, 224,
    227, 230, 233
World War One 8
World War Two 12, 21, 46,
    74, 110, 117
Wortley, T.H. 51
Wright, D. 161
Wyler, John 99
Yamaha 229, 240, 242
Young, R.B. 16, 29, 33, 52
Zeller, W. 92, 121, 125, 141,
    153
Zeller, Walter 92, 120, 152,
    164, 200, 202, 208–9
Zimbabwe 122

ND - #0350 - 270225 - C0 - 260/195/17 - PB - 9781780912189 - Gloss Lamination